D0847362

The International Origins of

the Federal Reserve System

The International Origins of the Federal Reserve System

J. LAWRENCE BROZ

Cornell University Press

ITHACA AND LONDON

HG
2563
B68
1997

First published 1997 by Cornell University Press

Printed in the United States of America

Cornell University Press strives to utilize environmentally responsible suppliers and materials to the fullest extent possible in the publishing of its books. Such materials include vegetable-based, low-VOC inks and acid-free papers that are also either recycled, totally chlorine-free, or partly composed of nonwood fibers.

Library of Congress Cataloging-in-Publication Data

Broz, J. Lawrence.
The international origins of the Federal Reserve System / J. Lawrence Broz.
p.   cm.
Includes index.
ISBN 0-8014-3332-0 (cloth : alk. paper)
1. Board of Governors of the Federal Reserve System (U.S.)—History.   2. Federal Reserve banks—History.   3. International finance—History.   4. Monetary policy–United States—History.   I. Title.
HG2563.B68   1997
332.1'1'0973—dc21   97-11932

Cloth printing   10   9   8   7   6   5   4   3   2   1

To my parents,

Carmen and Perry Broz

Contents

	List of Figures and Tables	ix
	Preface	xi
	Introduction	1
1	The Federal Reserve Act: Content and Contending Explanations	17
2	The Economics and Politics of International Currency Use	55
3	The International Economy, Patterns of Currency Use, and Domestic Politics	86
4	The Rise of the U.S. Economy and the Banking Reform Movement	132
5	Collective Action for Banking Reform	160
6	The Origins of Other Central Banks	206
	Summary, Observations, and Implications	245
	Index	263

Figures and Tables

Figure 1.1. Number of national banks, state banks, and trust companies, 1862–1913   22

Figure 1.2. Total assets of national banks, state banks, and trust companies, 1862–1913   23

Figure 1.3. Single- and double-name paper as a percentage of total loans and investments, all national banks, 1883–1913   44

Figure 1.4. Single- and double-name paper as a percentage of total loans and investments, New York City national banks, 1881–1913   44

Figure 1.5. Commercial paper as a percentage of total loans and investments, New York City national banks and all national banks, 1886–1913   45

Figure 4.1. Gold holdings of the U.S. Treasury, the Bank of England, the Bank of France, and the Reichsbank, 1878–1913   135

Table 1.1. Institutions not changed by the Federal Reserve Act   51

Table 1.2. The Federal Reserve Act's minor institutional changes   52

Table 1.3. The Federal Reserve Act's major institutional changes   53

Table 2.1. Functions of international money   58

Table 2.2. Necessary and supplementary characteristics of international currency countries   71

Table 2.3. International distributional effects of key currency status   75

Table 2.4. Domestic beneficiaries of international currency issue, ranked by intensity of preference   81

Table 3.1. Merchandise exports of the major trading states, 1872, 1899, 1913 91

Table 3.2. National export values, 1872, 1900, 1913 94

Table 3.3. National share of world exports, 1872, 1900, 1913 ... 96

Table 3.4. National share of world exports by product group, 1872, 1900, 1913 98

Table 3.5. Destination of national exports, 1872, 1899, 1913 ... 100

Table 3.6. National export share by area, 1872, 1899, 1913 102

Table 3.7. Destination of U.S. exports, 1872–1913 103

Table 3.8. U.S. balance of international payments, 1872–1913 ... 106

Table 3.9. Changes in the U.S. gold stock, 1890–1910 108

Table 3.10. Growth and composition of foreign-exchange assets, 1900–1913 114

Table 3.11. Stability and range of official discount rates in France, Germany, and England, 1878–1909 121

Table 4.1. Holdings of the U.S. Treasury 134

Table 5.1. Economic consequences of U.S. banking panics 166

Preface

From the Civil War to 1913, the United States suffered under one of the worst banking systems in the world. Major panics occurred about every ten years, and seasonal changes in the demand for credit created liquidity disturbances nearly every autumn. To many observers, the panic of 1907 was the last straw, prompting the rise of one of the great organs of American administrative government: the Federal Reserve System. Founded in 1913 by an act of Congress for the expressed purpose of reducing the propensity for panics, the Fed was given a mandate to provide society with one of its most basic public goods: a sound and efficient payments system. This book is an attempt to explain how American society overcame the collective action dilemmas that normally constrain the production of public goods to inadequate levels. In plain English, it is about how the nation produced one of the cornerstones of good government, in the face of disincentives that should have left few people with sufficient motivation to incur the large costs of institutional change.

I argue that Mancur Olson's familiar "joint products" model (also known as the "by-products" or "selective incentives" model) provides the key to understanding the voluntary collective action behind the Federal Reserve Act. The model postulates that a public good produced jointly with a private good can yield collective action in a large group setting, because the addition of the private good creates the necessary convergence between the individual and the social costs of collective action. In other words, if a person wants to enjoy a private good, and that enjoyment is contingent on the production of a public good, he or she will have incentives to contribute to an effort to produce both goods.

The Federal Reserve Act was a case of joint production, as it produced at least two important "goods." It was about solving the panic problem, to be sure, but, because this expected benefit approximated a pure public good, few people would invest in efforts to change the system, when they could enjoy any improvement for free. The Act also offered the means to fully internationalize the U.S. dollar and the operations of money-center banks, a benefit restricted to a far smaller segment of society. The New York financial community stood to gain the most, and the profits made possible through the attainment of international currency status created the necessary overlap between the private and social costs of institutional change. Bankers could not earn the rents associated with issuing an international currency without contributing to the overall effort to improve the general operation of the payments system. Moreover, the stimulus behind the entire process of institutional change was the rapidly advancing position of the United States in the world economy, a post-1870s trend that gave large bankers some incentives to absorb the expenses of domestic institutional innovation. In short, to its most ardent and organized proponents, the Federal Reserve Act was first and foremost a response to new international opportunities, previously unattainable because of the deficient organization of the domestic payments machinery.

This book began its life at the University of California, Los Angeles. UCLA offered a rich and stimulating environment for political economy research, and I am indebted to all those who attended presentations and commented on early drafts, especially Mark Brawley, David Lake, Karen Orren, and Ron Rogowski. Intellectually, I owe the most to my adviser and colleague, Jeffry Frieden, who diligently reviewed many drafts and uncovered numerous errors of commission and omission. Without his help and encouragement through every phase of the project, I doubt I could have completed it. Ken Sokoloff also conveyed sound advice on the full manuscript and introduced my project to other leading economic historians. Lance Davis was the most generous of this group, providing many pages of detailed evaluation and data on one of my presentations.

I also thank my colleagues at Harvard University for guidance and advice on parts of the manuscript. Marc Busch, Joel Hellman, Robert Keohane, and Lisa Martin offered important suggestions. Other scholars gave valuable counsel: Michael Bordo, William R. Clark, Benjamin J. Cohen, Barry Eichengreen, William Keech, Stephen Krasner, Charles Lipson, James Livingston, Robert Paarlberg, Louis Pauly, Frances Rosenbluth, George Selgin, Beth Simmons, Daniel Verdier, and Eugene N. White. I also had useful conversations with Vincent Carosso, Gary Gorton, Alex Leijonhufvud, Stephen Schuker, and Richard Sylla. Two anonymous reviewers provided first-rate advice, for which I am very grateful, and Roger Haydon deftly guided the manuscript to publication. Xenia Busch, Melissa Freeman, and Ilya Somin compiled the index and proofread the manuscript.

I received financial assistance from the National Science Foundation (grant no. SES-8819707), and UCLA's International Studies and Overseas Program. Research for this book was done while at the Center for International Affairs, Harvard University. The following institutions provided access to their libraries and archival assistance: The Rare Book and Manuscript Library of Columbia University, the Archives Division of the Federal Reserve Bank of New York, the Research Library of the Board of Governors of the Federal Reserve System, the Special Collections Department of the University of Virginia Library, the Archives Department of the Baker Library at Harvard University, the U.S. National Archives, and the Manuscript Division of the Library of Congress. Lastly, I thank my wife, Chris, and children, Adrian and Marina, for all their love and encouragement.

J. LAWRENCE BROZ

Cambridge, Massachusetts

The International Origins of

the Federal Reserve System

Introduction

hen Congress passed the Federal Reserve Act in December 1913, it established a new set of institutions governing the relationship between banks and credit markets and between banks, the government, and the production of money. The official rationale was to imbue the payments system with greater "elasticity," by way of central bank rediscounting facilities. Before 1913, there was no public-sector agency charged with management of the system in times of crisis, and private-sector remedies often proved inadequate to the task. Recurrent periods of shortage of a medium of exchange and severe banking panics were the result. Since the 1930s, no major disruption to the banking and payments systems has occurred, and scholars are virtually unanimous in attributing much of this success to prompt and aggressive interventions on the part of the Federal Reserve.[1] To explain the origins of the Federal Reserve System in terms of society's need for a credible lender of last resort—a desired institution that approximates a societywide public good—misreads the incentives that compelled the institutional changes. In this book, I argue that the rapid international advance of the American economy after the 1870s

[1] See, for example, Anna J. Schwartz, "Real and Pseudo-Financial Crises," in *Financial Crises and the World Banking System*, ed. Forrest Capie and Geoffrey E. Wood (London: Macmillan, 1986), pp. 11–31; Frederic S. Mishkin, "Asymmetric Information and Financial Crises: A Historical Perspective," in *Financial Markets and Financial Crises*, ed. R. Glenn Hubbard (Chicago: University of Chicago Press, 1991), pp. 69–108; and Gillian Garcia and Elizabeth Plautz, *The Federal Reserve: Lender of Last Resort* (Cambridge: Ballinger, 1988).

gave a specific *subset* of society concentrated (private) incentives to re-make the payments machinery along the lines of the Federal Reserve Act.

The Puzzle

The problem of reforming the American payments system can be cast in familiar collective action terms.[2] The term "payments system" refers to the instruments, institutions, operating procedures, and information systems used to initiate, transmit, and settle payments in an economy. It is the *infrastructure* upon which the soundness of the financial system, the effectiveness of monetary policy, and the functioning of the entire economy rests.[3] When payments institutions are efficient and operating smoothly, they are almost invisible. Transfers and advances of money take place between individuals and firms with little regard to the underlying infrastructure, facilitating exchange and maximizing aggregate social welfare. When a payments system is unreliable or prone to collapse, people become aware of it because the costs of its poor organization are made manifest in forgone everyday exchange. But simply because society gains from a sound payments system does not make its provision automatic. Provision is problematic because any effort to improve the payments infrastructure is itself a public good and, therefore, is subject to the constraints of collective action.

A good is public if it exhibits *nonexcludability*, meaning that once the good is provided, the producer is unable to prevent anyone from consuming it, and *nonrival consumption*, meaning that one person's consumption does not reduce its availability to anyone else. Production of public goods requires collective action; yet, since the benefits of concerted action are not excludable, it will be in the interest of each member of a community to "free-ride," contributing less to the effort than he would if he were the only one to gain from it. Any time individuals would benefit from cooperation but face powerful incentives to defect, a community may end up in a situation where the desired goods remain underprovided. As such, the provision of a reliable payments system presupposes the resolution of this collective dilemma.

The payments system in existence prior to the Federal Reserve Act was certainly unreliable, as major financial disruptions were common,

[2] Mancur Olson, *The Logic of Collective Action* (Cambridge: Harvard University Press, 1965).
[3] David B. Humphrey, ed., *The U.S. Payments System: Efficiency, Risk, and the Role of the Federal Reserve* (Boston: Kluwer, 1990).

and several were followed by severe recessions.[4] Hence, American society as a whole stood to gain from restructuring the system in a way that prevented financial crises like the major panic of 1907. From a collective action standpoint, however, cooperation among the individual beneficiaries for the purpose of improving the system could be expected to be very difficult, given the high costs of organizing such a large group, monitoring members' contributions to the provision of the good, and enforcing payment, should members attempt to free-ride. In more practical terms, people had to figure out how to allocate the costs of gathering information on the faults of the existing system, and on the economic and distributional consequences of changing any of its component parts. Society also had to determine how to distribute the burden of influencing policymakers to supply new institutions, since law and practice vested Congress with the authority to rule in this domain. Finally, society needed to ensure that each beneficiary paid into the collective effort an amount proportionate to the individual's expected gain from the improvement. Yet even if payoffs were symmetric and all people were made equally better off from an improvement in the payments system, there still would be a failure of supply, since the new institution would provide a public good and rational individuals would seek to secure its benefits for free.

It is intriguing is that there was no failure of collective action in this instance. Historians of the Federal Reserve have found evidence of pervasive collective activity on behalf of payments system reform. Although there is debate about the size and scope of this lobby's membership, not to mention its motivation, it is clear that a smaller subset of society—not all the potential beneficiaries—bore the brunt of the costs of reform.[5] With money-center bankers in the forefront, this subgroup drafted the initial reform legislation, made concessions to other organized factions, and funded most of the bill for a sophisticated public relations campaign aimed at securing the support of nonbanking constituencies and Congress. Through these efforts, society overcame the free-rider problem

---

[4] William Roberds, "Financial Crises and the Payments System: Lessons from the National Banking Era," *Federal Reserve Bank of Atlanta Economic Review* (May/June 1995): 15–31; O. M. W. Sprague, *History of Crises under the National Banking System* (Washington, D.C.: Government Printing Office, 1910).

[5] See, for example, James Livingston, *Origins of the Federal Reserve System: Money, Class, and Corporate Capitalism, 1890–1913* (Ithaca: Cornell University Press, 1986); Eugene N. White, *The Regulation and Reform of the American Banking System, 1900–1929* (Princeton: Princeton University Press, 1983); Robert C. West, *Banking Reform and the Federal Reserve, 1863–1923* (Ithaca: Cornell University Press, 1977); Gabriel Kolko, *The Triumph of Conservatism* (New York: Free Press, 1963); and Robert H. Wiebe, *Businessmen and Reform: A Study of the Progressive Movement* (Cambridge: Harvard University Press, 1962).

and produced major and lasting payments system reform in the shape of the Federal Reserve Act. Explaining why and how society surmounted collective dilemmas and produced the institutional public good is the central objective of this book.

Collective Action Theory

Collective action theory suggests two potentially relevant models for thinking about how large groups surmount the difficulties of collective action. The first is the "privileged group" approach, which relaxes the condition of uniform, symmetrical benefits.[6] If the gains of collective action are distributed unevenly within a community, then the benefit going to one or several members may be sufficient to justify this subgroup providing the public good singlehandedly, even if other beneficiaries free-ride. This line of reasoning is, of course, relevant to situations where a community is composed of agents of unequal size, such as a concentrated industry dominated by a few big firms. In fact, most political accounts of the Federal Reserve Act implicitly adopt a privileged group framework, arguing that New York bankers and other members of the coalition organized for political action because they would benefit disproportionately from payments system reform.

Various manifestations of the privileged group argument are examined in the next chapter, and found wanting. A common weakness is that the logical connections between asymmetric gains, institutional interests, and organized political action are not carefully specified, which makes it difficult to evaluate predictions and outcomes. Fortunately, theory offers a second approach relevant to collective action in large group settings—the "joint products" or "selective incentives" model.

The basic intuition of the joint products model is that collective action situations typically yield multiple benefits, public *and* private.[7] For example, coordinating an international alliance yields both a pure public good (deterring common enemies) and private, nation-specific benefits (alliance armaments can be used for patrolling coastal waters, protecting col-

[6] Olson, *Logic of Collective Action*; George J. Stigler, "Free Riders and Collective Action: An Appendix to Theories of Economic Regulation," *Bell Journal of Economics and Management Science* 5 (1974): 359–65.

[7] Olson, *Logic of Collective Action*; Russell Hardin, *Collective Action* (Baltimore: The Johns Hopkins University Press, 1982); Richard Cornes and Todd Sandler, *The Theory of Externalities, Public Goods, and Clubs* (Cambridge: Cambridge University Press, 1986), pp. 113–31; Todd Sandler, *Collective Action: Theory and Applications* (Ann Arbor: University of Michigan Press, 1992); Ezra J. Mishan, "The Relationship between Joint Products, Collective Goods, and External Effects," *Journal of Political Economy* 77 (May/June 1969): 329–48.

onies, providing disaster relief, curbing domestic unrest, pursuing nation-alistic goals, etc.).[8] Similarly, charitable organizations produce a public good (philanthropic activities), as well as private, agent-specific benefits (tax breaks for contributors).[9] The presence of joint products means that the relationship of the jointly defined goods plays a role when analyzing free-rider behavior: *the extent of free consumption associated with institution-building should be inversely related to the proportion of private outputs (selective incentives) involved in a given set of socially-desired rules.*

In this book, I build a case for a joint products understanding of the origins of the Federal Reserve Act. In addition, the framework is ex-tended, in Chapter 6, to explain the establishment of three other central banks: the Bank of England, and the First and Second Banks of the United States. Central banks are excellent cases, since they are com-monly understood as providing essential public goods, for example, fi-nancial system stability and a stable monetary environment. My objec-tive is to demonstrate that the joint products model offers a superior framework for understanding the collective dynamics behind the Fed-eral Reserve Act, as well as the charters of several earlier central banks.

The Argument

Before 1913, the United States faced not one, but two major problems of financial organization that distinguished it from other developed coun-tries. On the one hand, its payments system was deficient, the United States having been the only major country to experience panics and severe seasonal fluctuations in the nominal interest rate on a regular basis. In-deed, the United States experienced banking panics in a period "when they were a historical curiosity in other countries," the worst of which occurred in 1873, 1884, 1890, 1893, and 1907.[10] On the other hand, its currency lacked international status, as the U.S. was the only major indus-trial nation whose currency did not function as an international medium of exchange, unit of account, or store of value.[11] The U.S. dollar had no

[8] John A. C. Conybeare and Todd Sandler, "The Triple Entente and the Triple Alliance, 1889–1914: A Collective Goods Approach," *American Political Science Review* 84 (December 1990): 1197–1205.

[9] John Posnett and Todd Sandler, "Joint Supply and the Finance of Charitable Activity," *Public Finance Quarterly* 14 (April 1986): 209–22.

[10] Michael D. Bordo, "The Impact and International Transmission of Financial Crises: Some Historical Evidence, 1870–1933," *Rivista di Storia Economica* 2 (1985): 73.

[11] Peter Lindert, *Key Currencies and Gold, 1900–1913*, Studies in International Finance, Inter-national Finance Section, no. 24, Princeton University (1969); Vincent P. Carosso and Rich-ard Sylla, "U.S. Banks in International Finance," in *International Banking, 1870–1914*, ed.

status as an international currency, despite the strong and rising position of the United States' economy in the world trade and payments systems.

From a collective action standpoint, these two problems were quite distinct. The former was very much a domestic *public goods* problem, as the benefits of rendering the payments system more stable would extend undiminished to everyone in the nation connected to the money economy, regardless of individual contributions to the effort. The latter, however, was an *impure public goods* problem, as the benefits of internationalizing the dollar were more concentrated (agent-specific) and excludable. My claim is that the Federal Reserve Act was an example of joint production, in which the private output (internationalizing the currency) could not feasibly be separated from the associated collective output (improving the domestic payments system), creating the necessary convergence between the private and social costs of institutional change. The catalyst was the rapidly advancing position of the United States in the global economy, an international trend which gave to a subset of agents sufficient private incentives to internalize the wider benefits of lobbying for domestic institutional change.

Before 1913, the United States lacked the prerequisites of an issuer of international currency and an international banking center. Domestic financial markets were deficient in "breadth, depth and resiliency," all necessary conditions for the issue of international money.[12] The discount market was extremely narrow and bereft of instruments of the type held and traded internationally. In addition, secondary markets were extremely thin, as banks engaged in little rediscounting amongst themselves. Finally, in the absence of a reliable rediscounting mechanism, the entire payments system lacked resilience and was therefore prone to frequent bouts of illiquidity and panic.

The financial components of the Federal Reserve Act systematically addressed both deficiencies. The central goal was to develop broad and deep secondary markets for financial instruments that reflected commercial transactions, foreign and domestic. To add breadth, nationally chartered banks were for the first time authorized to "accept" bills of exchange arising out of international trade.[13] To add depth, bankers' acceptances,

---

Rondo Cameron and V. I. Bovykin (New York: Oxford University Press, 1991).

[12] George S. Tavlas and Yuzuru Ozeki, *The Internationalization of Currencies: An Appraisal of the Japanese Yen*, International Monetary Fund Occasional Paper, no. 90 (Washington, D.C.: International Monetary Fund, 1992), p. 2.

[13] "Bankers' acceptances" are financial instruments through which banks act as intermediaries between importers and exporters by guaranteeing to make payments to the exporter on a specific date. The purpose of the banker's acceptance, or guarantee, is to lower transaction costs in international exchange by adding a bank's creditworthiness to that of the less well-known importer. American bankers were prevented by law and custom from ac-

along with other commercial instruments, were made eligible for rediscount at the Federal Reserve banks. As an additional stimulus, Reserve banks were given powers to purchase acceptances and bills directly under the Act's open-market provisions. The Act's major provisions thus involved adding scope, depth, and resilience to the payments system, which served not only to enhance the stability of the banking system—the explicit domestic motivation—but also to develop the dollar for international use. In conjunction with this international financial goal, Reserve banks were also given explicit international monetary powers. This authority put the United States on equal footing with other major gold standard countries, who, through their central banks, influenced exchange rates at the margins and engaged in ad hoc multilateral stabilization efforts in crises. In short, the legislation produced multiple outputs, domestic and international.

The interdependence of these outputs explains how society overcame the dilemmas of collective action. When joint, complementary goods are at stake, collective action is more likely. I argue that the evolving international context altered the dynamics of institutional politics within the United States, making it possible to overcome the obstacles to collective action that stood in the way of change. It did so by transforming the situation at home from a *single issue* collective action problem (payments system stability) to a *multiple issue* problem (involving both financial stability and the global role of the dollar). As long as financial stability remained the exclusive issue, rational agents, either inside or outside of government, had little incentive to absorb the costs of generating improvements in the financial structure. But with the economic maturation of the United States, and the possibility of internationalizing the dollar and the joint-stock banking system centered in New York, a second incentive arose for remaking the domestic payments system. It was the addition of the new international goal that explains how and why the collective action barriers to institutional change were surmounted.

Testing the Argument

The argument ultimately rests on three testable assertions: (1) internationalizing the currency involved concentrated benefits of a kind suffi-

---

cepting trade bills prior to the Federal Reserve Act, and, as a result, the financing of American trade was intermediated almost entirely by foreign banks. Robert K. LaRoche, "Bankers Acceptances," *Federal Reserve Bank of Richmond Economic Quarterly* 79 (Winter 1993).

cient to generate collective action, (2) this output could not be produced independently of payments system reform, and (3) change in the international position of the U.S. economy was the stimulus for movement to the new Federal Reserve regime. To evaluate the first claim, I derive from the economics literature the domestic distributional implications of issuing an international currency. I show that the benefits and costs of issuing an international currency are not evenly distributed among domestic residents. The constituency expected to lobby for international currency status is composed of the following agents, ranked in terms of the share of benefits they consume: *Money-center financial firms* engaged in foreign trade finance, foreign exchange, and capital intermediation (inflows and outflows) derive the greatest share of the benefits, since they earn what are known as "denomination rents" from global use of the national currency.[14] Financing trade in the home currency also confers concentrated benefits upon exportables producers and importers, who no longer have to bear exchange-rate risk, and the benefit is greatest to producers most exposed to such risk. *Producers of differentiated manufactured products* for export rank highest here and, what is more, possess the market power to obtain invoicing in the local currency. *Producers of standardized manufactured goods* for export, while lacking market power, also face significant foreign exchange risk and are thus relatively strong supporters of currency internationalization. The actors with the least to gain and, therefore, the weakest positive preference, are *importers and exporters of raw materials and agricultural products*, since domestic prices for such products typically adjust for exchange rate changes. In short, unlike the beneficiaries of banking stability—a large and diverse group—international currency status confers large gains upon a far more restricted segment of society. Lobbying for institutions that underpin this status will thus be more likely than in the case of payments system stability.

To demonstrate that internationalizing the currency and reforming the payments system could not be separately accomplished, I again draw upon economics. Unlike the production of payments system stability, for which multiple institutional forms are possible (e.g., deposit insurance, deregulation of note issue, and branch banking), the structures required to issue an international currency are quite unique. Nonresidents need what Benjamin Cohen calls "capital certainty"—a low probability of loss

---

[14] Inasmuch as the banking sector of an issuing country has an effective monopoly over the issue of monetary liabilities denominated in the vehicle currency, expansion of such liabilities to meet the needs of nonresidents means that banks earn rents, which they would not have received if their liabilities were denominated in another currency. Alexander K. Swoboda, *The Euro-Dollar Market: An Interpretation*, Essays in International Finance, no. 64, International Finance Section, Princeton University (1968), pp. 105–6.

from selling assets at any time—before they utilize a currency for international purposes. Broad, deep, and flexible financial markets in the issuing country provide such certainty.[15] But improving the depth, breadth, and flexibility of national financial markets complements the production of domestic payments system stability almost by definition. The implication is that the Federal Reserve's joint products could not be independently produced, because the products were inherently *complementary in consumption*. The institutions required to enhance the standing of the dollar in international markets presupposed the production of financial stability, thereby giving the small group seeking the private benefits incentives to contribute to the production of the collective good. The failure to do so would have meant that the private good was not then available. Hence, banking reform addressed both objectives simultaneously.

To demonstrate that change in the international position of the U.S. economy was the dynamic element behind the movement to the Federal Reserve Act, I appeal once more to international currency economics. While not a theory, this analysis has specified the *necessary* and *supplementary* determinants of the choice and usage of national currencies for international purposes. The necessary prerequisites are domestic and institutional. As referred to above, an issuing nation must possess domestic financial markets that are broad, deep and resilient. In addition, it must maintain a credible commitment to low inflation and inflation variability. The supplementary factors, in contrast, are international: patterns of international currency use are associated with the relative positions of nations in the world economy. Specifically, a nation that has a large share of world exports of all kinds, a large share of world manufactured exports (especially differentiated manufactured exports), a large share of exports to developing countries, and enduring current account surpluses will experience enhanced demand for its currency for global invoicing, payments, and reserves purposes.

I add to these empirical findings the argument that *change* in the supplementary (international) factors is causally linked to change in the necessary domestic factors, by way of its impact on the size and preference intensities of the subgroup that benefits from internationalizing a currency.[16] Specifically, growth in a large nation's share of world exports, growth in that nation's share of manufactured and differentiated manufactured exports, growth in its share of exports to developing countries, and the onset of persistent current account surpluses, will feed back on

[15] Benjamin J. Cohen, *The Future of Sterling as an International Currency* (London: Macmillan, 1971), p. 27.
[16] This assumes zero transaction costs of collective action *within* the international currency coalition. The assumption is relaxed in Chapter 5.

domestic politics by adding new constituents to the internationalist coalition, as well as by intensifying the positive preferences of existing members.

These are testable propositions, and the analysis to follow consists largely of refining and evaluating the three-part argument. Suffice it to say here that the evidence is consistent with the joint products interpretation. Data on the international position of the U.S. economy between 1872 and 1913 show that, in each of the supplementary categories relevant to international currency use, the position of the United States changed in the direction presaging an expanded role for the U.S. dollar as global money. Data on patterns of international currency use in the period show, however, that, outside of Canada, the dollar did not serve any of the functions of money in the international realm, due to the absence of the necessary domestic preconditions. Finally, data on political organization and lobbying show that the demand for the Federal Reserve's joint products came specifically from the domestic agents expected to benefit directly from internationalizing the dollar and from globalizing the New York-centered banking system. Contradictory data, or the absence of the specified behaviors and outcomes in any one of these categories, would be sufficient to call into question the validity of the argument. I have explored the evidence deeply and systematically, and the evidence is compelling, as I hope to demonstrate.

To summarize, the construction of broader, deeper domestic financial markets, and the creation of a central bank of rediscount with the power to conduct international monetary operations, were the core financial features of the Federal Reserve Act. While justified as prophylactics against panics, these measures doubled as the institutional foundations for internationalizing the American payments system. This latter objective sufficiently explains the demand for institutional change, as well as the content of such demand. It was no accident that a subset of American society, led predictably by the New York banking community, was the main source of pressure to remake the U.S. payments system. It was also no accident that these proponents of change looked to Europe's key currency countries for a model of payments reform. For this small group, the benefits of the European system were concentrated—earning denomination rents and reduced risk of foreign exchange. This explains the group's willingness to undertake the costly intellectual, organizational, and financial burdens of developing a reform plan and moving it through Congress. It was also far more capable of overcoming the barriers to collective action that face all groups engaged in political activity. As a small, homogenous group with ongoing organizations (i.e., clearinghouse associations) capable of being transformed to coordinate the lobbying effort, bankers could act collectively to an extent that the very large and diverse group of beneficiaries of banking stability could not.

From the lobby's perspective, the societywide benefits of political entrepreneurship were external to the drive to internationalize the American banking system. Its incentives were to advance the role of the dollar as an international invoice, payments, and reserve currency, and thereby to allow New York City to become a worldwide financial center on par with London. The institutional agenda selected to attain these goals also enhanced broader social welfare by addressing the nation's internal financial shortcomings (e.g., insufficient liquidity in panics, seasonal credit market pressures), but this was a by-product created by the inseparable and complementary nature of the joint products: improving the depth and resiliency of short-term financial markets served both domestic and international purposes. The rise in America's global economic position gave certain groups within the U.S. incentives to redress these problems. Only then could they gain the concentrated advantages of key currency status. Society moved to a new, welfare-enhancing institutional equilibrium due to the complementary, interdependent nature of the dual objectives.

The Implications for Political Economy

Inasmuch as the Federal Reserve Act relates to the advancing position of the United States in the world economy, the argument touches on central themes in the study of international political economy. The financial side of the ascent of the United States in the early twentieth century, however, is a development that is remarkably absent from historical discussions of America's rise to global power, and from debates concerning "hegemony" (i.e., the leadership of a single dominant economic power), in this field. Most ignored are the domestic institutional underpinnings of U.S. international financial leadership.

History records an association between international economic stability and the existence of one dominant nation—a hegemonic power—on the world scene. The stability of the seventeenth-century world economy is ascribed to the centrality of the Netherlands, which provided a stable media of exchange, a central clearinghouse for international payments, and the protection of property rights on the high seas.[17] The mantle of leadership passed to Great Britain in the nineteenth century, whose singular importance in finance, trade, and naval power served to maintain the

---

[17] Mark R. Brawley, *Liberal Leadership: Great Powers and Their Challengers in Peace and War* (Ithaca: Cornell University Press, 1993).

classical gold standard and the relatively open trading system of the late nineteenth century. After a lag that encompassed the period between the two world wars of this century, the United States took over the role of hegemonic leader, establishing and maintaining the Bretton Woods system through 1971.[18]

Much of the theorizing about the necessity for a hegemon rests on Charles Kindleberger's privileged group argument.[19] Kindleberger posits that the global economy requires the provision of certain infrastructural collective goods to operate smoothly. In the trade and payments systems, the necessary goods are: (1) the provision of a market for distress goods, (2) the production of a countercyclical flow of capital, (3) the maintenance of a rediscount mechanism to provide liquidity when the monetary system freezes in panic, (4) the management of foreign exchange rates, and (5) the provision of a degree of coordination of domestic monetary policies. There is a tendency, however, for states to underproduce this infrastructure. Bargaining among two or more countries entails transaction costs, and enforcing cooperation in the provision of the public goods is problematic, due to the threat of defection (noncooperative free-riding). But when a hegemon is present, its dominance gives it incentives to act unilaterally, and to internalize the positive externalities associated with systemic stability, even if other nations free-ride. Hence, "for the world economy to be stabilized, there has to be a stabilizer, *one* stabilizer."[20]

These propositions are controversial, to be sure, but what is most important for present purposes is that all formulations of "hegemonic stability theory" posit a straightforward relationship between international conditions (e.g., the relative size, economic productivity, and degree of trade dependence of states) and the degree to which the infrastructural public goods are provided at the global level.[21] The implicit supposition is that a hegemonic structure is sufficient to explain the *capacity* of a dominant state to provide the necessary international services. Omitted are the domestic institutional structures that allow hegemonic states to serve in a stabilizing capacity.

While it is one thing to be positioned globally to take on the responsibilities outlined by Kindleberger, it is quite another to possess the domestic institutional means to do so. At minimum, the hegemon's domes-

---

[18] Charles A. Kindleberger, *The World in Depression, 1929–1939*, 2d ed. (Berkeley: University of California Press, 1986); Stephen D. Krasner, "State Power and the Structure of International Trade," *World Politics* 28 (April 1976): 317–47.

[19] Kindleberger, *World in Depression*.

[20] Ibid., p. 305.

[21] For a very good discussion, see David A. Lake, "Leadership, Hegemony, and the International Economy: Naked Emperor or Tattered Monarch with Potential?" *International Studies Quarterly* 37 (1993): 459–89.

tic currency must possess the qualities required of an international medium of exchange and store of value, if it is to serve as a focal point for exchange rate management and domestic macroeconomic coordination (Kindleberger's fourth and fifth functions). Moreover, domestic financial markets must maintain sufficient liquidity to perform Kindleberger's second and third requirements (as well as his first, since, as David Lake observes, a market for distress goods is a form of short-term financing).[22] Finally, the dominant nation needs an official agency with the power and legitimacy to act on behalf of the entire nation in international monetary affairs. These capabilities do not arise naturally or automatically from international forces. They are, instead, a function of domestic institutional and policy choices. In this sense, the value of this book lies in the fact that it provides a causal mechanism by which a nascent hegemonic power adjusted its internal institutions in accordance with its rising international position.

At the core of this mechanism bridging the international and domestic environments are rational, maximizing individuals. Rational behavior and methodological individualism are assumptions that lie at the heart of the rational choice paradigm, an expanding research program that yields insights into the sources of economic, political, and institutional outcomes.[23] Scholars interested in explaining domestic responses to foreign stimuli add the notion that self-interested individuals must also anticipate and respond to international pressures and opportunities deriving from conditions of global interdependence.[24] These pressures affect individuals unevenly, with repercussions for politics and political outcomes. Recent work shows that economic theory (trade theory, open economy macroeconomics) can provide a systematic basis for determining individual-level preferences, or the stakes involved in foreign economic policy.[25] Continuing in this vein, I employ international currency economics to extrapolate the stakes involved in the production of international money.

Determining the preferences of individuals is but the first step in the analysis of discrete changes in policies and institutions. Whenever individual goals must be sanctioned by institutions of collective choice (political institutions) to be realized, organization in support of such goals is

---

[22] Ibid., pp. 462–63.
[23] For overviews, see James E. Alt and Kenneth A. Shepsle, eds., *Perspectives on Positive Political Economy* (Cambridge: Cambridge University Press, 1990); and Kenneth A. Shepsle and Barry R. Weingast, "Positive Theories of Congressional Institutions," *Legislative Studies Quarterly* 19 (May 1994): 149–79.
[24] Peter Gourevitch, "The Second Image Reversed," *International Organization* 32 (Autumn 1978): 881–912.
[25] For an overview, see James E. Alt and Michael Gilligan, "The Political Economy of Trading States," *Journal of Political Philosophy* 2 (1994): 165–92.

necessary. Hence, it is necessary to know something about the individuals who will organize to act politically in support of these goals. Collective action cannot simply be assumed on the basis of common interests. Political action by groups is problematic, because it aims to produce collective goods—benefits that are often difficult to exclude from noncontributing members. Moreover, the suboptimal provision of the collective good is always a possibility because there are transaction costs involved—the costs of negotiating an agreement with other group members, bargaining over the distribution of the burden, monitoring group members to ensure they perform to the agreement, and punishing cheaters. The theory of collective action, however, is sufficiently well developed so as to allow a basis for predicting the likelihood of organized action. Group size, asymmetries among group members, the existence of organizational structures, and the possibility of offering (or denying) private benefits to noncontributors, compose a short list of the relevant factors.

Plan of the Book

The book's structure flows from my main objectives. First, I want to show that students of the Federal Reserve System have not paid enough attention to the role of international factors in explaining its creation. Chapter 1 thus provides the necessary background on the Federal Reserve Act and assesses alternative explanations and historiographic debates about its origins. A core purpose is to position the Act against the previous institutional baseline, so as to be specific about the difference to be explained. Quantitative and qualitative data profile the characteristics of the two regimes, the main empirical point being that the new regime contained innovations that were either explicitly, or indirectly, international in terms of function or objective.

Second, I endeavor to fill remaining gaps in the academic literature on the financial component of the global rise of the United States early in this century, and to develop theoretical arguments concerning the *domestic* institutional side of international economic leadership and the construction of hegemony. These issues are addressed in Chapters 2 and 3, which jointly compose the analytical heart of the study. Chapter 2 derives the domestic prerequisites of an international currency from economics, and specifies how social actors will align on these arrangements. Chapter 3 adds dynamism by positing a causal link between a nation's relative international position and domestic institutional change. Combining the two analyses yields the expectation that advances (and declines) in the international economic position of a nation, in areas relevant to international currency use, should be reflected in the political demands of previously identified social agents for (or against) the internationalization of the local currency.

Chapter 4 evaluates the link between the onset of payments system reform in the United States and change in the nation's international position, and thereby speaks to the general nature of the relationship between the international and domestic spheres. As expected, the social agents that stood to gain directly from the attainment of international currency status—money-center bankers and manufacturing exporters—were the most responsive. As revealed in their private and public papers, these actors understood the potential international change created for the dollar, and for New York City as a global banking center. As revealed in their intellectual, organizational, and lobbying efforts, these agents took the lead in designing and advancing payments system reforms consistent with the external signals. Moreover, they were aware of the fact that establishing the prerequisites of international money had complementary domestic benefits, which supports the joint products interpretation of the Federal Reserve Act.

Chapter 5 relaxes the assumption of zero organizational costs *within* the international currency coalition, and examines the relationship between the magnitude of these costs and the structure of political institutions. This approach is necessary, because (1) coalition lobbying is itself a public good for individual members, subject to the general constraints of collective action, and (2) the structure of collective choice institutions, with authoritative jurisdiction over policy, shapes collective action. I argue that the global currency coalition was "privileged" by the existence of a single dominant actor—the New York financial community—willing to shoulder a disproportionate share of the costs of the political campaign. Even as bank reform moved from the relatively closed committee setting to the majoritarian floor of Congress, where mass-based support was needed, New York banks absorbed the rising costs. They compromised with organized rivals, spreading the benefits more widely. They transformed their clearinghouse associations to coordinate the political effort, to enforce compliance among the wider set of beneficiaries, and to punish free-riders. And they founded an expensive nationwide public relations organization for the purpose of mobilizing a larger coalition.

My final objective is to evaluate the wider explanatory power of the joint products approach, by applying it to the formation of other central banks that produced collective goods. Chapter 6 adds the Bank of England and the First and Second Banks of the United States to the set of cases. The jumping-off point is the public goods rationale advanced recently in the literature.[26] I demonstrate, however, that private goods were also involved, and played a critical role in the origins of these institutions. Though the specific public and private goods were quite distinct from those involved in the founding of the Federal Reserve, the processes of institutional formation followed the same logic: institutions that promoted social efficiency were derivative of the private objectives of select members of the community.

The conclusion summarizes the findings, looks briefly at the Federal Reserve's early performance in respect to its multiple objectives, and further explores the analytical implications of the study.

[26] Douglass C. North and Barry R. Weingast, "Constitutions and Commitment: The Institutions Governing Public Choice in Seventeenth-Century England," *Journal of Economic History* 49 (December 1989); Philip T. Hoffman and Kathryn Norberg, eds., *Fiscal Crises, Liberty, and Representative Government, 1450–1789* (Stanford: Stanford University Press, 1994).

1 /

The Federal Reserve Act: Content and Contending Explanations

He pre-1913 financial regime is the baseline against which the Federal Reserve Act should be evaluated. Studies of institutional change that neglect the structural anteced-ents, or focus on a particular segment of a complex domain of interac-tions, run the risk of arbitrarily or imprecisely measuring the difference being considered. In this chapter, I position the Federal Reserve Act against existing rules and practices so as to identify what actually changed in 1913. I identify the structures that were important to the new regime by carefully separating radical institutional departures from minor rule modifications, as well as by isolating the features of the financial order that remained unaffected by the law. The chapter, however, is not merely descriptive. To enliven the exercise in institutional archaeology, I also evaluate existing causal arguments on the origins of the Federal Reserve Act. Conjoining descriptive analysis with the explanatory literature in this way produces joint benefits: rival arguments can be evaluated against institutional outcomes, yielding information on both.

Explanations designating the Federal Reserve's functional purposes—economic or political—should at minimum "fit" the institutional results. If the Act was a cartelization measure designed to insulate Wall Street bankers from competition, as some have proposed, then a second-order test would be evidence that the new law contained higher barriers to entry in banking than its predecessor.[1] Better still would be first-order

[1] Gabriel Kolko, *The Triumph of Conservatism* (New York: Free Press, 1963); Murray N. Roth-

17

evidence of a functional "feedback loop," wherein the processes of institutional change are tied in a systematic and intentional way to the functions specified in the argument.[2] If the Act was necessary to the corporate-capitalist mode of production, as James Livingston maintains, its existence cannot be accounted for simply on these grounds alone.[3] As Jon Elster points out, almost any social outcome can be rationalized by arguing that it serves either the interests of the capitalist class or capitalist institutions, thus making it difficult, if not impossible, to refute such claims.[4] Without solid microfoundations specifying the causal mechanisms whereby the intentional maximizing behavior of individuals is sufficient to yield predictable outcomes, including configurations of institutions, functional analysis will remain deficient.

The arguments assessed below differ in the explanatory role given to particular financial market arrangements, as well as to the weight of economic (efficiency) versus political (redistributive) factors in the rise of the Fed. Few, however, meet the criteria of effective functional analysis. Some fail to address critical elements of regime change directly, while others do not sufficiently specify the causal relationships involved. These shortcomings, I argue, result from the focus on *domestic* political-economic factors—a narrowness which leaves an uneasy fit between the arguments, the new regime of the Federal Reserve Act, and the mechanisms by which it was produced.

An Economic Equilibrium?

The most widely held view rationalizes the Federal Reserve Act as being necessary to offset domestic market failures that would otherwise plague the banking industry. This neoclassical story begins with the high incidence of banking panics and seasonal credit pressures that plagued the Federal Reserve System's predecessor, the National Banking System.[5]

---

bard, "The Federal Reserve as a Cartelization Device," in *Money in Crisis: The Federal Reserve, the Economy, and Monetary Reform*, ed. Barry N. Siegel (San Francisco: Pacific Institute for Public Policy Research, 1984).
[2] Arthur Stinchcombe, *Constructing Social Theories* (New York: Harcourt, Brace and World, 1968).
[3] James Livingston, *Origins of the Federal Reserve System: Money, Class, and Corporate Capitalism, 1890–1913* (Ithaca: Cornell University Press, 1986).
[4] Jon Elster, "Marxism, Functionalism, and Game Theory: The Case for Methodological Individualism," *Theory and Society* 11 (July 1982): 453–82.
[5] For analyses of panics in this period, see Charles W. Calomiris and Gary Gorton, "The Origins of Banking Panics: Models, Facts, and Bank Regulation," in *Financial Markets and Financial Crises*, ed. R. Glenn Hubbard (Chicago: University of Chicago Press, 1991); Jeffrey

The era began with the National Banking Acts of 1863 and 1864, and ended with the opening of the Federal Reserve Banks in 1914. Because small, isolated events such as a run on a single bank frequently triggered full-fledged panics, the logic is that the Fed was established to stabilize the fractional reserve banking system by acting as a lender of last resort. In other words, the Fed represented an "economic equilibrium" in which the government acted in neoclassical terms to provide the nation with the public good of financial stability, a good which the market had left underprovided.

Recent scholarship casts doubt on this interpretation and its more general premise that fractional reserve banking is inherently unstable. The market-failure logic is based on the special features of fractional reserve banking that supposedly set it apart from other industries; namely, the bulk of bank liabilities (deposits) are payable on demand, while bank assets (loans) are of longer duration. Borrowing short and lending long creates a maturities transformation (liquidity) problem wherein banks cannot repay depositors if they all ask for their money back simultaneously—unless banks can convert their sound assets into cash.[6] For a run confined to a single bank, this is not a problem since it can convert its assets into cash by borrowing from other banks on the collateral of its sound assets. Contagion, however, is possible since depositors are poorly informed about the condition of other banks: depositors *en masse* rush to make withdrawals from solvent banks as well as insolvent banks, because they have difficulty distinguishing between the two. Due to this informational problem, some outside source of liquidity is necessary, and "a central bank with the power to create outside money is potentially such a source."[7] Otherwise, banks are forced to curtail lending and suspend payments, an outcome that is socially suboptimal because the disruption in financial services reduces economic activity and increases business failures and unemployment.

Economists differ with respect to the process by which financial disturbances are transmitted to the real economy. In the monetarist view,

---

A. Miron, "Financial Panics, the Seasonality of the Nominal Interest Rate, and the Founding of the Fed," *American Economic Review* 76 (March 1986): 125–38; and George Kaufman, "Bank Contagion: A Review of the Theory and Evidence," *Journal of Financial Services Research* 8 (April 1994): 123–50.
[6] Douglas W. Diamond and Philip H. Dybvig, "Bank Runs, Deposit Insurance, and Liquidity," *Journal of Political Economy* 91 (June 1983): 401–19; Milton Friedman and Anna J. Schwartz, "Has Government Any Role in Money?" *Journal of Monetary Economics* 17 (1986); Milton Friedman, "Should There Be an Independent Monetary Authority?" in *In Search of a Monetary Constitution*, ed. Leland B. Yeager (Cambridge: Harvard University Press, 1962), pp. 219–43.
[7] Friedman and Schwartz, "Has Government Any Role in Money?" p. 55.

financial shocks influence real economic activity through changes on the liability side of the banking system's balance sheet. That is, changes in bank deposits impinge on aggregate spending, directly and indirectly, through changing interest rates and changes in the quantity of money. The alternative "credit rationing" view focuses on the asset side of the balance sheet, and the determinants of real fluctuations are changes in bank loans and other credit instruments.[8]

Either way, a paradox arises: the coexistence of optimal fractional reserve (debt) contracts and suboptimal banking panics. There is a large literature addressing the paradox,[9] but these efforts have foundered on the historical fact that not all banking systems offering the same debt contract have suffered banking panics.[10] Research shows that some countries with fractional reserve banking have been panic-free, and that "banking panics are not inherent in banking contracts—institutional structure matters."[11] Here "institutional structure" denotes the legal and economic framework within which banks operate, and the finding is that some frameworks clearly promote stability while others tempt panics. The Canadian experience is extremely relevant. Without a central bank, but with a nationwide system of branches, Canadian banks localized individual bank runs, thus containing the contagion problem.[12] The relevant implication is that, if existing regulations and structures were the cause of American financial instability, then the standard economic rationale for the Federal Reserve Act lacks intrinsic merit.

"Free banking" scholars have been at the forefront of the movement analyzing the destabilizing affects of government regulations in American banking. Free bankers presuppose complete laissez faire in banking, which means at minimum the absence of any central monetary authority

---

[8] See, respectively, Milton Friedman and Anna J. Schwartz, *A Monetary History of the United States, 1867–1960* (Princeton: Princeton University Press, 1963); and Joseph Stiglitz and Andrew Weiss, "Credit Rationing in Markets with Imperfect Information," *American Economic Review* 71 (June 1981): 393–410. For a test, see Michael D. Bordo, Peter Rappoport, and Anna J. Schwartz, "Money versus Credit Rationing: Evidence for the National Banking Era, 1880–1914," in *Strategic Forces in Nineteenth-Century American Economic History*, ed. Claudia Goldin and Hugh Rockoff (Chicago: University of Chicago Press, 1992), pp. 189–224.
[9] For a survey, see Calomiris and Gorton, "The Origins of Banking Panics."
[10] Michael D. Bordo, "Financial Crises, Banking Crises, Stock Market Crashes, and the Money Supply: Some International Evidence, 1870–1933," in *Financial Crises and the World Banking System*, ed. Forrest Capie and Geoffrey E. Wood (London: Macmillan, 1986), pp. 190–248.
[11] Calomiris and Gorton, "The Origins of Banking Panics," p. 110.
[12] Stephen D. Williamson, "Bank Failures, Financial Restrictions, and Aggregate Fluctuations: Canada and the United States, 1870–1913," *Federal Reserve Bank of Minneapolis Quarterly Review* 13 (Summer 1989): 20–40.

and the issuance of notes and deposits by private competing banks.[13] Their central conclusion is that there was nothing inevitable about the creation of the Fed. The panoply of welfare-reducing externalities that supposedly "explain" the rise of a central bank were, in fact, the direct consequence of public intervention during the National Banking period: "Were an evil dictator to set out purposefully to weaken a fractional reserve banking system and to increase its dependence upon a lender of last resort, he would (1) increase the risk exposure of individual banks to enhance the prospects of insolvency; (2) create an environment conducive to 'spillover' or 'contagion' effects, so that individual bank failures can lead to systemwide runs; and (3) obstruct private-market mechanisms for averting crises. Banking regulations in the United States . . . have unintentionally done all three things."[14]

Bank branching restrictions, bond-collateral restrictions on currency issue, and the legal reserve system for national banks were the main sources of "political market failure" in the United States. Section 8 of the National Banking Act of 1864 required that a national bank's "usual business be transacted at an office or banking house located in the place specified in its organization certificate," which federal regulatory authorities interpreted to mean a prohibition on branch banking.[15] State banking regulators were also generally hostile to branching for banks within their jurisdictions. This meant that the rising demand for banking services was filled by the establishment of new banks, rather than by existing banks opening new offices. Legal restrictions on interstate and intrastate branch banking thus explains the large number of "unit" (single-office) banks in existence, which in many cases approximated local monopolies. Many rural communities became one-bank towns, and banks in these areas could and did charge monopoly loan rates.[16]

Figure 1.1 shows the rapid growth of the unit banking system engendered by anti-branching laws and the relative importance of national banks, state banks, and trust companies in this system.[17] In terms of relative size, national banks (and trust companies) were generally larger

[13] The leading papers are collected in Lawrence H. White, ed., *Free Banking*, 3 vols. (Aldershot, England: Edward Elgar, 1993). For a critique, see Charles Goodhart, *The Evolution of Central Banks* (Cambridge: MIT Press, 1988).
[14] George A. Selgin, "Legal Restrictions, Financial Weakening, and the Lender of Last Resort," *Cato Journal* 9 (Fall 1989): 430.
[15] Cited in Eugene N. White, *The Regulation and Reform of the American Banking System, 1900–1929* (Princeton: Princeton University Press, 1983), p. 14.
[16] Richard Sylla, "Federal Policy, Banking Market Structure, and Capital Mobilization in the United States, 1863–1913," *Journal of Economic History* 29 (December 1969): 657–86.
[17] Trust companies are discussed below.

Figure *1.1.* Number of national banks, state banks, and trust companies, 1862–1913

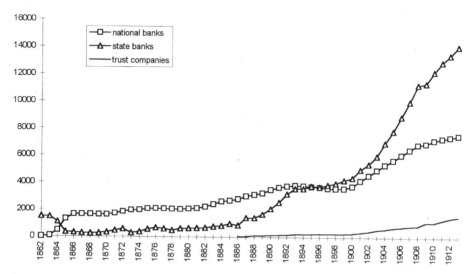

Sources: U.S. Department of Commerce, *Historical Statistics of the United States: Colonial Times to 1970* (Washington, D.C.: GPO, 1975), pp. 1024–31; U.S. Department of the Treasury, *Annual Report of the Comptroller of the Currency* (Washington, D.C.: GPO, various years).

than state "banklets," as shown in Figure 1.2. Between 1865 and 1874, national banks were in clear ascendance, due to fact that the federal government imposed a 10 percent tax on the bank-note issues of state banks in 1865. The levy was an attempt to "tax state banks out of existence," but by 1874, the more modern bank liability—deposits—had supplanted note issue, reducing the effective pressure of the tax on banks' choice of charters. Henceforth, banks were free to select their chartering agency— federal or state—according to the relative restrictiveness of the regulatory rules. After 1874, the number of state banks and trust companies rose more quickly than that of national banks, because states almost universally offered "easier" regulatory terms (e.g., lower capital, reserve, and investment requirements), which meant higher profits for banks.[18] This was particularly true for smaller banks in marginal, largely agricultural markets.

In addition to producing thousands of banks, restrictions on branch banking also affected the stability of the payments system. Branching prohibitions meant that banks were vulnerable to community-specific variation in the demand for currency and could not freely diversify this

---

[18] White, *Regulation and Reform of the American Banking System*, pp. 10–62.

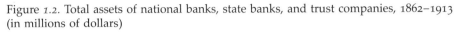

Figure *1.2*. Total assets of national banks, state banks, and trust companies, 1862–1913 (in millions of dollars)

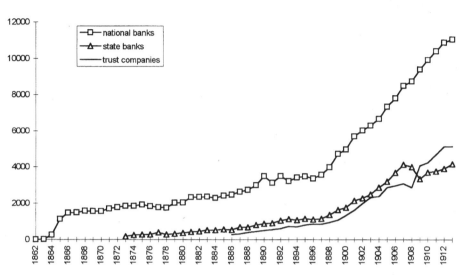

Sources: U.S. Department of Commerce, *Historical Statistics of the United States: Colonial Times to 1970* (Washington, D.C.: GPO, 1975), pp. 1024–31; U.S. Department of the Treasury, *Annual Report of the Comptroller of the Currency* (Washington, D.C.: GPO, various years).

risk by issuing deposits directly in other communities. If branching had been allowed, banks could have shifted reserves flexibly to those branches with the greatest demand for cash.[19] Anti-branching laws thus prevented banks from diversifying their liabilities (and assets) to reduce the risks associated with sudden changes in the public's deposit-to-currency ratio, making panics more likely. Indeed, Eugene White argues the counterfactual case that a system of nationwide branch banking modeled after the Canadian system would have been superior to the Fed as a path to stability.[20]

In Canada, where there were no restrictions on branching, the banking system was characterized by a small number of large banks (roughly 40 in the late nineteenth century, falling to 10 in 1929), each with many

[19] V. V. Chari, "Banking without Deposit Insurance or Bank Panics: Lessons from a Model of the U.S. National Banking System," *Federal Reserve Bank of Minneapolis Quarterly Review* 13 (Summer 1989): 3–19.

[20] White, *Regulation and Reform of the American Banking System.* For supporting evidence, see Charles W. Calomiris, "Regulation, Industrial Structure, and Instability in U.S. Banking: An Historical Perspective," in *Structural Change in Banking,* ed. Michael Klausner and Lawrence J. White (Homewood, Ill.: Business One Irwin, 1993), pp. 19–116.

branches. Without a central bank until 1935, Canada did not have a problem with panics, as runs on individual banks were contained. Canada experienced no banking panics after the 1830s, nor did Canada suffer a financial crisis during the Great Depression, even though its economic downturn was no less severe than that of the United States.[21] Furthermore, comparison with the United States indicates that the Canadian public did not suffer disproportionately from the oligopolistic structure of the Canadian system—stability did not come at the expense of nonprice competition, collusive rate setting, and other cartel-like behavior: "There is no evidence that cartel behavior among Canadian banks created gross differences in lending rates or other measures of bank behavior that would imply that Canada paid a high price for the stability it enjoyed relative to the United States."[22]

While branch banking may have been superior to the Fed as a stabilizing institution in a purely economic sense, it was a tough sell politically. Opposition in the United States has always come from smaller unit banks, which have an interest in preserving the regulations that protect them from head-to-head competition with larger, more efficient money-center banks. White analyzes the politics of branching through a collective action lens and concludes that the origins and persistence of anti-branching laws derived from the organizational and coalitional advantages which unit banks held over a divided and diffuse pro-branching lobby.[23] Charles Calomiris adds elements of the political structure to the explanation: "The protection of local interests ensured by federalism . . . gives disproportionate weight to regionally concentrated minorities, and the legal precedents established by the Supreme Court [not extending constitutional protection to banking as an activity involving interstate commerce] gives states great latitude in the chartering of banks."[24]

On the demand side, I would add that unit banks are not alone among the rural actors favoring unit banking rules; an anti-branching *coalition* is possible. Unit banks can rally support from local residents (farmers and businessmen) who might rationally fear having their finances controlled

[21] Canadian banks cooperated through the Canadian Bankers' Association to produce an informal lender-of-last-resort safety net to control the spread of bank runs. Williamson, "Bank Failures, Financial Restrictions, and Aggregate Fluctuations."

[22] Michael D. Bordo, Hugh Rockoff, and Angela Redish, "The U.S. Banking System from a Northern Exposure: Stability versus Efficiency," *Journal of Economic History* 54 (June 1994): 339. See also Michael D. Bordo, Angela Redish, and Hugh Rockoff, "A Comparison of the Stability and Efficiency of the Canadian and American Banking Systems, 1870–1925," *Financial History Review* (forthcoming).

[23] Eugene N. White, "The Political Economy of Banking Regulation, 1864–1933," *Journal of Economic History* 42 (March 1982).

[24] Calomiris, "Regulation, Industrial Structure, and Instability in U.S. Banking," pp. 90–91.

by a distant bank. Although bank customers in a community with a unit bank might pay monopoly loan rates, they also have better chances of securing credit from a local bank than from a branch of a money-center bank, should their city or town suffer a downward revision in expectations regarding the profitability of investments there. Say, for example, the terms of trade in agricultural activities are expected to decline over the long-term. If branching is allowed, farmers and farm-related businesses could expect their credit to be sharply curtailed, as branches of banks in rural communities head for marginally "greener pastures." A unit bank, on the other hand, has little choice but to go on lending to farmers and local firms, presumably even on reduced collateral. Indeed, Calomiris considers unit banking a form of "loan insurance" for local residents and thereby implies the coalitional basis of support for the restriction.[25]

In any case, the strength of the anti-branching lobby might suggest the logic of a "second-best" political argument for the founding of the Fed. If the political costs of removing the legal restrictions on branching were prohibitive, then the rise of the Fed might be explained according to some kind of political default logic. Such an argument is problematic for two reasons. First, legislating central banking was no cakewalk either, given the strong sentiment of the day against Wall Street and the popular opposition to financial centralization of any kind. As late as 1913, politicians could still rally constituents with the populist dictum: "Our people have set their faces like steel against a central bank."[26] Moreover, the nation had twice previously experimented with central banking, and in both cases, had rejected the institution (see Chapter 6). Secondly, there were other stability-enhancing alternatives available to policymakers, alternatives that could have been attained without threatening the unit banking system. Existing restrictions on the issue of bank currency, rules governing bank reserves, and extending *private* lender-of-last-resort arrangements are the salient examples.

Legal restrictions on the issue of banknotes were another source of instability under the National Banking System. Banks were required to purchase government bonds in the open market and to deposit them with the treasury in exchange for bank notes equal to 90 percent of the value of the bonds (raised to 100 percent in 1900). The practice was a Civil War measure designed to enhance the demand for government debt. This bond-collateral provision meant that the amount of bank cur-

[25] Ibid., p. 83.
[26] U.S. Congress, Congressman Everis Hayes of California, 63d Cong., 1st sess., *Congressional Record* 50 (1913), pt. 5: 4655.

rency in circulation tended to vary with the price of government bonds, rather than with the demand for currency. As a result, banks could not easily satisfy shifts in the public's ratio of deposits to currency. For example, when bonds went to premiums of up to 40 percent after 1880, as a result of the government's policy of eliminating its budget surplus by purchasing and retiring outstanding debt, the profitability of issuing notes was sharply reduced. Under these conditions, banks would have had to give up 40 percent more in lawful money (greenbacks, Treasury notes, specie, etc.), than they would receive in national bank notes, meaning that the money supply would actually *contract* by 40 percent due to the premium.[27] This was the antithesis of what was needed in a panic. Moreover, there were burdensome delays imposed by the treasury when it approved and shipped out currency—delays (of thirty days or more) that were most binding when the demand for currency was greatest and the state of panic most acute.[28]

In addition to panics, the resulting inelasticity of bank currency also created seasonal problems in the money market, which tended to coincide with the timing of panics.[29] Demand for currency and credit reached seasonal peaks in the fall and spring, owing to the annual agricultural cycle, and it was during these periods that spikes in nominal interest rates usually occurred. High seasonal withdrawals and low reserve-to-deposit ratios, while not the cause of banking panics, certainly left the banking system more vulnerable. Jeffrey Miron argues that an important justification for establishing the Fed was to eliminate this destabilizing annual pattern of interest rate fluctuations.[30] However, the Fed cannot be seen as a necessary or unique solution, since legal restrictions were a major cause of such seasonality in the first place. The harvest season drain on currency and reserves may well have led to interest rate fluctuations, but shifts in the currency-to-deposit ratio would have posed no

---

[27] Phillip Cagan, *Determinants and Effects of Changes in the Money Stock, 1875–1960* (New York: National Bureau of Economic Research, 1965); John A. James, "The Conundrum of the Low Issue of National Bank Notes," *Journal of Political Economy* 84 (April 1976): 362–67; Charles Goodhart, "Profit on National Bank Notes, 1900–1913," *Journal of Political Economy* 73 (October 1965): 516–22.

[28] Friedman and Schwartz, *A Monetary History of the United States*, p. 169; Steven Horowitz, "Competitive Currencies, Legal Restrictions, and the Origins of the Fed: Some Evidence from the Panic of 1907," *Southern Economic Journal* 56 (January 1990).

[29] Miron, "Financial Panics." See also Barry Eichengreen, "Currency and Credit in the Gilded Age," in *Technique, Spirit and Form in the Making of Modern Economies*, ed. Gary Saxonhouse and Gavin Wright (New York: JAI Press, 1984), pp. 87–114; and Edwin W. Kemmerer, *Seasonal Variations in the Relative Demand for Money and Capital in the United States* (Washington, D.C.: GPO, 1910).

[30] Miron, "Financial Panics."

problem if banks had been unrestricted in their ability to issue notes. George Selgin explains:

> When banks are unrestricted in their ability to issue bank notes, each institution can meet increases in its clients' demands for currency without difficulty and without affecting its liquidity or solvency. . . . The supply of currency is flexible under unrestricted note issue because bank note liabilities are, for a bank capable of issuing them, not significantly different than deposit liabilities. . . . The issue of notes in exchange for deposits merely involves offsetting adjustments on the liability side of the bank's balance sheet, with no change on the asset side.[31]

Further deregulation of note issue was thus a potential alternative to the Federal Reserve Act, as a way to smooth out seasonal interest rate movements and address the broader inelasticity problem.[32] If national banks had been given the freedom to issue currency unconstrained by bond collateral requirements, then their own profit-maximizing behavior would have led to an elastic currency.[33]

Legal reserve requirements were another source of trouble, since they helped create an unstable, inverted "pyramid of reserves" that was susceptible to breakdown during seasonal and panic demands for liquidity.[34] National banks were divided into three reserve classes: non-reserve "country" banks, "reserve-city" banks, and "central-reserve-city" banks. Country banks in the hinterlands were required to hold a 15 percent reserve against their deposit liabilities. Of this, three-fifths could be held as deposits in reserve-city banks, which typically paid interest. In turn, reserve-city banks, located in eighteen designated cities, had to maintain reserves equal to 25 percent of deposit liabilities, half of which could be held as interest-earning deposits in central-reserve-city banks, primarily New York City banks.[35] Partly as a result of this set-up, thou-

---

[31] George A. Selgin, *The Theory of Free Banking: Money Supply under Competitive Note Issue* (Totowa: Rowman and Littlefield, 1988), pp. 220, 226.

[32] Horowitz, "Competitive Currencies, Legal Restrictions, and the Origins of the Fed." For a skeptical view, see Calomiris, "Regulation, Industrial Structure, and Instability in U.S. Banking," pp. 34–36.

[33] Benjamin Klein, "The Competitive Supply of Money," *Journal of Money, Credit, and Banking* 5 (1974): 423–453; Lawrence H. White, "What Kinds of Monetary Institutions Would a Free Market Deliver?" *Cato Journal* 9 (Fall 1989): 367–91.

[34] The United States was the only major country in the world at this time to have legal reserve requirements. This is significant because minimum reserve requirements actually made it almost impossible for banks to use those reserves for redemption purposes. The intent was to ensure bank liquidity, but the opposite result was achieved since only reserves in *excess* of the minimum could be used to meet deposit withdrawals.

[35] Chicago and St. Louis were reclassified as central reserve cities in 1887. A good discus-

sands of unit banks throughout the country found it profitable to hold their legal reserves, as well as their excess or secondary reserves, in New York.[36]

At the pinnacle of the system were the large national banks of New York City, which held the nation's ultimate reserves and were expected to serve as lenders of last resort. The fact that central reserve city banks paid interest on correspondent balances meant that these banks invested these "reserves" in order to turn a profit. Their investment options, however, were constrained by the absence of a discount market such as existed in London (see below). Lacking the option of investing in highly liquid bills of exchange and bankers' acceptances, New York banks were compelled to employ their resources on the stock exchange "call loan market." Here, banks lent to stockbrokers and securities houses on call, meaning the loans were payable on demand, with stocks and bonds serving as collateral. The practice tied the money market to the capital market in ways that were destabilizing to both. When country and reserve city banks recalled some or all of their correspondent deposits due to demands for moving the crops or during a panic, New York banks were forced to meet the withdrawals by demanding payment on outstanding call loans. Although security loans are callable by a single bank, they cannot be called by all banks at the same time without producing a severe fall in stock values. "Consequently, a decline in bankers' balances produced a decline in reserves and a suspension of payments of New York banks was often the result."[37] The reserve system was consequently less able to withstand any increased demand for currency relative to demand deposits. Had the unit banks of the nation not been encouraged by reserve regulations to pyramid reserves as deposits in New York, they would have been better equipped to manage their own reserves and satisfy directly the seasonal and extraordinary demands for cash. New York banks, in turn, would have had little reason to invest funds in call loans.

Proponents of free banking also claim that, in spite of legal rules that served to concentrate reserves and currency demands in New York, the private market was capable of innovating institutional responses to the contagion problem, thereby precluding the need for a central bank for this purpose. A case in point are the lender-of-last-resort services of the clearinghouse associations. As mentioned above, New York sat at the

---

sion of reserve pyramiding is found in Richard F. Bensel, *Yankee Leviathan: The Origins of Central State Authority in America, 1859–1877* (New York: Cambridge University Press, 1990).
[36] John A. James, *Money and Capital Markets in Postbellum America* (Princeton: Princeton University Press, 1978), pp. 237–43; Richard Sylla, *The American Capital Market, 1846–1914* (New York: Arno Press, 1975); Leonard L. Watkins, *Bankers' Balances* (Chicago: A. W. Shaw, 1929).
[37] James, *Money and Capital Markets*, p. 118.

hub of the correspondent banking system and was expected to perform lender-of-last-resort services for the thousands of banks holding deposits there. The city's clearinghouse association, originally established to facilitate the settlement of interbank accounts, evolved in Coasian fashion in this direction.[38] In effect, the clearinghouse provided private mechanisms for coordinating reserve-center bank responses to panics. During panics, clearinghouses discounted bank assets for clearinghouse "loan certificates," thereby creating a market of last resort for illiquid bank assets. Member banks used these certificates in the clearing process in place of currency, thus freeing currency for payment of depositors' claims. In addition, small denomination certificates were issued directly to depositors and functioned as hand-to-hand currency. Since clearinghouse liabilities were liabilities of the association as a whole, depositors were insured against the failure of their individual banks. The risk-pooling arrangement imparted stabilizing expectations in the market.

The clearinghouse loan certificate system was successful in preventing some disruptions from developing into full-fledged panics (e.g., 1884 and 1890), but, in other cases, the issue of loan certificates was either too late or of insufficient quantity to reassure bank depositors (e.g., 1873, 1893, 1907).[39] The fact that the clearinghouse system failed to prevent all panics compels some analysts to challenge the laissez-faire argument on this point.[40] Charles Goodhart argues that conflicts of interest between banks can undermine the reliability of private quasi-central banking efforts: "Relationships between keen competitors are always subject to pressure, and the diversity of interest among the competing banks is liable to limit support to its lowest common denominator. It is *leadership*, rather than the direct financial assistance, provided by the Central Bank that has proved crucial."[41] The logic concerning interbank cooperation is quite valid. Serious coordination problems among banks arise in monitoring, regulating, and enforcing a private institutional arrangement for risk-pooling, and free-riding may limit individual bank contributions to the common safety net, resulting in suboptimal provision of the service. But there is no necessary reason why a central bank is required to solve the coordination problem. Other mechanisms for monitoring and en-

[38] Gary Gorton and Donald J. Mullineaux, "The Joint Production of Confidence: Endogenous Regulation and Nineteenth-Century Commercial Bank Clearinghouses," *Journal of Money, Credit, and Banking* 19 (November 1987): 457–68; Gary Gorton, "Clearinghouses and the Origin of Central Banking in the United States," *Journal of Economic History* 45 (June 1985): 277–84; Richard H. Timberlake Jr., "The Central Banking Role of the Clearinghouse Associations," *Journal of Money, Credit, and Banking* 16 (February 1984): 1–15.
[39] William Roberds, "Financial Crises and the Payments System: Lessons from the National Banking Era," Federal Reserve Bank of Atlanta *Economic Review* (May/June 1995): 15–31.
[40] Goodhart, *Evolution of Central Banks*.
[41] Ibid., p. 45.

forcement are certainly possible, and the United States did, in fact, innovate such a mechanism with the Aldrich-Vreeland Act of 1908.

The Aldrich-Vreeland Act followed on the heels of the 1907 panic. Its main provision was to legalize the previously illegal clearinghouse crisis activity, as associations of banks were given the authority to issue "emergency" currency on the basis of their normal assets. More importantly, the coordination and commitment problems that potentially undermined the private provision of last-resort credit were dramatically reduced by placing the new associations and their currency issues under the direct administration of a single dominant actor—the secretary of the treasury. Henceforth, the treasury retained the authority to determine which banks gave and received assistance in a crisis. This meant that all sound banks obtained the assurances they needed to work collectively toward their common interests, without the need for a central bank. The arrangement proved its effectiveness the only time it was used—during the war-related crisis of the summer of 1914, just before the Federal Reserve Banks went into operation.[42] Milton Friedman and Anna Schwartz argue that the Aldrich-Vreeland modification of established clearinghouse practice was preferable to the more far-reaching changes brought by the Federal Reserve Act, on the basis of a comparison of the performance of the two systems during the crises of 1914 and 1930.[43]

In summary, economic theory is underdetermining when it comes to the origins of the Federal Reserve. Logic and experience suggest that central banking was one of several regimes which could have been employed to maintain the interconvertibility of deposits and currency in normal and emergency periods. Legalizing branch banking (however difficult politically), liberalizing the restrictions on currency issue, and restructuring clearinghouse arrangements to minimize coordination problems were all economically viable alternatives to the Federal Reserve Act. If the Fed was not a spontaneous development in the evolution of fractional reserve banking in the United States, what was it?

A Political Equilibrium?

If efforts to specify an economic rationale are insufficient, distributional factors may explain the outcome. Previous attempts to identify the "political equilibrium" represented by the Federal Reserve Act, however,

---

[42] Alexander D. Noyes, *The War Period of American Finance* (New York: G. P. Putnam's Sons, 1926), pp. 77–82; Stanley Markowitz, "The Aldrich-Vreeland Bill: Its Significance in the Struggle for Currency Reform" (master's thesis, University of Maryland, 1965).
[43] Friedman and Schwartz, *A Monetary History of the United States*, pp. 170–72.

founder because they fail to make strong logical and empirical connections between the relevant actors, their institutional interests, collective action, and the actual structures of the Federal Reserve System. This problem is particularly acute in the cartelization hypothesis.[44]

The thesis is that rent-seekers pushed for government regulation in order to control entry and competition in the banking industry. The rapid growth of state-chartered banks and trust companies, whose less rigorous capital, reserve, and investment regulations gave them a competitive edge over nationally chartered Wall Street banks, provided the fundamental challenge (Figure 1.1). Yet, while documenting Wall Street's major role in banking reform, supporters of this view fail to sufficiently specify the relationship between this activism and the onset of the Fed. While virtually all scholars, from Lloyd Mints to Robert West, recognize that the reform movement was led by bankers after the panic of 1907, there is scant evidence linking bankers' desire to control entry with the basic institutional features of the Federal Reserve Act.[45] The Act did many important things, but it did *not* disturb the right of banks to choose between state and national charters—the very source of Wall Street's competitive woes.[46] Leveling the regulatory playing field was simply not the primary objective of the Act, nor was it the focus of the lobbying campaign that demanded it. Although national banks were allowed to enter some new fields of business after 1913—the trust business being one example—these were extremely minor rule changes that could have been effected without the massive restructuring entailed in the Federal Reserve Act.

The argument also ignores evidence that the largest and most powerful state-chartered "competitors" of Wall Street were actually owned and operated by Wall Street's national banks themselves. Indeed, the "largest trust companies were directed by the same men who directed the largest National Banks, and the largest industrial and railroad corporations."[47] As John James notes, "One response to the threat posed by the trust

---

[44] Kolko, *Triumph of Conservatism*; Rothbard, "The Federal Reserve as a Cartelization Device."

[45] Lloyd W. Mints, *A History of Banking Theory in Great Britain and the United States* (Chicago: University of Chicago Press, 1945); Robert C. West, *Banking Reform and the Federal Reserve, 1863–1923* (Ithaca: Cornell University Press, 1977).

[46] For several years after 1913, state banks and trust companies almost universally refused to join the Federal Reserve System. White attributes this to the fact that the Fed's main benefit—access to the discount window—could be had by nonmembers in roundabout fashion through the correspondent system. White, *Regulation and Reform of the American Banking System*, p. 134.

[47] Larry Neal, "Trust Companies and Financial Innovation, 1897–1914," *Business History Review* 45 (Spring 1971): 51.

companies was combination, so that it was not uncommon to see a national bank and a trust company operated and controlled by the same stockholders, frequently in the same building."[48] In 1911, for example, J. P. Morgan and Company, First National Bank, the National City Bank, and the [Morgan-controlled] Bankers and Guaranty Trust Companies, held 118 directorships in 34 banks and trust companies with total resources of $2.7 billion.[49] Uncovering this web of interlocking financial relationships was what the "Money Trust" investigations of 1912–13 were all about.[50] That banks innovated around the legal restrictions imposed by their national charters undermines the notion that the Federal Reserve Act was a cartelization device pure and simple. Why then did the institutional preferences of the financial community change? What explains bankers' activism in the reform movement?

In a recent study, James Livingston challenges the relevance of these questions.[51] From a class-analytic framework, Livingston maintains that the central banking movement "was a historical phenomenon that transcended the social and cultural-intellectual limits of an interest group."[52] Livingston links the origins of the Fed to the emergence of the modern corporation and the decline in "competitive-entrepreneurial" capitalism. From the premise that competition in the American economy was declining (contra Kolko) and in the process of being replaced by the corporate form of organization, Livingston argues that the capitalist class as a whole "understood that the point of restructuring the banking system was to validate or stabilize an investment system dominated by and organized around the new industrial corporations."[53] Financial crises arising from the poor organization of the payments system meant not only short-term losses for corporations, but the potential for "economic anarchy and political unrest, if not revolution."[54]

There is much to admire in Livingston's carefully researched study, yet the core logic of the argument is unclear. Much hinges on whether financial instability is more debilitating to a corporate economy (and corporations) than to an economy organized around smaller firms. Livingston assumes that a corporate economy fares much worse, although from an industrial organization perspective, it is quite possible to infer

---

[48] James, *Money and Capital Markets*, p. 40.
[49] Fritz Redlich, *The Molding of American Banking*, vol. 2 (New York: Johnson Reprint Company, 1968), p. 189.
[50] U.S. Congress, House of Representatives, *The Money Trust Investigation before the Subcommittee on Banking and Currency*, 62–63d Cong., 16 May 1912–26 February 1913.
[51] Livingston, *Origins of the Federal Reserve System*.
[52] Ibid., p. 21.
[53] Ibid.
[54] Ibid., p. 27.

just the opposite.[55] Consider an economy composed of many small firms, maintaining few, if any, formal or informal ties with each other. In this setting, a reliable payments system is essential, since the large number of "arm's-length" transactions requires an equally large number of monetary transfers to settle payments. In contrast, in a corporate economy characterized by a small number of very large, vertically or horizontally integrated firms, a large share of these transactions is *internalized* within the firm, reducing the need for money transfers. Market transactions that would otherwise require offsetting money transfers are taken inside the corporation, thereby *reducing* the importance of the payments system, and payments system instability, on the overall economy. Livingston does not address this simple and compelling alternative logic, nor does he supply sufficient reason why the advent of corporations should imply greater concern for the payments system.

Despite the logical leap, Livingston's historical discussion is extremely rich, especially on the issue of who organized to lobby for the Fed. Had he not tried to squeeze this material into a class-analytic framework, my work would have been in some ways redundant. For example, in an apparent effort to synchronize the timing of the reform movement with the rise of corporations (circa 1894), Livingston conflates two distinct and contradictory reform movements that pitted sections of the capitalist class against one another. The first proposal called for *deregulation* along the "real bills" line envisaged by free bankers. It emanated from Chicago in the mid-1890s and sought to replace the government bond-secured note issue with "asset currency," whereby banks would issue bank notes freely on the basis of their commercial assets.[56] The second movement began after the assets currency/branch banking movement had withered (circa 1900), due to opposition from small, rural banks—the usual defenders of unit banking—and Wall Street, which feared incursions into the New York capital market by Chicago-based banks.[57] This new program called for central banking, with the English system as its model and New York bankers as its original champions.

[55] Oliver E. Williamson, *The Economic Institutions of Capitalism* (New York: Free Press, 1985).
[56] George A. Selgin and Lawrence H. White, "Monetary Reform and the Redemption of National Bank Notes, 1863–1913," *Business History Review* 68 (Summer 1994): 205–43; Mints, *A History of Banking Theory.*
[57] "Plans allowing all banks to issue notes were no longer considered. Instead, the tendency was toward some sort of central agency with the power to issue notes and to require member banks to centralize reserves." West, *Banking Reform and the Federal Reserve,* p. 66. See also Robert H. Wiebe, *Businessmen and Reform: A Study of the Progressive Movement* (Cambridge: Harvard University Press, 1962); Robert H. Wiebe, "Business Disunity and the Progressive Movement, 1901–1914," *Mississippi Valley Historical Review* 44 (March 1958): 664–85.

It is true that most prominent spokesmen for asset currency and branch banking ended up joining ranks with the proponents of central banking after about 1910. Yet this union in itself does not necessarily validate the corporate class-consciousness thesis. My view holds that it was an example of coalition-building, where interest groups with *hetero-geneous* preferences on payments reform compromised and made conces-sions with one another, so as to build broader support for reform. The majoritarian nature of political institutions dictated such a strategy. New York could not go it alone in Congress, creating the necessary incentive for spreading the benefits of reform more widely. I leave it to the reader to assess the relative explanatory performance of the two accounts.

Livingston also considers some elements of the international environ-ment that shape my interpretation of the Federal Reserve Act, but these are not central to his thesis.[58] In coming chapters, I take special care to develop the relationship between international economic structure, do-mestic preferences, and payments system reform, specifying the social cleavages that are expected to arise. My subsequent findings do seem to confirm that coalitional patterns broke down along *sectoral* lines, wherein industries having clear stakes in the global economy supported "interna-tionalizing" the domestic financial machinery by way of English-styled institutions, while actors whose interests were primarily domestic op-posed the agenda.

In sum, the literature on the Fed does not generate nonarbitrary solu-tions to the puzzles that surround this case of institutional change. Eco-nomic theory suggests a range of institutional possibilities for maintain-ing the interconvertibility of deposits and currency, but cannot explain the particular choices made in 1913. Politically grounded investigations, in contrast, have tried to make the link between material interests and the legislation, but have either failed to address the Fed's institutional structure directly, or failed to clearly specify the causal relationships in-volved. In the following section, a systematic comparison of the pre- and post-Fed financial regimes elucidates the substantive explanatory issues. The conclusion is that many of the important institutional changes that occurred had an international component that has not been sufficiently recognized.

Continuity and Change

Much of financial structure existing before 1913 remained untouched by the Federal Reserve Act. The "unit" banking system (single-office, as op-

---

[58] Livingston, *Origins of the Federal Reserve* System, pp. 153, 193, 202–3.

posed to branch banking) and the "dual" banking system (banks chartered, regulated, and supervised by both federal and state governments) remained essentially unaffected by the Act. Some minor alterations in national banking laws were made in respect to the competitive relationship between national- and state-chartered banks, but these could have been separately produced without involving the overarching reorganization of the Federal Reserve Act. The significant changes involved the organization, encouragement, and deepening of a modern discount market similar in make-up to those of Europe, the establishment of a central bank discount window, and the vestment of Federal Reserve banks with both domestic and foreign powers—a set of reforms that brought the U.S. payments system up to worldwide standards.

The unit banking system and the dual banking system were largely unaffected by the legislation. The Act did not affect the regulations prohibiting branch banking, nor did it alter the right of banks to arbitrage between state and federal charters.[59] The only chink in the armor of anti-branching statutes came in the form of allowances made for *overseas* branching. Section 25 gave the largest national banks—those with a capital and surplus of $1 million or more—the freedom to set up branches in foreign countries for the "furtherance of the foreign commerce of the United States."

The correspondent banking structure (interior banking markets linked to money-center markets by contractual arrangement), though a focus of concern in the legislation, was not dislodged by the Act. While changes in reserve requirements (see below) were intended to eliminate reserve "pyramiding," which channeled interbank deposits to New York and placed these funds in the hands of stock exchange speculators, the correspondent system and pyramiding persisted after 1913. The new law only required national banks to transfer their legal reserves to Federal Reserve banks, so interior banks remained free to continue holding correspondent balances as before. And though the Federal Reserve banks took over the clearing and collection services performed by the correspondent system and clearinghouses (section 16), interior banks continued to find advantages in dealing with city correspondents after 1913, particularly in regard to the investment services that banks in the financial centers offered.[60]

While these important components of the financial system remained unaltered, other rule changes affected the National Banking System only at the margins. Regulations affecting the competitive position of national

---

[59] The authoritative study is White, *Regulation and Reform of the American Banking System.*
[60] Watkins, *Bankers' Balances*, pp. 245–90, 370–72.

banks vis-à-vis their state-chartered rivals fall into this category. Capital requirements were not changed at all for national banks, even though this was an area in which they were at a clear competitive disadvantage.[61] Reserve requirements, however, were adjusted downward, and national banks were allowed for the first time to separate time and demand deposits and to hold smaller reserves against the former. Separating time deposits was important, because thirty states either did not require reserves to be held against time deposits or set them lower than the national banks' 15 percent rule. There was, however, nothing to stop state regulators from lowering reserve requirements to maintain the competitive equilibrium of the old system. Indeed, by 1915, fifteen states had already lowered reserve requirements in the ongoing game of competitive deregulation.[62]

Portfolio restrictions were also eased a bit. Under section 10 of the Act, national banks could apply for permits to engage in trust banking (that is, to serve as executors and administrators of estates), so as to compete more effectively with trust companies. In addition, section 24 gave national banks outside the central reserve cities the ability to lend on real estate collateral, defined explicitly as "improved and unencumbered farm land," so long as such loans did not exceed 50 percent of the value of the land nor exceed in the aggregate 25 percent of the lending bank's capital and surplus, or one-third of its time deposits. This, too, was an attempt to regain the eminence of national banks, particularly in rural agricultural markets where lending on real estate collateral was an important part of the banking business. Under the old regime, as George Barnett noted, "there is no more characteristic difference between the state banking laws and the national-bank act than the fact that, in almost all States, state banks and trust companies may make loans on the security of real estate, whereas national banks are prohibited from doing so."[63] But like the easing of reserve requirements, there was nothing in these changes that required the *major* institutional innovations stipulated in the Act, to which we now turn.

The major new elements involved the Act's provisions for transforming the commercial paper market into a modern discount market, establishing an official rediscounting mechanism, and vesting the newly-created central bank with domestic and international rediscounting and

[61] White, *Regulation and Reform of the American Banking System*; James, *Money and Capital Markets*; Watkins, *Bankers' Balances*.
[62] White, *Regulation and Reform of the American Banking System*, pp. 142–49.
[63] George Barnett, *State Banks and Trust Companies since the Passage of the National-Bank Act* (Washington, D.C.: GPO, 1911), p. 99.

open-market powers.[64] Moreover, there was a coherence to these innovations suggesting a high degree of interdependence. According to Paul Warburg, a key player in the banking reform movement and one of the original governors of the first Federal Reserve Board: "The central bank system and the discount system cannot be separated; they are absolutely interdependent. The discount system cannot exist without a central bank to which it may resort in case of need and, on the other hand, the central bank cannot exist without an efficient bank rate—that is, without the means of protecting itself and the nation through its powers to influence upward or downward the general interest rates of the country."[65] A brief definitional and descriptive discussion of discounting will set the stage for demonstrating the centrality of these institutions in the new regime.

A "discount" is distinguished from a "loan" in that the interest charge on a discount is taken in advance, whereas the interest charges on a loan are payable at specific intervals and at maturity. That is, with a discount, the investor purchases notes at less than face value and receives the face value at maturity. A discount is generally unsecured, made on the basis of the general creditworthiness of the borrower and/or the borrower's endorsers, while a loan is secured by collateral of some form, such as stocks and bonds, and may be payable on demand (i.e., "call" loans).

Banks and banking houses generally discount two kinds of commercial paper: *single-name* and *double-name* paper. With single-name paper, only the original maker is liable for payment at maturity. There is no second-party endorser, or guarantor, to be held liable should the maker fail to settle the contract at maturity. In effect, single-name paper is a form of unsecured promissory note involving only two parties, the drawer and the bank, with the bank necessarily relying upon the general credit of the drawer for security. Double-name paper, in contrast, is a negotiable bill of exchange involving at least three parties: the drawer, the drawee, and the payee. In this contractual relationship, the drawer commands the drawee to remit a specific sum to the payee (or to the final bearer of the bill) at a specific time in the future; that is, A commands B to pay C a specified sum of money at a certain future time. The drawer (A) is the person who makes out the order and directs the drawee (B) to pay a specific sum to the payee (C) on a certain date. To be legally bound by the agreement, the drawee must stamp the word "Ac-

---

[64] Commercial paper is the summary name for short-term negotiable instruments used and traded in the money market: promissory notes, bills of exchange, and drafts. More details will follow.

[65] Paul M. Warburg, *The Discount System in Europe* (Washington, D.C.: GPO, 1910), reprinted in Warburg, *The Federal Reserve System: Its Origin and Growth*, vol. 2 (New York: Macmillan, 1930), p. 205.

cepted" across the face of the bill and then sign it. By doing so the drawee unconditionally guarantees to pay the face value of the bill at maturity, shielding the payee from default risk. The bill thus becomes known as an *acceptance* and the drawee becomes known as the *acceptor.* This instrument is two-name paper, since it carries the names and legal liability of at least two parties: the drawer and the acceptor.

We also need to distinguish between two types of acceptances—*trade acceptances* and *bankers' acceptances.* A trade acceptance is a bill of exchange drawn by the seller on the purchaser of goods sold, and unconditionally accepted in writing on the face of the bill by the latter. It is a negotiable instrument representing money receivable by the payee for goods sold or services performed. The drawee in this instance is the seller of goods: the seller draws a time bill of exchange (trade acceptance) on the buyer, and can then discount the acceptance at his or her bank to receive cash immediately. When the discount matures, payment to the bank is the primary obligation of the drawer (buyer) and the contingent obligation of the drawee (seller). Thus, if the drawer fails to make payment at maturity, the seller, who obtained the discount, is liable to the bank for the amount involved.

The transaction cost advantages over promissory notes are straightforward: To the seller the trade acceptance creates a definite obligation on the purchaser, which can be discounted at a bank for cash. By the same token, the buyer is in a better position to make favorable terms and secure the lowest prices since he or she is legally bound to a definite date of payment and unconditionally obligated to pay on the stated terms. Finally, the bank that discounts the bill is further protected from default risk by the addition of the drawee's contingent liability. These advantages make the secondary market for acceptances deeper than for single-name promissory notes, which tend to be held by the purchaser until maturity. As a general rule, two-name acceptances are more liquid than single-name promissory notes, since they can be sold and resold by banks in need of cash with less fear of loss of principle or interest.

The bankers' acceptance, is perhaps the most liquid and reliable form of commercial paper. With the bankers' acceptance, a bank or banking house acts as the drawee (acceptor) of the time bill of exchange. When a bank stamps "Accepted" on the bill and endorses the instrument, it unconditionally guarantees to pay the face value of the acceptance at maturity. The bank, in effect, replaces the seller of goods as the guarantor of the bill. This is important because a bank, or at least a major bank, is generally far better known than the many thousands of individual firms and merchants that endorse trade acceptances. This reduction in informational costs makes bankers' acceptances eminently suitable for financing international trade, since the reputations of individual traders are even more uncertain across national boundaries. Thus bankers' acceptances arise most often in connection with international trade. The process of securing a bankers' acceptance in foreign trade goes as follows:

An American importer may request acceptance financing from its bank when, as is frequently the case in international trade, it does not have a close relationship with and cannot obtain financing from the exporter it is dealing with. Once the importer and the bank have completed an acceptance agreement, in which the bank agrees to accept drafts for the importer and the importer agrees to repay any drafts the bank accepts, the importer draws a time draft on the bank. The bank accepts the draft and discounts it; that is, it gives the importer cash for the draft but gives it an amount less than the face value of the draft. The importer uses the proceeds to pay the exporter. The bank may hold the acceptance in its portfolio or it may sell, or rediscount, it in the secondary market. In the former case, the bank is making a loan to the importer; in the latter case, it is in effect substituting its credit for that of the importer, enabling the importer to borrow in the money market. On or before the maturity date, the importer pays the bank the face value of the acceptance. If the bank rediscounted the acceptance in the market, the bank pays the holder of the acceptance the face value on the maturity date.[66]

Furthermore, the guarantee of a bank enjoying a solid reputation makes bankers' acceptances the "most liquid type of investment available."[67] Unlike single-name paper or even the trade acceptance, the holder of a bankers' acceptance need not be concerned with the success or failure of the underlying transaction, since the bank's liability to the holder is absolute and must be discharged irrespective of the performance or nonperformance of contracts on the part of others.[68] Furthermore, should the bank default, the holder has several other legal remedies: recourse to the drawer, a preferred claim to any collateral lodged with the acceptor as security for its acceptance, and finally, the double liability of stockholders.[69] The result of all this security against default

[66] Robert K. LaRoche, "Bankers' Acceptances," *Federal Reserve Bank of Richmond Economic Quarterly* 79 (Winter 1993): 75–76.
[67] First National Corporation of Boston, *Acceptances as Attractive Short Term Investments* (Boston: First National Corporation of Boston, 1928), p. 12.
[68] The rise of bills of exchange and their centrality to economic growth is considered in Douglass C. North, *Institutions, Institutional Change, and Economic Performance* (New York: Cambridge University Press, 1990), pp. 122, 125–26.
[69] First National Corporation of Boston, *Acceptances as Attractive Short Term Investments*, p. 11.

risk is that bankers' acceptances are prime quality money market instruments and are actively traded among banks, other financial institutions, corporations, and securities dealers as high quality, short-term investments and a ready source of cash.

American discounting practices before the founding of the Fed were, as Warburg put it, "as backward as Europe at the time of the Medicis, and Asia, in all likelihood, at the time of Hammurabi."[70] The discount market in double-name paper was in steep decline, banks were not empowered to accept bills of exchange, and "the short-term, unsecured promissory note [single-name paper] became the dominant credit instrument for financing the credit needs of merchants and farmers."[71] Moreover, the market for call loans secured by stock exchange collateral was "considerably more important than the commercial paper market" in New York City, the nation's financial center.[72] In contrast, in England, as well as on the continent, the double-name bill of exchange and bankers' acceptance predominated (see Chapter 3).

Until the Civil War, the American discount market had actually evolved in the direction of European markets. In the standard view, the war, along with certain legal restrictions, disrupted this evolution: "The trade acceptance was widely used in the antebellum period to finance commercial transactions . . . [but] the Civil War put an end to this system of conducting business based on long credit terms."[73] The problem was the monetary uncertainty caused by the issue of greenbacks. Fluctuations in the value of credit contracts fixed in dollars led sellers to try and arrange business on a cash basis. Sellers did so by offering substantial discounts for immediate payment in cash, discounts ranging from 13 to 18 percent per year. To take advantage of the system of cash discounts, buyers got used to borrowing at banks on promissory notes and then paying sellers in cash, rather than issuing trade acceptances. Consequently, by 1900, only about 3 percent of all domestic credit transactions were financed through trade acceptances.[74]

While the literature generally gives emphasis to the role of the Civil War and cash discounts as the causes of the decline in two-name trade

[70] Paul M. Warburg, "Defects and Needs of Our Banking System" [1907], in Warburg, *The Federal Reserve System*, 2:9.

[71] James, *Money and Capital Markets*, p. 57.

[72] Charles A. E. Goodhart, *The New York Money Market and the Finance of Trade, 1900–1913* (Cambridge: Harvard University Press, 1969), p. 20.

[73] James, *Money and Capital Markets*, p. 55. See also Albert O. Greef, *The Commercial Paper House in the United States* (Cambridge: Harvard University Press, 1938), p. 70.

[74] Greef, *The Commercial Paper House*, p. 66. For evidence, see West, *Banking Reform and the Federal Reserve*, pp. 155–62; James, *Money and Capital Markets*, pp. 55–66; and Goodhart, *New York Money Market*, pp. 18–24.

acceptances, other factors were also important. Margaret Myers, for example, notes that for most of the antebellum period, the trade acceptance was the exception, not the rule: "The promissory note was the usual form of business paper discounted by banks during the first quarter of the nineteenth century."[75] What seems to be clear from the sketchy data on bank portfolios is that the use of trade acceptances reached a peak during the reign of the Second Bank of the United States (1812–1836), especially while Nicholas Biddle served as the bank's president (1823–1832). This is important, since it raises a possible relationship between the structure of the discount market and central banking—the "interdependence" noted by Warburg. Biddle actively encouraged the development of acceptances by maintaining a market for acceptances purchased by other banks (rediscounting acceptances) and by discounting acceptances based on the bank's own account (open-market purchases). Myers concludes that the "history of the Second Bank of the United States showed what a determined effort to push the acceptance could accomplish. The central bank was essential to the development of an acceptance market, not only for the influence which it could exert in its favor, but for the discounting facilities which it could provide."[76] After 1836, when the bank lost its charter, the trade acceptance began to fall into disuse. In this view, the Civil War, and the rapid price changes that accompanied it, reinforced the trend begun with the demise of the Second Bank: cash payments went to a premium and the system of cash discounts financed by promissory notes brought about a further displacement of the time bill of exchange.

Unlike trade acceptances, bankers' acceptances were simply prohibited by law: "American joint-stock banks—national and state—were either legally forbidden or (what amounted to the same thing) lacked specific authorization to accept drafts or bills of exchange."[77] The Supreme Court held to a restrictive interpretation of banking law, and, since the National Banking Act did not explicitly authorize banks to accept bills (a reasonable omission, given the lack of demand for dollar acceptances at the time), federal and most state courts refused to legalize the activity.[78] Hence, it is "substantially correct to say that American joint-stock

---

[75] Margaret G. Myers, *The New York Money Market: Origins and Development*, vol. 1 (New York: Columbia University Press, 1931), p. 48.
[76] Ibid., pp. 51–52.
[77] Vincent P. Carosso and Richard Sylla, "U.S. Banks in International Finance," in *International Banking, 1870–1914*, ed. Rondo Cameron and V. I. Bovykin (New York: Oxford University Press, 1991), p. 53.
[78] A Supreme Court ruling stated that "It is settled that the United States statutes relative to national banks constitute the measure of the authority of such corporations, and that they

banks did no accepting before 1914."[79] By the turn of the century, there *was* demand for dollar acceptances, and the prohibition put American banks at a disadvantage vis-à-vis European banks in the financing of international commerce, since bankers' acceptances were the main instrument (due to lower transaction costs) by which banks participated in trade finance.

The postbellum American commercial paper market did have certain advantages, however. Lance Davis argues that the open market in commercial paper helped integrate the national financial market and, like the correspondent system, served as a substitute for an interstate branch banking system.[80] Borrowers no longer had to rely upon local banks and pay monopoly rates for credit since they could turn to the extensive system of note brokers who sold paper to banks throughout the nation. Here, the spread of an open market in commercial paper was a factor in the narrowing of inter-regional interest rate differentials that occurred in the second half of the century.

But what of the effect on payments system stability? In one respect, the rise of commercial paper was a good thing for commercial banks, as it proved to be a safe investment for reserves in excess of legal requirements. Although critics pointed to the lack of transparency and/or security in single-name paper relative to acceptances, the fact of the matter was that the paper had a very low risk of default.[81] Albert Greef attributes this to the thorough credit analysis note brokers and, later, banks performed on prospective borrowers. The end result was that the notes were nearly always paid off at maturity. For the banking system as a whole, however, liquidity of open-market paper depended upon the ease with which earning assets could be shifted from individual banks to other banks in the system. Here, commercial paper proved to be an illiquid asset for banks, as there was not a functioning rediscount market in pre-Fed America—at least not since the passing of the Bank of the

---

cannot rightfully exercise any powers except those expressly granted." Cited in J. Laurence Laughlin, *Banking Reform* (Chicago: National Citizens' League, 1912), pp. 93–94.

[79] Carosso and Sylla, "U.S. Banks in International Finance," p. 53. See also Clyde W. Phelps, *The Foreign Expansion of American Banks: American Branch Banking Abroad* (New York: Ronald Press, 1927), pp. 91–92; H. Parker Willis, "The Origin of the Acceptance Provisions of the Federal Reserve Act," *Economic World* (28 May 1921).

[80] Lance E. Davis, "The Investment Market, 1870–1914: The Evolution of a National Market," *Journal of Economic History* 25 (September 1965): 355–99. See also James, *Money and Capital Markets*, pp. 174–235.

[81] Greef, *The Commercial Paper House*, pp. 56–57, 307–25. For contemporary criticisms of promissory notes, see Laurence M. Jacobs, *Bank Acceptances* (Washington, D.C.: GPO, 1910); and Warburg, *The Discount System in Europe*.

United States. There was a strong customary bias against rediscounting among banks: "Any attempt by a bank to rediscount such paper was looked upon as a clear sign of that bank's weakness and would be objected to strenuously by the original borrower, who would dislike seeing his paper 'hawked' about. As a result, there was no market for the bulk of such paper."[82] Because banks had no way of disposing of their paper when in need of cash, a loan made to a commercial borrower involved the complete absorption of that portion of the bank's loanable funds until the maturity of the loan; to be too heavily loaned up on commercial paper meant vulnerability to sudden depositor shifts into currency. Banks thereby sought out an alternative investment that was more marketable than commercial paper, and the call loan fit the bill. In the absence of rediscounting, call loans, payable on demand, "were the most liquid asset in which a bank could invest."[83]

There is evidence supporting this view. While the rise of the commercial paper market was bringing about a change in the kind of discounts being made by banks (from two-name to single-name paper), there was also an overall decline in the volume of commercial paper in bank portfolios—commercial paper of all varieties was losing ground to other forms of investment for bank funds. Discounts, as an investment for the funds of commercial banks, had to compete against both call loans and securities in terms of return and marketability, and "on the whole they ran a losing race with other earning assets."[84] Figure 1.3 shows the decline in two-name paper relative to single-name paper for all national banks. In New York City, the trend was more dramatic, as Figure 1.4 illustrates. But the most striking feature of the portfolio characteristics of commercial banks was the decline in the ratio of commercial paper to other loans and investments. As Figure 1.5 demonstrates, commercial paper of both varieties lost ground to other investments for bank funds, particularly in New York City. This confirms Goodhart's finding that in New York, "the market for loans secured by collateral, especially the call loan market, was considerably more important than the commercial paper market."[85]

---

[82] Goodhart, *New York Money Market*, p. 22. City banks rediscounted a small amount of paper for their rural correspondents. See also James, *Money and Capital Markets*, p. 153; and Greef, *The Commercial Paper House*, pp. 304–5.

[83] James, *Money and Capital Markets*, p. 118.

[84] Myers, *The New York Money Market*, p. 335; Anna Youngman, "The Growth of Financial Banking," *Journal of Political Economy* 14 (1906): 435–43.

[85] Goodhart, *New York Money Market*, p. 20.

Figure 1.3. Single- and double-name paper as a percentage of total loans and investments, all national banks, 1883–1913

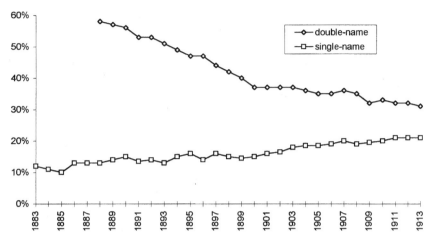

Source: U.S. Department of the Treasury, *Annual Report of the Comptroller of the Currency* (Washington, D.C.: GPO, selected years).

Figure 1.4. Single- and double-name paper as a percentage of total loans and investments, New York City national banks, 1881–1913

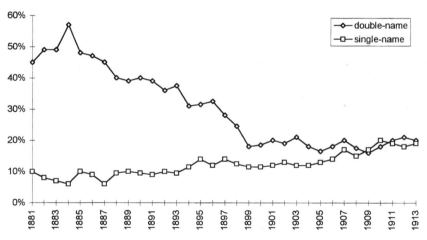

Source: U.S. Department of the Treasury, *Annual Report of the Comptroller of the Currency* (Washington, D.C.: GPO, selected years).

Figure 1.5. Commercial paper as a percentage of total loans and investments, New York City national banks and all national banks, 1886–1913

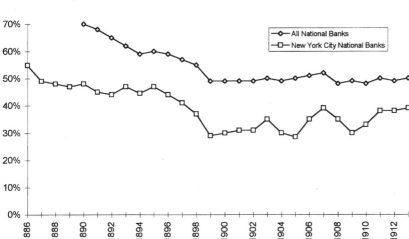

Source: U.S. Department of the Treasury, *Annual Report of the Comptroller of the Currency* (Washington, D.C.: GPO, selected years).

The Discount Market and Central Banking

The heart of the Federal Reserve Act involved discounting and rediscounting, and the basic thrust was to make commercial paper—rather than call loans—the most liquid asset in bank portfolios. Bankers' acceptances were particularly favored among the various forms of paper, since only these instruments were made eligible for both rediscounting and direct purchase by the Federal Reserve banks. In turn, the primary function of central banking was to add *resilience* through rediscounting, and *guidance* through rediscounting and open-market operations, to the newly invigorated discount market. Moreover, the powers granted to reserve banks had a distinct international orientation, which recognized the advantages of European central banks in influencing exchange rates and international movements of gold through discount rate policy, gold purchases and sales, the purchase and sale of foreign bills of exchange, and occasionally, international cooperation.

As part of the machinery meant to eliminate reserve pyramiding in New York, the Act required member banks to hold legal reserves with the Federal Reserve banks or in their own vaults, rather than with city correspondents.[86] The law also provided for a new currency form—the Federal Reserve note—that could be expanded to meet public shifts out of deposits and into currency. But the centerpiece of the new framework was the mechanism enabling banks to convert their assets readily into such currency—rediscounting. A member bank could accommodate an increase in loan demand or currency withdrawals by rediscounting "eligible" commercial paper with its Federal Reserve bank. The Federal Reserve bank would provide the commercial bank with reserves or currency, and charge its discount rate. This liquidity function, however, was not simply heaped on top of the existing organization of credit markets. Instead, by defining and limiting the types of assets that were eligible for rediscounting, the Act sought to remake the American payments system in the image of European discount markets.

The eligibility rules with the most obvious intentions were those restricting rediscountable assets to commercial, as opposed to speculative, instruments and those that dealt with bankers' acceptances. Section 13 of the law provides that upon the endorsement of a member bank, a Federal Reserve bank may rediscount "notes, drafts, and bills of exchange arising out of actual commercial transactions . . . but such bills shall not include notes drafts, or bills covering or trading in stocks, bonds, or other investment securities," except those of the U.S. government. Eligible paper "drawn of agricultural, industrial, or commercial purposes" was limited to a maturity of ninety days, with the exception of agricultural paper which could run for six months. By restricting access to the discount window to paper representing actual commercial transactions, it was hoped that banks would be drawn away from the call loan market and other securities-backed lending: "It was to minimize the importance of the call loan market that some concentration of reserves in the Federal Reserve banks was provided and that the bill market was established. Instead of adjusting their daily "cash" requirements through the call loan market, it was expected that banks would make use of the bill market . . . The bill market would have direct access to the Reserve banks . . . so that temporary periods of tension could be relieved."[87]

Of all credit instruments dealt with in the new law, bankers' acceptances were the most favored. National banks were finally given permis-

[86] A three-year transitional period allowed for the gradual transfer of reserves previously held as interbank deposits. In 1917, the Act was amended to require all legal reserves to be held as deposits in Federal Reserve Banks; vault cash could no longer be counted as legal reserves.
[87] Benjamin H. Beckhart, *The New York Money Market: Uses of Funds*, vol. 3 (New York: Columbia University Press, 1932), pp. 257–58.

sion to accept bills of exchange involving foreign trade, thereby super-
seding the various court rulings that had denied them the authority to
do so under the National Banking Act. By the terms of section 13, a
member bank was permitted to "accept drafts or bills of exchange drawn
upon it and growing out of transactions involving the importation or
exportation of goods having not more than six months to run," with the
total amount limited to one half of the accepting bank's capital and surplus. Permission to accept bills involving domestic transactions was not
included since the primary purpose of this section was to allow national
banks to engage in international trade finance. Dislodging established
practice in domestic finance was apparently seen as too difficult at this
juncture.[88] According to Benjamin Beckhart:

> Indispensable though the acceptance is in foreign trade, by virtue of the
> difficulty of securing information on the credit standing of foreign buyers,
> there is little justification for its extension to domestic transactions. The
> domestic trade of the United States for a long period had been financed by
> means of the open-book account and the cash discount system. To attempt
> to change this would involve an overcoming of the lethargy and habits of
> the American business man which would be a Herculean task as com-
> pared with the substitution in foreign transactions of the dollar for the
> sterling bill. The latter substitution would involve simply the use of one
> type of currency instead of another, since importers and exporters were
> fully acquainted with the use of the bill of exchange.[89]

In addition, bankers' acceptances were made eligible for rediscount at
the Federal Reserve banks. Under section 13, the reserve banks were
authorized to rediscount bankers' acceptances, if maturing within three
months and if endorsed by at least one member bank, to an amount not
to exceed one half the capital and surplus of the bank for which the
rediscounts were made. In this respect, bankers' acceptances were treated
similarly to other instruments at the discount window. The greatest dis-
tinction, however, was that bankers' acceptances were among the instruments that reserve banks could purchase directly, under the Act's open-
market provisions. Promissory notes were denied this benefit.

The reserve banks' open market powers reveal that contemporaries
clearly understood that a pure discount policy would not allow the Fed
to achieve all conceivable monetary policies in the context of the international gold standard. In some cases it would need to use open-market

---

[88] The acceptance system was extended to domestic trade by amendment in 1916. Beckhart,
The New York Money Market, pp. 267–69.

[89] Ibid., pp. 263–64.

operations to "make its discount rate effective"—that is, to ensure that it succeeded in influencing market rates of discount, and the gold flows on which they acted.[90] For this purpose, section 14 allowed reserve banks to "purchase and sell in the open market, at home or abroad, either from or to domestic or foreign banks, firms, corporations, or individuals, cable transfers and bankers' acceptances and bills of exchange of the kind made eligible for rediscount, with or without the endorsement of a member bank." In addition, every reserve bank had the power to buy and sell, at home or abroad, U.S. government securities, and certain classes of state and local government securities.

The section specifying the nongovernmental instruments available for purchase and sale did not authorize the reserve banks to engage directly in domestic business to any great extent; the emphasis was clearly on international instruments. Cable transfers, like bankers' acceptances, involve foreign transactions: they are orders sent to or from a foreign country for the immediate delivery of cash. The power to make such purchases and sales not only provided reserve banks with a convenient means to transfer funds to or from a foreign country, but also allowed them to become active players in the foreign exchange market.[91] Second on the list of instruments reserve banks could deal in directly was the bankers' acceptance, which included (1) acceptances by American banks, drawn in dollars in connection with foreign trade and, (2) acceptances of foreign banks or individuals, drawn in foreign currencies. The idea behind granting reserve banks the power to purchase bankers' acceptances by American banks was to sponsor the dollar acceptance in foreign trade finance: reserve banks could make a market in these instruments should commercial banks find other investments (e.g., call loans) more profitable. The idea behind granting reserve banks the power to purchase bankers' acceptances of foreign banks was to allow the reserve banks to build up a portfolio of acceptances, denominated in foreign currencies, for the purpose of intervening on the foreign exchange market and influencing international flows of gold, as was common practice among European central banks.[92] The final instrument eligible for open-market operations was the bill of exchange drawn within the United States—the trade acceptance—which, as we have seen, was not used extensively to finance domestic transactions. The objective was to foster its growth.

[90] Edwin W. Kemmerer, *The ABCs of the Federal Reserve System* (Princeton: Princeton University Press, 1919), p. 42.
[91] Thomas Conway and Ernest M. Patterson, *The Operation of the New Bank Act* (Philadelphia: J. B. Lippincott, 1914), p. 174.
[92] Arthur I. Bloomfield, *Monetary Policy under the International Gold Standard: 1880–1914* (New York: Federal Reserve Bank of New York, 1959).

Promissory notes were not included, apparently in an effort to promote the development of two-name paper: "The framers of the Act desired to sponsor the use of two-name paper in domestic finance which it was hoped, would come to occupy as important a role as it did prior to the Civil War, in the days when Nicholas Biddle threw the weight of his influence in favor of financing on this basis."[93]

The open market provisions reveal an emphasis on international operations in another sense as well. Since the resumption of the gold standard in 1879, the United States had perhaps the freest market for gold in the world, not having a central bank capable of "protecting" the national gold supply or dealing with foreign central banks in the event of a crisis. Contemporaries recognized that the gold standard did not operate automatically nor entirely within the "rules of the game"; policy discretion and the artificial manipulation of gold flows were commonplace features.[94] "The leading countries of the world employ numerous devices to control their supplies of gold and to attract more in times of need. Gold does not flow from one nation to another in response to trade demands, nor does it move merely when exchange rates are favorable. At times it is attracted by inducements that have no immediate connection with commercial needs. To offset foreign operations our new law introduces a number of features which are intended to aid us in conserving our stock of gold and even to make possible additions to the supplies on hand."[95] Moreover, the gold standard regime involved a modicum of international cooperation among central banking nations, a function also recognized by contemporaries.[96] According to Warburg, one of the "chief features and advantages of a central bank system is the fact that it creates a central institution able to deal with other nations, in case exceptional measures become advisable, and with which other nations, even in times of the worst panic, can negotiate to furnish or obtain loans of gold, as has frequently been the case between France and England."[97]

The open-market features of the Act do indeed reveal the intention to confer upon the United States the international monetary advantages of central banking. In addition to the power of intervening in the foreign exchange market, reserve banks were given the authority to deal directly in the international gold market and the power to "open and maintain

---

[93] Beckhart, *The New York Money Market*, p. 274.
[94] Bloomfield, *Monetary Policy under the International Gold Standard.*
[95] Conway and Patterson, *The Operation of the New Bank Act*, p. 178.
[96] Barry Eichengreen, *Golden Fetters: The Gold Standard and the Great Depression* (New York: Oxford University Press, 1992).
[97] Paul M. Warburg, "A Central Bank System and the United States of America," [1908] in Warburg, *The Federal Reserve System*, 2: 99–100.

accounts in foreign countries, appoint correspondents, and establish agencies" for the purpose of dealing in bills of exchange and government bonds.[98] The effect of these provisions was to permit the reserve banks to liquidate foreign bills or obtain gold abroad when exchange rates approached the gold export point, thereby avoiding the general contraction in business that would follow an advance in the discount rate. This put the United States on par with the major European central banking nations, which maintained portfolios of foreign bills and cooperated during crises to avoid extreme actions on interest rates.

Taken as a whole, the open-market features of the Act sought "to permit the Regional banks . . . to make their own discount rates effective; to control international movements of gold; to rectify the exchanges; to assist in the financing of America's foreign trade, in the development of a discount market in New York, and in the use of bankers' acceptances."[99] When combined with the other financial innovations of the legislation—its discount market rules, the legalization and encouragement of bankers' acceptances for financing foreign trade, the creation of a rediscounting authority, the legalization of overseas branch banking—it is clear that international objectives permeated the legislation. Tables 1.1–1.3 provide a convenient summary of the institutional impact of the Federal Reserve Act.

In summary, the core innovations of the new regime involved both domestic and international objectives. Domestically, the goal was to improve the depth and breadth of the payments system so that bank runs and seasonal pressures could be accommodated with less financial and real destabilization. Internationally, the goals were to facilitate the development of the dollar as an international currency (whose value would be subject to central bank policy on the margins) in conjunction with the foreign expansion of American joint-stock banks. Moreover, financial internationalization went hand-in-hand with monetary internationalization, as the Act explicitly gave the new reserve banks the capacity to engage in international monetary operations, with the objective of minimizing international financial crises. In short, the Act was an exercise in "joint production," and previous studies have given insufficient attention to the international outputs. In the next chapter, I draw upon economics to show that (1) the joint products could not be separately pro-

---

[98] The gold policy tools included the power "to deal in gold coin and bullion, at home and abroad . . . and to contract for loans of gold coin and bullion, giving therefore, when necessary, acceptable security, including the hypothecation of United States bonds or other securities which Federal reserve banks are authorized to hold."

[99] Benjamin H. Beckhart, *The Discount Policy of the Federal Reserve System* (New York: Henry Holt, 1924), p. 167.

Table 1.1. Institutions not changed by the Federal Reserve Act

	National Banking System	Federal Reserve System
Unit banking system	Anti-branching restrictions produced a system of thousands of single-office "unit" banks.	Domestic anti-branching provisions retained.
Dual banking system	Banks allowed to chose between federal and state charters.	Banks retain the right to chose between federal and state charters.
Correspondent system	Rural unit banks linked to money centers by correspondent relationships. Reserve regulations encouraged the correspondent system.	No prohibition implied. Institution prevails since correspondents in money centers continue to offer valuable benefits to rural bankers, notably investment services.
Capital requirements	Capital requirements determined by the size of the community in which a bank operated. Banks in towns with populations of up to 6,000, needed a capital base of $50,000*; banks in communities of up to 50,000 people were required to have $100,000 in capital; and for the larger cities, a minimum capital of $200,000 was mandated. *Lowered to $25,000 for the smallest towns (under 3,000 people) in 1900.	Capital requirements remain in place.
Gold standard	The U.S. returned to a de facto gold standard in 1879, codified with the Gold Standard Act of 1900.	Section 26 reaffirms the Gold Standard Act of 1900.

Table 1.2. The Federal Reserve Act's minor institutional changes

	National Banking System	Federal Reserve System
Reserve requirements	Reserve requirements differed for urban and city national banks. Banks in "central reserve" and "reserve" cities maintained reserves of 25 percent; "country" banks required to hold reserves of 15 percent. No distinction between demand and time deposits.	Reserves on demand deposits reduced to 18 percent for central-reserve-city banks, 15 percent for reserve-city-banks, 12 percent for country banks, and 5 percent on time deposits for all classes of banks. After an interim period, reserves to be kept on deposit without interest at the Federal Reserve Banks.
Reserve "pyramiding"	Country banks could hold up to three-fifths of required reserve with reserve-city and central-reserve-city banks. Reserve-city banks could carry a maximum of one half their reserve with central-reserve banks. Central-reserve banks had to carry full reserves in their vaults.	Banks can continue to carry balances with city correspondents, although such balances no longer count as legal reserves.
Portfolio restrictions (real estate lending)	Courts prohibited national banks from lending on real estate collateral, which gave state banks a competitive edge in rural markets.	National banks outside the central reserve cities given the ability to lend on real estate collateral, up to 50 percent of the value of the land and limited in total to 25 percent of the lending bank's capital and surplus, or one-third of its time deposits.
Portfolio restrictions (trust banking)	National banks prevented from managing the estates of wealthy individuals.	National banks can serve as executors and administrators of estates, thus enabling direct competition with trust companies.
Foreign branching	All branching by national banks, foreign or domestic, forbidden by the courts.	Any national bank possessing a capital and surplus of $1 million or more may establish foreign branches for the "furtherance of the foreign commerce of the United States."

Table 1.3. The Federal Reserve Act's major institutional changes

	National Banking System	Federal Reserve System
Rediscounting	Rediscounting among banks very rare.	Creates twelve Federal Reserve Banks whose primary function is to rediscount for member banks.
Discounts and loans	Single-name commercial paper and promissory notes eclipsed two-name bills of exchange (trade acceptances) in bank portfolios. Bankers' acceptances prohibited. Demand loans on securities (call loans) the most liquid assets banks held.	Eligibility rules governing Federal Reserve rediscounting aim to create a modern discount market. Notes, drafts, bills of exchange, and bankers' acceptances arising from commercial transactions are eligible. Instruments backed by stocks, bonds, or other securities (e.g., call loans) are not. Two-name bills of exchange particularly favored by virtue of the Act's open-market provisions.
Bankers' acceptances	National banks forbidden from accepting bills of exchange drawn against either international or domestic transactions	Legalizes bankers' acceptances drawn to finance international trade only. Bankers' acceptances for domestic transactions legalized in 1916.
Open-market operations	U.S. Treasury endeavored to influence credit market conditions, but was highly constrained, both domestically and internationally (discussed later).	Federal Reserve Banks given broad powers to influence domestic credit markets, foreign exchangerates, and international gold flows.
Note issue	National banks issued notes backed by government bonds. If a bank failed to redeem its notes on demand in lawful money, the bonds were sold and the proceeds used for this purpose. National bank currency was widely regarded as "inelastic."	Creates the Federal Reserve banknote, issued by the Reserve Banks at the discretion of the Federal Reserve Board. To meet the need for elasticity, Reserve Banks can issue notes against commercial paper and bills rediscounted. Reserve banks maintain a 40 percent reserve in gold or lawful money against notes.

duced, and (2) that the benefits of producing the international outputs were sufficiently concentrated to generate collective action. This roughly corresponds to an insight offered by Vincent Carosso and Richard Sylla: "Growing perceptions of defects in American banking arrangements—especially their periodic tendency to collapse in financial panics—created a movement for banking reform starting in the mid-1890s. During the subsequent two decades the internationalist minority used this movement to create openings for greater involvement in international banking."[100]

[100] Carosso and Sylla, "U.S. Banks in International Finance," pp. 70–71.

2 /

The Economics and Politics of
International Currency Use

The Federal Reserve Act brought comprehensive reform to the payments system to further domestic *and* international objectives. Its major provisions were for overhauling the stunted discount market, which served not only to add liquidity to the internal payments system, but to develop the U.S. dollar for international use. In addition, legalizing bankers' acceptances and foreign branching had the direct and obvious intention of facilitating the financing of international trade by large American banks in dollar-denominated bills of exchange. Furthermore, the newly created Reserve Banks were given powers to influence internal credit markets, exchange rates, and gold flows. In short, the legislation produced multiple outputs, domestic and international. The purpose of this chapter is to demonstrate that (1) the domestic and international outputs were difficult, if not impossible, to produce independently, and (2) the international output involved enough narrowly distributed private gains to generate lobbying for comprehensive reform by a subset of society. The fundamental purpose is to explain how the collective action problems inherent in generating a more efficient payments system were overcome.

Demonstrating that the Fed's joint products could not be separately produced means demonstrating that internationalizing the currency and stabilizing the domestic banking system had a common, and perhaps unique, institutional foundation. For this purpose, I draw on the economics literature on international currency use, which is quite explicit in terms of the prerequisites required of an issuer of an international currency. Unlike the production of domestic banking stability, for which a range of institutional forms are possible, these prerequisites are quite unique and conform closely to the Federal Reserve Act's core innovations. Demonstrating that internationalizing the currency can generate the kind of excludable, agent-specific benefits that are the basis of successful collective action requires analysis of the distributional consequences of international currency use. Again, I look to the economics literature on international currencies to derive these implications. The benefits and costs accruing to the issuing nation are not evenly distributed among domestic residents, as some agents reap direct concentrated benefits, while others obtain little benefit but are fully exposed to the costs. Mapping the preferences, relative preference intensities, and collective action capabilities of resident social actors follows from the distributional effects of international currency issue.

The chapter begins with a short discussion of the functions of international money, followed by a review of the factors that contribute to the use of a particular national currency as international currency. These factors conveniently divide along level-of-analysis lines: the necessary prerequisites are purely domestic, while other factors involve the international economic position of a nation. As we shall see, the domestic preconditions overlap quite closely with the major financial changes of the Federal Reserve Act. The next section explores the distributional issues involved in international currency use, beginning with the international effects and progressing to the domestic level. The latter analysis allows for specification of domestic agents' preferences and incentives in regard to internationalizing the currency. Two rival coalitions are identified—currency internationalists and nationalists—along with the relative preference intensities of actors within these broad coalitions. The result is a set of political economy propositions regarding how society divides up politically on the issue.

These propositions, however, are but the first cut of the analysis. Since the objective is to explain institutional *change*, specifying the fixed preferences of individuals, groups, and potential coalitions is necessary but insufficient. As preferences are not allowed to vary within the framework, additional factors must be incorporated into the analysis. Chapter 3 addresses this issue by adding a second dynamic cut, which links the processes of institutional change to change in the relative international economic position of the country.

Functions and Characteristics of International Currencies

What distinguishes the functions of currency in the international monetary system from the role of currency within the domestic realm? Very little, in fact, except greater complexity. Regardless of the domain in which it is used, money serves three basic functions: it is a medium of exchange, a unit of account, and a store of value. The international use of a currency happens whenever a national currency performs these functions outside the borders of the nation that issues it. As a medium of exchange, an international currency is used to settle foreign trade transactions and to discharge international financial obligations. As a unit of account, it is used to invoice merchandise trade and to denominate financial instruments. International currencies are also used by official agents in expressing exchange-rate relationships. As a store of value, it serves as an investment asset held by nonresidents: both official and private agents may hold international currencies and financial assets denominated in such currencies as reserve assets.

An international currency is also typically used as a *vehicle*—that is, to denominate and execute foreign trade and international capital transfers that do not involve direct transactions with the issuing country.[1] For example, in the pre-Fed era, U.S. exports to Latin America were denominated and paid for in sterling, so sterling was the vehicle currency. Here, sterling served as both a unit of account and a medium of exchange, but a vehicle currency can also be used to fulfill the store of value function of money. Moreover, it can fulfill any of these functions with respect to both official agents and private transactors. For example, during the gold standard period, central banks and private transactors used sterling to settle international payments, to fix prices, and to hold as a liquid asset. Table 2.1 summarizes the three roles of an international currency.

What factors contribute to the choice of a particular national currency as an international currency? Students of international money have isolated transaction costs as the overriding consideration: "A currency is used as a vehicle currency when the transaction costs (e.g., the costs of information, search, uncertainty, enforcement, and negotiation) involved in using it are less than the transactions costs involved in using other currencies."[2] Put more generally by Paul Krugman, "The microeconomics of money, whether domestic or international, is fundamentally about frictions . . . Frictions—costs of transacting, costs of calculation—cause agents to use national monies as international media of exchange, units of account, stores of value."[3]

---

[1] George S. Tavlas, "Vehicle Currencies," in *The New Palgrave Dictionary of Money and Finance*, ed. Peter Newman et al. (London: Macmillan, 1992), pp. 754–57.
[2] George S. Tavlas and Yuzuru Ozeki, *The Internationalization of Currencies: An Appraisal of the Japanese Yen*, International Monetary Fund Occasional Paper, no. 90 (Washington, D.C.: International Monetary Fund, 1992), p. 2.
[3] Paul Krugman, "The International Role of the Dollar: Theory and Prospect," in *Exchange-Rate Theory and Practice*, ed. John F. O. Bilson and Richard C. Marston (Chicago: University

Table 2.1. Functions of international money

	Private agents	Official agents
Medium of Exchange	Currency used to settle international trade and to discharge international financial obligations	Intervention currency in foreign exchange markets and currency used for balance of payments financing
Unit of Account	Currency used to invoice foreign trade and denominate international financial instruments	Currency used in expressing exchange-rate relationships
Store of value	Currency used to denominate deposits and liquid assets	Reserve asset held by central banks and governments

Source: Adapted from Peter Kenen, *The Role of the Dollar as an International Currency*, Group of Thirty, Occasional Paper no. 13 (New York: Group of Thirty, 1983), p. 16.

The literature seeks to identify the factors that raise or lower the transaction costs associated with the use of national monies for international purposes. Although no comprehensive theory is available to accurately predict whether a currency will become an international currency, there is broad agreement on the conditions necessary for it to do so. George Tavlas breaks these conditions into two categories: (1) the general or necessary prerequisites, which involve domestic institutional and policy considerations, and (2) the supplementary factors, which involve the relative position of nations in the global economy.[4]

Domestic Prerequisites of International Currency Use

There are two necessary characteristics required of an international currency. First, there needs to be confidence in the value of the currency, so as to reduce the information costs to international transactors. According to Tavlas and Yuruzu Ozeki, "In order to serve as an international unit of account, means of payment, and store of value, a currency should be stable in value, so that its price relative to other currencies provides sufficient information to make it generally accessible to market participants,

---

of Chicago Press, 1984), p. 262. See also Charles Goodhart, *Money, Information and Uncertainty*, 2d ed. (London: Macmillan, 1989); and Karl Brunner and Allan H. Meltzer, "The Uses of Money: Money in the Theory of an Exchange Economy," *American Economic Review* 61 (December 1971): 784–805.

[4] Tavlas, "Vehicle Currencies"; George S. Tavlas, *On the International Use of Currencies: The Case of the Deutsche Mark*, Essays in International Finance, no. 181, International Finance Section, Princeton University (March 1991).

making it unnecessary for them to conduct costly investigation."[5] The most prominent gauge of currency stability is thus the inflation rate. A rate of inflation that is relatively high or variable usually generates nominal exchange-rate depreciation and variability, thereby raising the costs of using a currency internationally. When the value of a currency is uncertain, due to high and variable inflation rates, the costs of acquiring information and making efficient calculations about prices, bid and offered, for tradable goods increase. Put another way, currency uncertainty lowers the information content of prices, as agents must decompose price variations into changes owing to shifts in demand or supply in world markets, and changes owing to exchange-rate variations in the vehicle currency country. Furthermore, inflation increases the costs of holding assets denominated in a currency by eroding its purchasing power, thereby degrading the currency as an international store of value. Purchasing power uncertainty also negatively affects a currency's role as a medium of exchange, since international transactions entail a lapse of time between initiation and completion of the contract. All else equal, a country that successfully limits inflation and inflation variability stands a better chance of seeing its currency assume international functions.

The importance of stable currency, in connection with the emergence of sterling as an international currency during the gold standard era, is widely noted. According to Benjamin Cohen, "No other currency offered such a high degree of certainty as did sterling."[6] More systematic evaluations of the relationship between price stability and the choice of international currencies have produced the finding that "the safest currency for all investors, regardless of their country, is the currency of the country with the least unpredictable inflation. In the absence of capital controls and restrictions on the use of foreign currencies, we would expect the safe currency to gain increasingly widespread use as the unit of denomination for financial instruments."[7] Thus, the first necessary precondition for the internationalization of a currency is stable and consistent government macroeconomic policies, particularly monetary policy.

---

[5] Tavlas and Ozeki, *The Internationalization of Currencies*, p. 2. Some authors consider "political stability" in the issuing country a necessary precondition, but since this factor is usually discussed in the context of currency stability (i.e., political stability contributes to currency stability), it will not be treated separately here. See Robert Mundell, "International Monetary Options," *Cato Journal* 2 (1989): 189–210.

[6] Benjamin J. Cohen, *The Future of Sterling as an International Currency* (London: Macmillan, 1971), p. 61. See also David Williams, "The Evolution of the Sterling System," in *Essays in Money and Banking in Honour of R. S. Sayers*, ed. C. R. Whittlesey and J. S. G. Wilson (London: Oxford University Press, 1968).

[7] Pentti J. K. Kouri and Jorge Braga de Macedo, "Exchange Rates and the International Adjustment Process," *Brookings Papers on Economic Activity* 1 (1978): 111–50.

Recent work on the political economy of macroeconomic policy identifies factors that promote stable and consistent monetary policies, and one central finding is that institutional structure matters. Although a benevolent policymaker that does not deviate from a time-consistent policy path is considered the optimum, empirical work suggests that certain "second-best" institutions also promote stable prices.[8] Typically, countries with one or more of the following institutions tend to have relatively low rates of inflation: (1) an independent central bank, (2) a binding commitment on policymakers to preserve price stability, as in present-day New Zealand, (3) rules that severely constrain policy discretion, like strict monetary growth rules, and (4) a credible commitment to fixed exchange rates.[9] These may be alternative means to the same end and the details need not concern us. The important point is that internationalizing the currency requires institutions that promote low levels of inflation and inflation variability.

In the United States during the nineteenth century, the issue of price stability revolved around commitment to the gold standard and fixed exchange rates.[10] Uncertainty regarding the future of the monetary regime was a central feature of American political and economic life in the second half of the century, but the commitment to gold—and hence low inflation and inflation variability—was firmly established by 1896.[11] From 1862 to 1879, the United States operated on a greenback standard, with no convertibility maintained between the greenback and gold. In January 1879, following a decade of bitter political rivalry over the resumption of convertibility, the greenback became convertible at a parity equal to that of the pre-Civil War dollar. But with convertibility, a new threat to the dollar emerged in the form of the "free silver" movement. The goal of this movement was to reestablish a bimetallic standard, which would

---

[8] For the time inconsistency problem and the inflationary bias of discretionary policymaking, see Finn Kydland and Edward Prescott, "Rules versus Discretion: The Inconsistency of Optimal Plans," *Journal of Political Economy* 85 (June 1977): 473–92; Torsten Persson and Guido Tabellini, "Designing Institutions for Monetary Stability," *Carnegie-Rochester Series on Public Policy* 39 (December 1993): 53–84; and Alex Cukierman, *Central Bank Strategy, Credibility and Independence: Theory and Evidence* (Cambridge: MIT Press, 1992).

[9] For a review of alternative institutional paths to price stability, see Charles Goodhart and Jose Vinals, "Strategy and Tactics of Monetary Policy: Examples from Europe and the Antipodes," Federal Reserve Bank of Boston Conference Series, no. 38 (Boston: Federal Reserve Bank of Boston, 1994), pp. 141–87.

[10] For the view that a fixed exchange rate regime operates as a commitment mechanism, see Michael D. Bordo and Finn E. Kydland, "The Gold Standard as a Rule: An Essay in Exploration," *Explorations in Economic History* 32 (October 1995): 423–64.

[11] Charles W. Calomiris, "Greenback Resumption and Silver Risk: The Economics and Politics of Monetary Regime Change in the United States, 1862–1900," in *Monetary Regimes in Transition*, ed. Michael D. Bordo and Forrest Capie (Cambridge: Cambridge University Press, 1994), pp. 86–132.

have led to a de facto switch to a depreciated silver dollar standard. These struggles were the defining feature of national politics from the 1870s to 1896, and culminated when William J. Bryan decried before the Democratic Convention the "cross of gold" that threatened the crucifixion of America.

After the 1896 election and the defeat of the bimetallic challenge, the gold standard ceased to be a pivotal political issue. The Gold Standard Act of 1900 gave de jure basis to the commitment to gold payments and was not controversial.[12] The United States attained a credible commitment to low inflation and inflation variability by committing to the gold standard monetary regime a decade and a half before the passage of the Federal Reserve Act. As a result, the Act merely reaffirmed the gold standard, and did so in the most casual terms. The only reference to the regime appears in the Act's final provision (section 26), which reads: "All provisions of law inconsistent with or superseded by any provisions of this Act are to that extent and to that extent only repealed: *Provided*, nothing in the Act contained shall be construed to repeal the parity provision or provisions contained in the Act approved March fourteenth, nineteen hundred. . . ." In short, the Federal Reserve Act was not primarily about establishing price stabilizing institutions. Although the subject was broached in debates over who would manage monetary policy (i.e., the central bank "independence" issue), price stability emerged earlier by virtue of the victory of gold standard advocates over greenback and silver supporters.

The second prerequisite for a currency's international use involves the character of the issuer's internal financial markets, and it is here that the analysis is most relevant to the founding of the Fed. According to Tavlas and Ozeki, "a country whose currency is used internationally should possess financial markets that are broad (i.e., with a large assortment of financial instruments traded), deep (i.e., including well-developed secondary markets), and substantially free of controls (such as trade restrictions and capital controls)."[13] The primary issue is liquidity. For example, controls that restrict the convertibility of a currency result in higher transfer costs (e.g., a greater likelihood of illiquidity), thereby impeding its use as an international currency. However, a country that is free of controls—and the United States kept capital controls low throughout the period—must also possess broad and deep financial markets to ensure that assets and liabilities denominated in that currency will always have a ready home market.

---

[12] Timberlake, *Monetary Policy in the United States*, pp. 167–70.
[13] Tavlas and Ozeki, *The Internationalization of Currencies*, p. 41.

The liquidity issue relates to the three functions of international money. For a currency to be used as a medium of exchange and unit of account internationally, a nation needs well-developed markets in the types of financial instruments that are suitable for international transactions purposes. A bankers' acceptances market, for example, is necessary for a currency to be used in this respect, since, as we have seen, this instrument reduces the informational costs of short-term cross-border finance to a minimum. Hence, "a well-developed bankers'-acceptance market in a country contributes to the amount of trade financed in its currency and, thus, to the amount of trade invoiced in that currency."[14] Ronald McKinnon notes the role London's acceptance market played in securing sterling's global role: "A very high proportion of international trade among countries other than Britain was financed by sterling bills, drawn on importers by exporters, which were due in 90 days or 6 months. If these commercial bills were guaranteed against default by an acceptance house, exporters, in turn, could freely sell these sterling bills to a London bank (discount house) at the world's lowest open-market rates of interest."[15] Similarly, the relatively restricted international use of the yen in recent years is explained partly because Japan's "bankers' acceptance market is thin, curtailing the yen's international use as a unit of account and medium of exchange."[16]

The breadth and depth of the domestic financial market is also critical to the store of value function of international money. To settle trade contracts, to service long-term loans, to conduct private interbank transactions, and to intervene in foreign exchange markets, nonresidents (foreign banks, firms, and central banks) maintain working balances denominated in the currency. The term "working" connotes that these balances are invested in short-term financial instruments, and the safety and reliability of such instruments requires that the center country's financial markets be well developed and exhibit "capital certainty"; that is, the probability of loss from selling assets is reasonably low:

> A currency has capital certainty to the extent that the issuing country's financial markets exhibit the favorable characteristics of depth, breadth and resiliency. Capital certainty here does not refer to the price of the currency per se—that is what exchange convenience and convertibility is all about—rather it refers to the price of assets denominated in such a currency. Potential store-of-value holders do not usually hold cash. They

[14] Ibid.
[15] Ronald McKinnon, *Money in International Exchange* (New York: Oxford University Press, 1979), p. 84. See also Williams, "The Evolution of the Sterling System," p. 269.
[16] Tavlas and Ozeki, *The Internationalization of Currencies*, p. 3.

prefer to hold interest-earning assets. But they also want to minimize the possibility of capital loss should such assets have to be sold off at short notice in order to honor commitments. Consequently, to the extent that they find it convenient to hold international assets in their reserve balances, investors prefer to acquire them in the countries with the best-organized and most efficient financial institutions and markets. These are the countries with the most capital-certain currencies.[17]

As a final institutional source of capital certainty, a center country needs some form of rediscounting facility to give foreigners greater confidence that the assets they hold in that country's currency will always have a ready home market of last resort. Private individuals, foreign banks, central banks, and governments will not hold substantial working balances in a foreign market without the assurance that these assets can be rediscounted—that is, converted into currency—at any time. Before gold or other convertible currencies can be obtained and/or repatriated, it is first necessary to convert working balances into currency, and no matter how broad and deep financial markets are, there are times at which they become illiquid. A primary function of central banks is to provide liquidity to the market during such periods. This last mechanism is crucial, since it implies that a high degree of certainty as to the value of a nation's currency and articulated domestic markets in internationally accessible financial instruments are not enough. To serve as an international financial center, a country must also provide a central banking agency capable of convincing foreigners that their balances are perfectly liquid and that, under any circumstances, they can get these assets rediscounted *before* the proceeds are converted into other currencies or gold for shipment abroad.

Of the Bank of England's rediscounting role, for example, Barry Eichengreen observes that "The [London] discount market's attraction was its safety, and it was safe because the discount houses could turn in the last resort to the Bank of England."[18] "The Bank of England's readiness to rediscount bills on behalf of discount houses and provide gold on demand were critical for the development" of the London market in foreign bills.[19] I will show later that this prerequisite was clearly recognized by advocates of modern American central banking (see Chapter 4).

[17] Cohen, *The Future of Sterling as an International Currency*, p. 27.
[18] Barry Eichengreen, "Conducting the International Orchestra: Bank of England Leadership under the Classical Gold Standard," *Journal of International Money and Finance* 6 (March 1987): 9.
[19] Barry Eichengreen, *Golden Fetters: The Gold Standard and the Great Depression* (New York: Oxford University Press, 1992), p. 42.

With respect to the second prerequisite, the U.S. financial system was seriously deficient before 1913. The domestic discount market was narrow and bereft of the type of instruments held and traded internationally. In addition, secondary markets were notoriously thin, as banks engaged in little rediscounting amongst themselves. Finally, in the absence of a central bank rediscounting mechanism, the entire financial system lacked resilience, and was thereby prone to frequent bouts of illiquidty and crisis. As seen in the previous chapter, the Federal Reserve Act systematically addressed these weaknesses. To add breadth to financial markets, banks were finally given permission to accept bills of exchange arising out of international trade. In addition, a central goal of the legislation was to aid in the development of secondary markets for the range of financial instruments that reflected commercial transactions, foreign and domestic (i.e., acceptances, notes, drafts, and bills of exchange). To do so, these instruments were given legal status and made eligible for rediscount at the Federal Reserve banks. Call loans were discriminated against at the discount window by virtue of the speculative and uncertain character of these instruments. Moreover, as an additional stimulus to secondary markets in internationally accessible instruments, reserve banks were given the power to purchase acceptances and bills directly, under the Act's open-market provisions. In short, the Act sought to transform the commercial paper market into a modern discount market by extending the range of instruments banks could deal in, by setting up a rediscount window, and by vesting the newly created Federal Reserve banks with domestic and international rediscounting and open market powers.

The point of Chapter 1 is primarily empirical: the Act involved multiple outputs, international and domestic. The key point here is theoretical: the dual goals of internationalizing the U.S. dollar and stabilizing the internal payments system were closely *interdependent,* as both were attainable through the installation of a common set of institutions. Moreover, the goals may have been *inseparable,* in the sense that the attainment of the former necessarily required attainment of the latter. Improving the sophistication and integration of domestic financial markets for international reasons cannot help but complement the production of financial stability in the home market. This is due to the fact that well-developed domestic markets improve "capital certainty" for both non-resident and resident agents alike. A broader home market means that agents can diversify risk by selecting from a wider range of financial instruments to invest in. Deeper secondary markets mean that asset holders seeking liquidity can sell assets easily, with less chance of capital loss in normal times. A reliable rediscounting facility—a lender of last resort—means that markets have a liquidity guarantee in crises. In short, greater capital certainty means confidence that financial assets will be liquid and safe, a prerequisite of international currency issue and a complement to domestic financial market stability. In Chapter 4, I present evidence supporting the proposition: the architects of banking reform understood the dual outputs to be interdependent, and therefore linked them to a common set of institutional innovations.

In summary, an international currency requires (1) certainty of the currency's value and, therefore, low and stable inflation performance on the part of macroeconomic policymakers, and (2) a wide range of safe and liquid financial instruments denominated in that currency. It is useful to think of these requirements in terms of demand and supply: the former contributes to the *demand* for an international currency, while the latter is required to *supply* assets appropriate for international currency use. Lacking these attributes, a currency cannot be used internationally— they are the essential prerequisites for internationalizing a national currency. The U.S. dollar was well positioned with respect to price stability after 1896, but lacked domestic financial markets characterized by "breadth, depth, and resiliency." The assertion that core features of the Federal Reserve Act (as distinguished from, say, its foreign branching provisions) were internationally motivated derives from the basic complementarity of the two products. A well-developed domestic market meant not only the ability to supply assets appropriate for international currency use, but greater internal stability. Because the international output of globalizing the use of the dollar could be obtained only with institutions that also served to impart stability to the domestic payments system, it may have been impossible to have produced the outputs separately. Other reform measures, such as the Aldrich-Vreeland modification of the clearinghouse emergency currency mechanism or deregulation of the note issue and branch banking, might have been sufficient to forestall panics, but would not have provided the infrastructure necessary for the dollar to serve as an international payments and reserve currency. Banking reform, by necessity, had to address both objectives simultaneously.

Later in this chapter, I show that the benefits of internationalizing the financial system were sufficiently concentrated on a specific subset of social agents to motivate collective action on behalf of the joint, inseparable goods. But before turning to this matter, it is relevant to consider the additional factors that affect the global use of national currencies. While stable currency and well-developed financial markets are essential, several "supplementary" factors have been found to be influential. The factors in this category involve a nation's relative position in the global system: the extent, composition, and direction of the issuing country's foreign trade and the nation's balance of payments position.

Supplemental Factors Contributing to International Currency Use

Once the "essential" conditions are met, an additional factor that promotes the emergence of a dominant international currency is the *extent* of a nation's trade. Generally, the larger a nation's trade, the more likely it is that trade contracts will be invoiced in its currency. Being important in world trade necessarily means being important in world payments; the final demand for a nation's currency reflects the relative size òf the markets in it. In terms of transaction costs, the larger the volume of transactions conducted in a currency, the lower the costs of using that currency. As S. A. B. Page notes, "the larger a country's trade, the more likely are its currency, and probable movements in it, to be already familiar to traders."[20] Furthermore, a virtuous cycle can kick in once a currency emerges as a vehicle, enhancing that currency's international use even more: "Once a currency emerges as a vehicle, economies of scale enter into play, further decreasing transaction costs and enhancing the currency's position as a vehicle. For example, the more a currency is used, the greater the familiarity with it and the lower the costs of information and uncertainty—the greater, also, will be the probability of finding a matching transaction and thus the lower the search costs."[21] Kindleberger's analogy between international language and international money is relevant here: "The optimum language and currency areas today are not countries, nor continents, but the world; and because, for better or worse—and opinions differ on this—the choice of which language or which currency is made not on merit, or moral worth, but on size."[22]

Studies of invoicing decisions have also found several other patterns related to the composition and direction of trade. First, trade between developed countries in manufactured products tends to be invoiced in the currency of the exporter. Second, invoicing in the exporter's currency is more recurrent for differentiated manufactured products with long production lags. Third, trade between developed and less developed

[20] S. A. B. Page, "The Choice òf Invoicing Currency in Merchandise Trade," *National Institute Economic Review* 98 (November 1981): 60–72.

[21] Tavlas, *On the International Use of Currencies: The Case of the Deutsche Mark*, p. 6. See also Krugman, "The International Role of the Dollar."

[22] Charles P. Kindleberger, *The Politics of International Money and World Language*, Essays in International Finance, no. 61, International Finance Section, Princeton University (August 1967), p. 11.

countries tends to be denominated in the currency of the developed country. Fourth, trade in primary products and transactions in financial investments are usually denominated in the dominant international currency.[23]

At base, these patterns reflect agents' exposure to foreign exchange risk. Note that both exporters and importers prefer to avoid invoicing in foreign currencies, since their revenues, costs, and profits in terms of domestic currency will be affected if the exchange rate changes. Hence, the home currency is always the trader's "preferred monetary habitat."[24] Covering this risk by hedging in forward markets is possible, but these markets are typically thinner than spot markets and thus entail higher costs. Nevertheless, an important finding is that the exposure to exchange risk varies across sectors and regions. For example, the reason why trade in manufactured products tends to be invoiced in the exporter's currency is that exporters of such products are more exposed to exchange-rate risk than importers:

> Both the importer and the exporter consider the variance of their respective profits in making invoicing decisions. The covariance between revenue and costs, however, is likely to be higher for the importer than the exporter of manufactured products, the costs for which are determined early in the production process. Consequently, it is harder for exporters to cut their factor costs in response to a depreciation of their currencies [the longer the production lag, the greater the exporter's exchange risk]. They have to absorb unfavorable exchange-rate movements in lower profit margins. Exporters, therefore, have an incentive to invoice in their own currencies.[25]

Importers, in contrast, are more insulated from exchange risk, since they can often pass through a depreciation by charging a higher price for the product in the domestic market. This is more likely in small, open economies where a large, domestic import-competing industry does not exist, "which helps to explain why trade between a developed and a developing country is usually denominated in the currency of the developed country."[26] In the case of trade between developed countries with import-competing industries, this is typically not an option; hence, the importer must bear some exchange risk by contracting in the exporter's currency. However, importers in small open economies gain experience

[23] See the summary discussion in Tavlas and Ozeki, *The Internationalization of Currencies.*
[24] McKinnon, *Money in International Exchange*, p. 68.
[25] Tavlas, *On the International Use of Currencies*, p. 7.
[26] Tavlas and Ozeki, *The Internationalization of Currencies*, p. 5.

in dealing with the exchange risk of invoicing in foreign currencies. As Krugman states, "the importer . . . has to deal with exchange markets as a matter of course. . . . In small countries, everyone is obliged to be sophisticated about foreign exchange."[27] Additionally, importers sometimes receive open-account credits directly from exporters, thereby allowing "discretion in the timing of repayments as a quid pro quo for bearing currency risk."[28]

The reason why invoicing in the exporter's currency is more common for differentiated manufactured products with long production lags reflects the same currency risk factors, but also involves the market power of these exporters. Remember that all traders prefer to invoice in their home currency, but, as McKinnon points out, differentiated manufactured products are produced by firms possessing some degree of monopolistic power. Since exporters of these products "almost certainly possess more market power than the importer," exporters are typically in a position to guard against exchange risk by stipulating that invoicing be done in their own currencies. In effect, the monopolistic power of such firms enables them to shift exchange risk to importers. This market power can be put to use on the accounts payable side as well: should they deal with foreign suppliers for inputs, producers of differentiated goods can stipulate that import contracts be denominated in their own currency.

Another pattern is that the invoicing of trade in primary products and financial assets is typically done in the most important international currencies. These markets are characterized by low levels of product differentiation and are competitive; products are homogeneous, and prices are determined by global demand and supply conditions. Wheat, oil, and bonds, for example, are standardized goods whose prices are very much internationalized. Producers of such goods face less risk if they invoice in the most important currency, even when it is not their own, because the exchange rate and the domestic price of the product are likely to be highly correlated. If the producer's home currency depreciates against the vehicle currency, the price of the commodity—in terms of the producer's currency—is likely to be bid up by a similar amount, due to the law of one price: "International commodity arbitrage would be nearly perfect."[29] Hence, the most efficient procedure for homogenous goods is to have all contracts in the world written in the same currency, since this minimizes costs of information and calculation: "The choice of an invoic-

---

[27] Krugman, "The International Role of the Dollar," p. 271.
[28] McKinnon, *Money in International Exchange*, p. 79.
[29] Ibid., p. 83.

ing currency in competitive markets usually narrows to a single currency (or, at most, several vehicle currencies), since it is more efficient to transmit price-change information about homogenous products in a single currency than through many currencies."[30] The dominant vehicle currency is the obvious candidate, since it is the currency with which most participants are familiar.

These patterns indicate that the two necessary conditions for the international use of a nation's currency do not fully explain why a particular currency emerges as a dominant international currency. Switzerland, for instance, possesses both stable money and deep, articulated financial markets, but the Swiss franc is not used extensively as an international currency. Based on the preceding analysis, the global importance of a currency also reflects (1) the issuing country's share of world exports, (2) its share of differentiated manufactured product exports, and (3) its share of trade with developing countries. The larger a country's share of world exports, the more its exports are composed of differentiated manufactured products, the larger its share of products that are imported by developing countries, the greater the likelihood that its currency will be used internationally.

A final consideration concerns the nation's balance of payments position. Given the essential conditions, a persistent pattern of current account surplus, offset by capital outflows, can serve as a "promotional mechanism for the international use of a nation's currency."[31] The promotional effect accrues due to the fact that (1) the export of capital will induce foreigners to acquire balances denominated in the capital-exporting country's currency to service the obligations, and (2) because the transfer of liquidity from the capital-exporting country to the deficit country is accompanied by a transfer of goods and services in the same direction, so that foreigners demand claims in the currency of the exporter to pay for imports from the surplus nation. In short, the current account surplus/capital outflow pattern increases the demand for a currency, as foreigners acquire short-term claims denominated in that currency both to service long-term loans and to pay for imports from the surplus country. There is also a reinforcing feedback mechanism underlying this process: the surplus nation's ability to attract short-term capital enhances its capacity to supply longer-term loans to the rest of the world, as net short-term inflows mean the surplus country can borrow short in order to lend long. Furthermore, the longer-term capital supplied to the rest of the world, denominated in the surplus nation's cur-

---

[30] Tavlas and Ozeki, *The Internationalization of Currencies*, p. 5.
[31] Tavlas, *On the International Use of Currencies*, p. 11.

rency, also facilitates the international use of its currency. With respect to London's role as world banker in the nineteenth century, David Williams observes that foreigners held short-term claims in sterling, partly "to meet sterling obligations in London."[32]

Consequently, a nation running a current account surplus over a protracted period of time is in a position to serve as a "world banker." When a nation serves as a world banker, it imports short-term capital and exports longer-term capital, denominated in its own currency, thereby supplying liquidity to the international financial system. This is exactly the process that underpinned the use of sterling and, later, the dollar: "Banks in these nations provided liquidity—denominated in sterling and the U.S. dollar, respectively—to the rest of the world and used the funds (i.e., short-term capital inflows) so acquired to make longer-term investments in the rest of the world, which were also denominated in sterling or the U.S. dollar."[33]

The status of world banker, however, does not develop automatically from a persistent current account surplus. The ability to serve as world banker is, in fact, directly related to the necessary conditions for international currency use listed above:

> In particular, the capacity of a nation's banks to attract short-term capital denominated in its own currency depends importantly upon the certainty of the currency's value (and, therefore, on the nation's inflation performance) and the availability of a range of safe, liquid financial instruments denominated in that currency. For example, if foreigners are acquiring short-term claims (i.e., supplying short-term capital), on a net basis, in the currency of a particular country, it implies (1) the country possesses a large supply of short-term, relative high-yielding financial instruments denominated in its own currency; (2) access to these instruments is relatively free from controls; and (3) foreigners attach a relatively high degree of certainty to the value of that nation's currency (and, therefore, that the nation has a relatively low and stable inflation rate)."[34]

Table 2.2 summarizes the necessary and supplementary factors that determine international currency use. In regard to the essential domestic factors, the United States had attained price stability by commitment to the gold standard, but lacked well-developed financial markets. Evidence on the supplemental international factors is presented in Chapter

---

[32] Williams, "The Evolution of the Sterling System," p. 268.
[33] Tavlas and Ozeki, *The Internationalization of Currencies*, p. 18.
[34] Ibid.

Table 2.2. Necessary and supplementary characteristics of international currency countries

Necessary (domestic) characteristics	Supplementary (international) characteristics
1. Issuing nations typically have proven low inflation and inflation variability records. Price stability may derive from central bank independence, a binding commitment to fixed exchange-rates, strict monetary growth rules, etc. 2. Issuing nations typically have broad, deep, and resilient domestic financial markets.	1. Issuing nations are typically major trading nations in the world system; nations that command a large relative share of world exports. 2. Issuing nations are typically large developed nations; nations that command a large relative share of world manufactured-product exports (of both differentiated and standardized goods). 3. Issuing nations typically trade heavily with developing countries, and command a large relative share of exports to the developing world. 4. Issuing nations typically register persistent current account surpluses, and offsetting capital outflows.

3, and the findings indicate that by 1913, the U.S. economy had advanced to a position where the dollar should have acquired a major international standing. That it failed to do so reflected the underdevelopment of domestic financial markets. The remainder of this chapter explores the distributional implications of internationalizing the currency, the goal being to identify the domestic agents with preferences for or against international currency institutions.

International Distributional Effects

The distributional implications of international currency use are typically discussed in international terms—the relative gains and losses accruing to issuing versus nonissuing nations. In this accounting, the nation-state is the unit of analysis, and national welfare is defined in terms of net social benefits and costs. Literature on the *domestic* distributional issues is virtually nonexistent. In the following sections, however, I demonstrate that it is possible to derive domestic political propositions from the welfare implications of international currency use. The starting point is still the existing literature, with its focus on the international distribution of benefits and costs. I merely add the recognition that the benefits and costs are not distributed symmetrically among domestic residents, which suggests the possibility of both collective action and interest group conflict over internationalizing the currency.

International currency status confers three major benefits and one important cost on the issuing nation. The first benefit is that the issuing country earns *seignorage* on the other countries' holdings of its currency: other countries have to give up real goods and services in order to add to their key currency balances. The second benefit involves economic *rents*. Since the banking sector of the issuing country has an effective monopoly over the issue of monetary liabilities denominated in the vehicle currency, the nation earns "denomination" rents from the international use of its currency.[35] The third benefit involves the risks and expenses of transactions involving foreign exchange. Since cross-border transactions are denominated in the local currency, residents of the issuing country are able to shunt exchange risks and costs on nonresidents. The major disadvantage of international currency status is diminished scope to control the domestic money supply. Due to the foreign use of a nation's currency, macroeconomic conditions may be subject to larger fluctuations than before, and international credibility must be maintained, even at the expense of domestic monetary conditions. International currency status thus constrains domestic macroeconomic independence.

Seignorage—the difference between the value of the money issued and its costs of production—accrues to the issuing country because the foreign claims built upon the country are denominated in its own currency. According to Cohen: "The seignorage benefit takes the form of a greater cumulative deficit in the country's balance of payments than would otherwise be possible—in effect, a kind of 'free' command over foreign goods, services and assets—owing to the willingness of other states to accumulate the reserve center's currency as reserves. The center country would be able to finance deficits simply by issuing liabilities . . . rather than by giving up reserves."[36] In short, foreigners extend credit to the issuing country, but at the prevailing interest rate. This gain accrues to the issuing country, since it issues the currency held as international reserves by official agents. Alexander Swoboda also notes that the concept can be extended to the currency holdings of private nonresidents, which result from the vehicle status of a currency.[37] As Tavlas notes, however, "The temptation to exploit seignorage can lead to higher inflation in the key-currency country and can thus eventually undermine one

[35] Alexander K. Swoboda, *The Euro-Dollar Market: An Interpretation,* Essays in International Finance, no. 64, International Finance Section, Princeton University (1968), pp. 105–6.
[36] Benjamin J. Cohen, *Organizing the World's Money* (New York: Basic Books, 1977), p. 71.
[37] Swoboda, *The Euro-Dollar Market,* p.104.

of the essential prerequisites for using its currency internationally."[38] During the Bretton Woods era, for example, the United States exploited this benefit and ultimately eroded confidence in the value of the dollar.

Economic rents also accrue to the issuing country, specifically to its banking sector. Inasmuch as the banking system of the center country has an effective monopoly over the issue of monetary liabilities denominated in the vehicle currency, expansion of such liabilities to meet the needs of nonresidents means that the banking sector earns supernormal profits, which it would not have received had their liabilities been denominated in another currency. In other words, "the average level of profits of the banking system of an issuing country will tend, other things equal, to be higher than that of the banking systems of other countries."[39] In more practical terms, "as the international use of currency expands, loans, investments, and purchases of goods and services will increasingly be executed through the financial institutions of the issuing country. Thus, the earnings of its financial sector are likely to increase [relative to the financial sectors of non-issuing nations]."[40] Cohen provides a lucid description of the process:

> A direct benefit of an international currency derives from the fact that when a currency begins to be used internationally, purchases and sales, and loans and investments, will most likely have to be executed through banks or brokers in the issuing country. Consequently, the earnings of the banking sector and its ancillary activities, including the foreign exchange market, are likely to rise. These extra earnings will include not only the commissions charged for the increased volume of foreign exchange transactions, but also the fees charged for investment services, such as the placement of foreign securities and the purchase of domestic financial assets for foreign accounts. In addition, they will include the interest earned on the higher total of foreign loans and investments.[41]

When a nation's currency is used internationally, there is simply "more business for the country's banks and other financial institutions."[42]

Another benefit for the issuing country comes in the form of reduced foreign exchange costs and risks. Assume that all foreign trade is settled

---

[38] Tavlas, *On the International Use of Currencies*, p. 13.
[39] Ibid., p. 106. Swoboda shows how the rise of the Euro-dollar market eroded the monopoly position of American banks and distributed denomination rents to banks of other countries.
[40] Tavlas, *On the International Use of Currencies*, p. 12.
[41] Cohen, *The Future of Sterling as an International Currency*, p. 37.
[42] Jeffrey A. Frankel, "Still the Lingua Franca: The Exaggerated Death of the Dollar," *Foreign Affairs* 74 (July/August, 1995): 11.

in a single vehicle currency. Here, the residents of the issuing country require no foreign cash in their working balances and are, therefore, able to bypass the costs of exchanging domestic for foreign currency assets. Also, to the extent that they are concerned with the domestic-currency value of their net worth, residents of the issuing country need bear no part of the risk of exchange-rate uncertainty, since they never have to leave the local currency domain.[43] Only nonresidents must transact in a foreign currency (the vehicle currency), which means that they must bear the costs and exchange risk. In effect, residents of the issuing country are able to shunt the costs and risks of dealing in foreign exchange to nonresidents. In speaking of the present role of the dollar, for example, Jeffrey Frankel notes: "It is certainly more convenient for a country's exporters, importers, borrowers and lenders to be able to deal in their own currency rather than in foreign currencies. The global use of the dollar, as with the global use of the English Language, is a natural advantage that American businesspeople tend to take for granted."[44]

The most serious cost to international currency status is that it constrains domestic monetary independence: extensive foreign holdings of a currency reduce the degree of control over the money supply. Underlying this approach is the view that substantial swings in capital flows can interfere with domestic stabilization, though the loss of control is related to how open an economy is.[45] A move by a central bank to tighten or loosen monetary conditions could be undermined by capital inflows or outflows, and by the consequent expansion or reduction of liabilities to nonresidents. Between the late 1960s and the early 1980s, for example, both Japan and Germany sought to limit the international use of their currencies for precisely this reason. A specific case in point occurred in 1972, when the Bundesbank, following restrictive monetary policies aimed at lowering inflation, was frustrated by the capital inflows induced by the policies. This led the Bundesbank to intervene in support of the U.S. dollar. To offset the effects of this intervention on the money supply, the Bundesbank had to initiate even more restrictive monetary measures, "which led to more capital inflows, and so on."[46] To end the vicious cycle, the Bundesbank eventually imposed strict controls over

---

[43] Swoboda, *The Euro-Dollar Market*, p.103.

[44] Frankel, "Still the Lingua Franca," p. 11. The language metaphor is from Kindleberger, *The Politics of International Money and World Language.*

[45] According to optimal currency area theory, exchange rate fluctuations induce larger domestic price changes in more open economies, thereby complicating the task of domestic stabilization polices and contributing to the preference for stable exchange rates. See, for example, Paul R. Masson and Mark P. Taylor, "Common Currency Areas and Currency Unions: An Analysis of the Issues," *Journal of International and Comparative Economics* (1992).

[46] Tavlas, *On the International Use of Currencies*, pp. 16–19.

the issue of deutsche mark liabilities in international markets, thus limiting the use of the currency internationally. In effect, Germany chose to sacrifice the growing internationalization of its currency—and the gains that would accrue to German residents—in order to maintain its grip on domestic monetary conditions. To the extent that international currency status and national monetary autonomy are incompatible, all potential vehicle currency countries must resolve this trade-off. Table 2.3 summarizes the benefits and costs of international currency status.

Domestic Distributional Effects

The preceding section discussed the distributional effects that occur at the international level when a national currency attains global currency status: certain benefits and costs accrue to the issuing nation that do not accrue to nonissuing countries. This background can also serve as the basis for a systematic evaluation of the domestic politics intrinsic to international currency use.[47] With the exception of seignorage, the benefits and costs accruing to the issuing nation are not distributed symmetrically among domestic residents: some residents gain direct (private) ben-

Table 2.3. International distributional effects of key currency status

Benefits	Costs
1. The issuing country gains seignorage, or the "automatic" access to short-term foreign credit.	1. The issuing country loses some of its monetary independence, since extensive foreign holdings of a currency reduces the issuer's control over the domestic money supply.
2. The issuing country earns denomination rents, as the monopoly over the issue of cross-border monetary liabilities means its banking sector obtains an above-normal rate of return.	
3. The issuing country benefits from reduced foreign exchange costs and risks, because residents do not have to deal in foreign exchange when transactions with nonresidents are conducted in the home currency.	

[47] This section builds on two previous works: Jeffry Frieden, "Invested Interests: The Politics of National Economic Policies in a World of Global Finance," *International Organization* 45 (Autumn 1991): 425–51; and C. Randall Henning, *Currencies and Politics in the United States, Germany and Japan* (Washington, D.C.: Institute for International Economics, 1994).

efits from the international use of the local currency while being relatively insulated from the costs, while others obtain little benefit but are fully exposed to the costs. (Since seignorage accrues directly to the government of the issuing country, any distributional effects fall out of prevailing transfer mechanisms. For simplicity, I treat seignorage as distributionally neutral in the domestic context). In this section, I map out the domestic distributional effects of international currency use and, from these effects, infer the preferences and the relative preference intensities of resident actors for currency internationalization.

A preliminary framework designates preferences along a single dimension: the extent to which an actor is engaged in international economic activity (internationalists-nationalists). This simple framework is then refined in order to draw inferences on relative preference *intensities* of actors within these broad constituencies. Since the benefits and costs of international currency status are concentrated, it is possible to identify the agents with the most at stake. To look ahead, banks and financial firms in national financial centers, and exporters of differentiated manufactured products, are expected to have the strongest incentives for internationalizing a currency and, therefore, the most intense motives to install the necessary domestic institutions.

Consider first the denomination rents that accrue to the issuing country. As noted above, the country issuing an international currency derives rents vis-à-vis other nations because its banking sector has an effective monopoly over the issue of monetary liabilities denominated in the vehicle currency. Although this point is about global redistribution, a more subtle distributional effect arises *inside* the vehicle currency country. First and most obviously, it is the banking sector that benefits directly, since there is no necessary reason why rents earned by banks must be distributed more widely. In fact, to the extent that foreign demands divert financial resources away from domestic economic activity, other sectors might be left worse off from international currency status. Second, rents are likely to be unevenly distributed *within* the banking sector. When a currency is used internationally, foreign purchases and sales, and loans and investments, are typically executed through a small number of highly specialized banks, brokers, and underwriters located in the issuing country's main financial centers. As is well known, economies of scale, external economies, and transaction cost factors give rise to the dominance of a financial center within a nation, and to the centralization and concentration of international financial activity within this center.[48] International banking and financial services are not carried out

---

[48] Charles A. Kindleberger, *The Formation of Financial Centers*, Studies in International Finance, no. 36, International Finance Section, Princeton University (1974).

by *all* banks and financial firms in the issuing country—indeed, the rank and file of banks in the hinterlands of an issuing country do little business which would give rise to such transactions. Instead, a small group of large, specialized firms with detailed knowledge of these activities and well-developed connections to foreign markets typically handle the foreign financial business of the entire nation.

In the American context, for example, "no more than a score" of leading private banks (unincorporated partnerships with European connections, such as J. P. Morgan & Co., Kuhn, Loeb & Co., Kidder, Peabody & Co., and Alexander Brown & Sons) conducted most of the nation's foreign banking and securities business between 1870 and 1914: "They financed most of the country's foreign trade that was not foreign financed, and were involved in negotiating nearly all the international loans raised to refund the United States government's Civil War debt and to help pay for the expansion, consolidation, and reorganization of the nation's rail system."[49] They also intermediated the foreign capital that helped establish the industrial giants of the era. In short, the provision of international financial services is a concentrated, oligopolistic affair, characterized by significant barriers to entry arising from economies of scale and transaction cost factors. Hence, if monopoly rents accrue to a nation issuing an international currency, it is this small group that most directly reaps them.

Consider the actual processes by which rents are generated. First, having the home currency serve as the international vehicle currency gives money-center banks positioned to engage in international financial activity the ability to earn the commissions, fees, and interest associated with the relatively safe and lucrative business of financing world trade and payments. Secondly, as foreign banks, central banks, and businesses come to regard the center country's currency as a store of value (i.e., as suitable for holding private assets and official reserves), large inflows of short-term funds enter the nation's central money market as working balances, maintained in preparation for making future payments. The overall increase in the demand for national banking services that derives from the use of the currency for vehicle, reserve, and asset purposes is thus of decided advantage to banks that have the resources and connections to attract foreign balances and lend abroad. Therefore, large money-center financial firms with international orientations should have relatively intense preferences for installing the domestic institutions that underpin international currency status.

---

[49] Vincent P. Carosso and Richard Sylla, "U.S. Banks in International Finance," in *International Banking, 1870–1914*, ed. Rondo Cameron and V. I. Bovykin (New York: Oxford University Press, 1991), p. 55.

Next consider the exchange-rate benefit that accrues to an international currency country. In a global perspective, one of the main benefits accruing to the nation issuing an international currency is a reduction in the risks and costs of foreign exchange. This gain, however, does not accrue to *all* domestic residents evenly: it is concentrated specifically upon those agents who are heavily involved in world trade and payments—importers, exporters, and foreign lenders. Consider the case where a currency is used extensively for global invoicing and medium of exchange purposes: it is resident importers and exporters that are freed of the costs and risks of foreign exchange dealings since they are the specific agents who no longer have to worry about the vagaries of foreign exchange. By financing the country's foreign trade at home in bills denominated in the home currency, these actors benefit directly, as they no longer have to deal in other currencies. Whatever exchange risks exist are effectively transferred to foreigners, who must receive or make payments in a currency other than their own. Resident exporters in a potential issuing country benefit in an additional way. Financing exports through domestic banks in the local currency reduces the total costs of financing, since exporters are no longer obligated to pay "double" commissions—one to the domestic bank which draws the original bill and the other to the foreign bank that "accepts" it (guarantees payment) in a currency of international standing. This savings can be passed on to foreign purchasers in the form of lower prices, making exporters more competitive in global markets.[50]

The exchange benefit also accrues to resident foreign investors. As foreign loans are denominated in the center country's own currency, all exchange risks and hedging costs are shouldered by foreign borrowers, since they must make payments in that currency. For lenders in the center country, exchange risk is virtually eliminated, as they have no need to deal in foreign exchange. This advantage, of course, accrues to all types of foreign lending, whether for 30 days or 30 years, and thus benefits international banks lending short, as well as international financiers lending long. To the extent that short-term financing paves the way for the expansion of long-term lending—the normal sequence of events leading to the rise of a "world banker"—resident investment bankers, who underwrite and distribute foreign securities, and the broader investing public, who purchase and hold foreign bonds, benefit from international invoicing and medium of exchange roles of the local currency.

The exchange benefits that accrue specifically to actors with overseas

[50] Robert S. Mayer, *The Influence of Frank A. Vanderlip and the National City Bank on American Commerce and Foreign Policy, 1910–1920* (New York: Garland, 1987), pp. 89–90.

investments (short-term, portfolio, or direct), producers of manufactured and primary products with large foreign markets, internationally-oriented merchants and shippers, and consumers of foreign imports as inputs or final products, provide the basis for identifying the coalition that supports the internationalization of a currency. As these actors are heavily engaged in world trade and payments, it is accurate to term this the "international currency coalition." Not only do these agents gain from the reduction of exchange-rate risk implied by conducting foreign transactions in the home currency, they are also relatively insulated from the central cost of key currency status—reduced domestic monetary policy flexibility. As Jeffry Frieden points out, internationalists typically conduct business in a host of countries, so they can respond to unfavorable domestic economic conditions by shifting more business abroad.[51] In other words, their ability to buy, sell, or invest in more than one market protects internationalists from having to suffer the effects of reduced domestic monetary autonomy. As these agents gain directly from international currency status and are relatively protected from the costs, they should align with money-center bankers in support of foundational domestic institutions.

While foreign traders are expected to support efforts to globalize the domestic currency, preference *intensities* within this broad coalition need not be symmetrical. The home currency is all traders' "preferred monetary habitat"; yet, some internationalists prefer it more than others. Specifically, exporters of manufactured products—especially differentiated manufactured goods—can be expected to have the strongest incentives to see the home currency internationalized. In contrast, importers of all types of goods and exporters of raw materials and agricultural products will be relatively less motivated. These distinctions reflect variance in traders' exposure to foreign exchange risk, as detailed above.

Recall that production of manufactured goods typically involves long lags which expose manufacturers to high exchange-rate risk when exporting. Since the costs of production are determined early in the production process, it is difficult for manufacturers to adjust factor costs in response to exchange-rate variations. Instead, they typically have to absorb unfavorable exchange-rate movements in the form of lower profits. Exporters of differentiated manufactured products not only bear high exchange risk, but are also in a position to do something about it: they can leverage their market power vis-à-vis nonresidents into the requirement that invoicing be done in their home currency. Resident importers, on the other hand, are protected in one of two ways: (1) When an im-

---

[51] Frieden, "Invested Interests," p. 445.

port-competing industry does not exist, importers can often pass through exchange-rate changes to purchasers. (2) Even in the presence of competing domestic industries, importers are relatively insensitive to invoicing in a foreign currency, since they are required to be sophisticated about foreign exchange as a matter of course. Exporters of primary and agricultural products are relatively less exposed for a somewhat related reason. As they produce homogeneous tradable goods, the prices of which are determined by global market conditions, they face less exchange risk in invoicing exports in a foreign currency, since commodity prices adjust readily to the exchange rate.

Though it is difficult to rank precisely the relative preference intensities of internationalist coalition members, the foregoing does suggest that globalizing the currency and the payments system should be most highly valued by exporting producers of specialized and standardized manufactured products, while importing merchants and exporting producers of primary and agricultural products should be more or less indifferent. They all benefit from having international transactions denominated in the home currency, but the benefits are inversely related to the degree of exchange-rate risk specific to each sector.

To summarize, internationalists benefit from international currency status, but preference intensities will vary within the coalition. The small group of money-center banks and financial firms engaged in foreign trade finance, foreign exchange, and capital intermediation (inflows and outflows) is expected to have the strongest preference for international currency status, since the rents accrue specifically to them. Globalizing the currency should also be relatively highly valued by exporters of specialized manufactured goods, because they are most exposed to foreign exchange risk and have the market power to obtain invoicing in the local currency. Exporters of standardized manufactured goods, while lacking market power, also face significant exchange risks and should thus be relatively strong supporters of the institutions necessary for the currency to obtain global status. The coalition members with the least to gain, and, therefore, the weakest positive preference, are importers and exporters of raw materials and agricultural products. They are least exposed to exchange risk, as domestic prices typically adjust for exchange rate changes. Table 2.4 summarizes preference intensities within the internationalist coalition.

On the other side of the spectrum, and with institutional preferences in conflict with internationalists, stand "economic nationalists": individuals and firms whose market activities take place primarily within national borders. Among those so restricted are uncompetitive tradables producers servicing the home market, and producers of nontradable

Table 2.4. Domestic beneficiaries of international currency issue, ranked by intensity of preference

The international currency coalition				
strongest preference --weakest preference				
Money-center banks	Exporters of specialized manufactured products	Exporters of standardized manufactured products	Importers of foreign inputs or finished products	Exporters of homogenous primary and agricultural products

goods and services. Since the well-being of these actors depends first and foremost upon the health of the domestic economy, they gain little, if at all, from the internationalization of the currency. Their money dealings are primarily in the local currency, which means that reduced exchange risk is a benefit that is largely irrelevant to them. Likewise, denomination rents accrue not to firms engaged in domestic financial activity but to institutions intermediating international business. While the seignorage benefit may offer the near-term advantage of reducing the balance of payments constraint on national macroeconomic policy, it is a double-edged sword. In the long run, a nation issuing a global currency must give priority to maintaining currency stability over competing domestic goals. Because the nominal interest rate on debt is comprised of a real component and an expected-inflation component, countries with international currencies can inflate away a portion of the real purchasing power of the claims held by foreigners through policies that raise inflation above its expected level. However, exploiting seignorage in this fashion has definite limits. During the Bretton Woods era, for example, the United States was able to run chronic balance of payments deficits and avoid internal adjustment, because Europeans were willing to accumulate dollars in their central banks. By electing to hold reserves in dollars rather than gold, Europeans, in effect, chose to underwrite expansive American policies. As the deficits increased, however, and outstanding dollar holdings abroad became too large in relation to gold reserves, the constraint ultimately emerged—confidence in the dollar eroded and the United States lost whatever "flexibility" it had in dealing with payments imbalances.[52] In the long run, currency internationalization imposes hardships on nationalists, since it concentrates upon these actors the brunt of the major cost of international currency status: reduced national monetary independence.

[52] See Robert Triffin, *Gold and the Dollar Crisis* (New Haven: Yale University Press, 1960).

Nationalists' first concern is with the condition of the domestic economy; hence, their institutional preferences are for reducing the exposure
of the national economy to the rigors of maintaining stable currency.
That is, these groups have interests in structures that place domestic economic considerations above ensuring the stability of the currency. And
because the adjustment costs associated with maintaining external equilibrium in the context of stable currency weigh heavily upon these actors, their institutional interests lie in promoting agendas that enhance
the prospects for national monetary policy autonomy. Insular structures
are preferred because they can accommodate policies that support a rising price level, economic growth, and unemployment at full employment levels, even in the face of balance of payments pressures. Nationalists favor floating exchange rates, for example, as free rates give national
monetary authorities more flexibility in dealing with balance of payments constraints.[53] Other favored institutions include rules that expand
or eliminate the commodity base that backs the currency (e.g., bimetallism, "free silver," etc.), weak or nonexistent monetary growth rules, politically controlled central banks, and exchange and capital controls.

Obtaining few benefits, but fully exposed to the costs, economic nationalists can be expected to oppose efforts to internationalize a national
currency. The reason is that center countries must usually subordinate
domestic objectives to the external goal of maintaining confidence in the
soundness and convertibility of the currency. Since the well-being of the
domestic economy depends in some measure on the depth, breadth, and
resilience of the national financial system—the second prerequisite of an
international currency country—nationalists' opposition may be tem-
pered or uneven. Specifically, nationalists' preferences should be most
intense on the issue of currency stability, but relatively muted on measures aimed at the fuller development of national financial markets and
the establishment of a rediscounting facility to ensure the liquidity of
these markets. This is because enhancing the scope and liquidity of the
domestic financial system has dual and complementary effects. On the
one hand, it promotes the global use of the home currency, generating
the concentrated benefits that accrue specifically to members of the internationalist coalition. On the other hand, it adds stability to the domestic
banking system—a genuine public good for all domestic residents. Nationalists gain from domestic banking stability, so they should be relatively less concerned about these liquidity-enhancing institutions. Nevertheless, the basic conflict between internationalists and nationalists

[53] Frieden, "Invested Interests."

should be observable in the particulars. On the matter of where central bank policymaking power should reside, nationalists should tend to prefer more "democratic" authority structures, in which key policymaking offices are staffed by politicians or political appointees. In all but the most open economies, nationalists greatly outnumber those agents with large stakes in the international economy; hence, a government-controlled central bank is more likely to be responsive to popular pressures for policies that promote domestic economic prosperity and full employment. Internationalists, by contrast, want the central bank to maintain a stable currency orientation above all else and, as a means to this end, demand structures that shelter the agency from democratic influences. There are, of course, several institutional ways to achieve this, from establishing the central bank as a private or quasi-private corporation, to formulating strict monetary growth rules that constrain the central bank to act in an orthodox manner. In any event, we can expect the issue of central bank "autonomy" to be controversial, as it goes to the very heart of the conflict between internationalists and nationalists.

The discord may also be observed in debates over the types of assets that are eligible for purchase or rediscount by the central bank. Eligibility rules are important because they encourage or discourage alternative forms of lending and, thereby, shape the structure of the money market. For example, if credit instruments suitable for use in international exchange are favored among the types of paper eligible for rediscount or purchase by the central bank, not only will open market credit be channeled in this direction, but the overall discount market will be encouraged to develop along cosmopolitan lines. Conversely, if the rules give priority to domestic paper, open market credit will gravitate toward these instruments, and the market will tend to develop along parochial lines. Internationalists should thus have a distinct preference for rules that give bills of exchange based on international transactions (acceptances) a privileged position at the discount window, while nationalists should prefer eligibility rules that favor the range of credit instruments which carry domestic transactions—such as internal bills, commercial paper, and agricultural credit instruments.

These arguments suggest patterns of social and political activity on institutions that promote the internationalization of a currency. One issue is whether monetary policy and the credit system shall be managed toward the fulfillment of currency stability, or toward domestic economic growth, rising prices, and full employment. If a nation is to serve as an international banking center, priority must be given to the former. In addition, an international currency country must also be able to offer financial instruments suitable for use in global trade and payments, articulated secondary markets for such instruments, and a rediscount window capable of making a market for these assets in times of distress. Predictions about politics are inferred from the domestic distribution of benefits and costs arising from international currency status. In short, the basis of support for global currency institutions comes from internationalists in general, but financial firms in the nations' banking centers and exporters of manufactured products have the most intense preferences. Conversely, domestically bound economic actors have strong preferences against institutions that promote stable currency at the expense of domestic monetary policy autonomy, but will be relatively mute on the other key prerequisite of an international issuer—well-developed home financial markets. This anticipated pattern of social preferences is summarized in the following propositions.

1. The basic social division on institutions required to develop the national currency for international use will fall between internationalists and nationalists. Internationalists favor international currency status because the benefits are concentrated among their members, while the costs are borne largely by others.
2. Among internationalists, money-center financial firms and exporters of manufactured products (especially differentiated products) will have the most intense preference for installing the institutions that stand behind the international use of the currency. These are the agents expected to act collectively in support of such institutions.
3. Economic nationalists will have stronger preferences on institutions that involve the stability of the currency, than on institutions that involve the depth, scope, and liquidity of the domestic financial system. Both are essential to international currency use, but the latter has a positive complementary effect on the provision of financial stability—a public good—which mitigates the opposition of nationalists.

By extrapolating from the economics, I have identified the likely pattern of social preferences regarding the internationalizing of a national currency. The overall framework, however, is quite static—preferences on international currency institutions are fixed and do not vary across time and place—and hence is ill-suited to explaining institutional *change*. To address the causes of institutional variation, something in the framework must vary. Building such dynamism into the framework is the objective of the next chapter. The argument is that the critical factor involves the international economic position of a nation. Like the political reasoning of this chapter, this claim is founded on existing empirical findings, which show that the extent, composition, and direction of a nation's foreign trade, as well as its overall payments position, influence the use of currencies internationally. By extension, change in the international position of an economy systematically effects the domestic politics of international currency use.

3 /

The International Economy,
Patterns of Currency Use,
and Domestic Politics

The literature on international currencies specifies the necessary and supplementary determinants of international currency use. The necessary characteristics are domestic, while the supplementary factors involve the relative international economic positions of nations. The argument of this chapter is that change in the latter is causally linked to change in the former by way of its impact on the preferences of domestic actors. Specifically, growth in a large nation's share of world exports, growth in its share of manufactured exports, growth in its share of exports to developing countries, and the onset of persistent current account surpluses feed back on domestic politics by motivating the beneficiaries of international currency use to demand the installation of the necessary domestic institutions. The first section of the chapter fleshes out the causal processes involved, the second provides empirical support for the view that the changing international economic situation after the 1870s implied greater use for the U.S. dollar as an international currency, and the third presents data on international currency use before World War I. The final section evaluates the domestic financial characteristics of existing key currency countries (England, Germany, and France) and assesses how accurately the framework maps domestic politics within these countries. Full treatment of the U.S. case is the subject of Chapters 4 and 5.

The supplementary factors effecting international currency use involve the relative extent, direction, and composition of trade, as well as balance of payments considerations. Consider first the relationship between the *extent* of a nation's foreign trade and the global use of its currency. Clearly, not all economies have the size and scope in global markets to generate international demand for their currencies, regardless of their records for currency stability and the depth and breadth of their domestic financial markets. Switzerland possesses both domestic prerequisites, but the Swiss franc is not a major international currency because Switzerland is not a large country in world trade and payments. The point is that use of a nation's currency internationally reflects, in part, the relative size of markets in it; it is the currencies of countries that loom large in the world economy that will be demanded on that account. This explains why a country's share of world exports has been found to be an important determinant of invoicing patterns. By extension, *growth* in a large country's share of world exports should generate pressures within that nation to develop its currency for invoicing purposes.

To simplify matters, a secular rise in a nation's relative export position can develop in one of two ways: either more producers become internationally competitive, entering new product markets abroad, or existing exporters increase their foreign market shares. Either way, a change in the domestic political balance will occur. When new producers conquering new product markets overseas account for a rising share of world exports, the ranks of the internationalist coalition will swell, while the nationalist bloc will lose some members. When the rising share of world exports is due to an expansion of existing exporters' foreign markets, these actors' preference for internationalizing the currency should become more intense, further redressing the coalitional balance. In other words, an advance in a large nation's international economic position, as marked by an increasing share of world exports, should strengthen the internationalist currency coalition by increasing its *size* relative to that of the rival nationalist coalition, and/or by increasing the *intensity* of its members' preferences.

Next consider change in the *composition* of a large nation's exports. Should exports shift from an agricultural/primary product basis to a mix favoring manufactured products, exporters of the latter will become a more important part of the international currency coalition. That is, a parallel shift will occur within the currency coalition, as the ratio of manufactured goods exporters to traditional product exporters turns in favor of the former. Since exporting manufacturers are among the most vulnerable to exchange-rate risk, the political implication is that the coalition will have stronger incentives to press for internationalizing the currency, since this result will mitigate exchange risk. (Note, however, that producers of manufactured goods need not be "internationalist" in respect to all aspects of foreign economic policy; e.g., the tariff). Should the export mix also show a rise in differentiated manufactured products, the intensity of this local currency preference should be even stronger. Here again, change at the global level feeds back on domestic institutional politics by way of its effect on preference intensities.

Change in the *direction* of trade is also relevant to the analysis. As seen in Chapter 2, trade between developed and developing countries tends to be denominated and settled in the currency of the developed country. The choice of invoicing and settlement currency reflects the relative exchange-rate risk and exposure of the parties to this trade. Invoicing and payment is denominated in the developed country's currency because (1) importers in developing countries can "pass through" the exchange-rate costs inherent in invoicing in a foreign currency, (2) developing-country exporters of traditional goods are insulated from exchange risk, because the exchange rate and the domestic price of undifferentiated products produced in competitive markets tend to track one another, and (3) developed-country exporters of manufactured products prefer to invoice in their own currency, because they are most exposed to exchange-rate risk. All else equal, the equilibrium result is that trade is financed in the currency of the developed country.

Now consider the domestic political effects of change in the international position of the developed trading state. A rise in that nation's share of exports going to developing countries should be reflected in more manufacturers joining the international currency coalition and/or stronger preferences among existing exporting manufacturers for doing all that is necessary to attain invoicing currency status. In other words, as a large country's exports shift to developing countries, we should expect to see a parallel shift in the size and the intensity of the key currency coalition. For manufacturers whose trade with developing countries was previously financed and invoiced in a foreign currency, the desire to reduce exposure to exchange risk should translate into political action aimed at developing the home currency for international use. For this to happen, the domestic prerequisites must be established, and the expectation is that a rise in the nation's share of exports headed to developing country markets should contribute to manufacturing exporters' demand for these prerequisites.

Finally, consider changes in the large nation's balance of payments position. Recall that a protracted period of current account surpluses has a positive impact on the use of that nation's currency internationally. When a nation exports more goods and services than it imports, capital flows out from the surplus nation to provide deficit countries with liquidity to finance imports. The promotional effect results specifically from the fact that the export of capital induces nonresidents to acquire balances denominated in the capital-exporting country's currency, both to service the obligations and to pay for imports from the surplus nation. That is, foreigners seek financial instruments denominated in the surplus country's currency to make payments and settle trade. Furthermore, the surplus nation's ability to attract short-term capital enhances its capacity to supply longer-term loans to the rest of the world, thereby facilitating its rise to the position of world banker.[1]

Within the surplus nation, the enhanced demand for financial instruments denominated in that nation's currency is felt most directly by financial firms in national money centers. These are the firms with the scale, resources, and connections necessary to offer foreigners the short-term claims they desire for liquidity and payments purposes. They are thus the direct beneficiaries of the enhanced demand for financial services (i.e., they earn the denomination rents accruing to vehicle currency countries). Their ability to offer foreigners short-term claims denominated in the home currency depends first and foremost, however, on the existence of the domestic prerequisites for international currency use. Hence, a shift to persistent current account surpluses should compel banks and other financial firms in the surplus nation's central financial markets to demand the installation of these institutions. When a large country advances to a position where it is selling goods abroad while buying foreign securities and making direct investments, financial firms should respond to the enhanced demand for liabilities denominated in the home currency by pressing harder for international currency status. To borrow short from the rest of the world, the key currency nation needs a stable currency and well-developed domestic financial markets. Only when these necessary conditions are established can the nation serve as world banker, enhancing the liquidity of the international financial system by borrowing short from, and lending long to, the rest of the world.

In summary, the process of institutional change within a nation is expected to be driven by change in that nation's international economic position. While the pattern of social agents' preferences on international currency status is assumed to be fixed, changes in the global position of an economy affect the size and preference intensities of the competing coalitions. The claim is that the rise of a nation to the upper strata of the world economy—as measured by an increasing share of world trade, an increasing share of the world's manufactured product exports, an in-

---

[1] For a good discussion of the concept of "world banker," see George S. Tavlas and Yuzuru Ozeki, *The Internationalization of Currencies: An Appraisal of the Japanese Yen,* International Monetary Fund Occasional Paper, no. 90 (Washington, D.C.: IMF, 1992), pp. 17–21.

creasing share of its exports going to developing countries, and the onset of enduring current account surpluses—will have a positive effect on the relative size of the international currency coalition and on the political enthusiasm of its members. I now turn to the empirical evidence to see whether the global position of the U.S. economy was moving in the directions stipulated above, implying greater demand for internationalizing the payments system from the domestic beneficiaries.

The Global Position of the United States

The preceding section identifies the "supplementary" international variables that contribute to the international use of currencies, and derives domestic political propositions from changes in these systemic variables. The argument is that change in a country's relative international position in a direction presaging greater use of its currency will strengthen currency internationalists at home. The coalition may both gain members and develop stronger incentives to install the domestic institutional prerequisites of international currency use. To facilitate the investigation of these factors with respect to the United States and the role of the dollar, the following discussion assesses the period between 1872 and 1913 in terms of (1) the U.S. share of world exports, (2) its share of manufactured and differentiated manufactured product exports, (3) its position with respect to exports going to developing countries, and (4) its evolving balance of payments position. Since the potential of the dollar as an international currency depended upon the performance of the United States relative to other countries, the discussion considers—to the extent the data permit—the changing position of the United States relative to that of other major industrial countries.

A growing share of world exports is found to influence the international use of a currency, and the data show that the U.S. economy advanced significantly in terms of its share of world exports between 1872 and 1913. Although comparative statistics on truly worldwide trade in the nineteenth century are not available, data are available for the largest exporting countries—the industrial nations of western Europe, the United States, Canada, and Japan. This is a reasonable substitute, since the United States and Europe together accounted for about 65 percent of world trade in all goods, and for about 80 to 90 percent of world trade in manufactures during this period.[2]

The data strongly suggest a rising potential for the dollar as an inter-

[2] Mary L. Eysenbach, *American Manufactured Exports, 1879–1914* (New York: Arno Press, 1976), pp. 39, 51–53.

national currency. American exports rose from 14.1 percent of this "total trade" in 1872 to 22.1 percent in 1913 (Table 3.1). Because a country's share of world exports is an important determinate of invoicing behavior, the potential of the dollar as an invoicing medium appears to have been advanced significantly between 1872 to 1913. Specifically, these data show that America's share of "world" exports rose 57 percent above its 1872 level, more than any other large country. Indeed, Britain's share fell by 36 percent (from a share of 35.8 percent in 1872 to 22.8 percent in 1913), and, by 1913, Britain held a share virtually identical to that of the United States and Germany. France also experienced a contraction in its share of world exports, falling by 42 percent over the period. All else equal, the pound and the franc should have experienced a diminution in their global roles as units of account and media of ex-

Table 3.1. Merchandise exports of the major trading states, 1872, 1899, 1913 (in millions of dollars at contemporary prices)

Exporter	1872	1899	1913
United Kingdom	1,246	1,604	2,556
Germany	544	1002	2,405
France	726	816	1,359
Other Western Europe[a]	473	911	1,679
United States	492	1,204	2,484
Canada	—	164	432
Japan	—	113	315
Total	3,481	5,814	11,230

Share of Total (percent)	1872	1899	1913
United Kingdom	35.8	27.6	22.8
Germany	15.6	17.2	21.4
France	20.9	14.0	12.1
Other Western Europe[a]	13.6	15.7	15.0
United States	14.1	20.7	22.1
Canada	—	2.8	3.8
Japan	—	1.9	2.8

Sources: Charles P. Kindleberger, *The Terms of Trade: A European Case Study* (Cambridge: Technology Press of MIT, 1956), table 3–4a, pp. 58–59; Alfred Maizels, *Industrial Growth and World Trade* (Cambridge: Cambridge University Press, 1963), table A1, pp. 426–27; U.S. Department of Commerce, *Historical Statistics of the United States, Colonial Times to 1970* (Washington, D.C.: GPO, 1975), pt. 2, table U317–334, pp. 903–4.
[a]Includes Belgium-Luxembourg, Italy, Netherlands, Norway, Sweden, and Switzerland. Excludes goods consigned from the Netherlands. Switzerland and Norway are not included in the 1872 figures.

change. Like the United States, Germany's share of global exports rose, but at a pace slower than that of the United States (37 percent). The U.S. economy simply outperformed all others in terms of the rate of expansion of its share of world exports. These data suggest a rising invoicing potential for the U.S. dollar (and, to a somewhat lesser degree, the German mark), conditioned, of course, upon the existence of the necessary domestic factors.

A second supplementary determinant of international currency use is a nation's share of world manufactured exports. As detailed above, manufacturing exporters are relatively more vulnerable to exchange-rate risk and prefer to invoice in the home currencies. A rise in a nation's share of world manufactured exports should thus be associated with greater use of that nation's currency as an invoicing and settlements medium. It should also have the political effect of motivating manufacturers to seek to develop the national currency for international use. Tables 3.2, 3.3, and 3.4 present evidence of the advancing position of the United States in the export of manufactured products that is strongly supportive of a greater role for the dollar.

Table 3.2 gives the export figures, by value, for the major exporting countries at three dates, broken down by product group. For convenience, product Categories I and II (food, drink, tobacco and raw materials) are classed as "primary products," taken to encompass the range of nonmanufactured exports in a country's trading profile, while Categories III through VIII are classed as manufactured exports. This division, however, may understate the proportion of manufactured products in a country's export mix. One problem is that Category I includes *manufactured* food, drink, and tobacco products, along with such crude renewable resources as food grains, feed crops, meat, and animal products.[3] Comparable data on the ratio of manufactured food exports to crude food exports are not available, but statistics for the United States are available. These data reveal that, in all but four years between 1872 and 1913, the United States exported more manufactured food products than crude food products, suggesting a somewhat higher proportion of manufactured to primary products for the United States.[4] Indeed, in 1913, U.S. exports of manufactured food products accounted for 62.6 percent of all food, drink, and tobacco exports. A similar problem involves the raw materials category, which includes such manufactured products as refined petroleum, cement, and newsprint. Though it is impossible to

---

[3] For the exact specification of each product category see Eysenbach, *American Manufactured Exports*, appendix table 6, pp. 265–68.

[4] U.S. Department of Commerce, *Historical Statistics of the United States, Colonial Times to 1970* (Washington, D.C.: GPO, 1975), pt. 2, table U213–224, pp. 889–90.

eliminate completely the tendency of these data to understate national shares of manufactured exports, the table is accurate enough for the purpose of determining broad trends in the composition of U.S. exports, relative to those of other exporting nations.

Table 3.3 reports statistics on national shares of world exports for each product category. As is clear, England experienced a steep relative decline in all categories of manufactured goods, with textiles holding up somewhat better than other sectors. What England lost in these export markets was made up for by the gains of others, particularly the United States and Germany. For the United States, the areas of fastest growth were in metals and metals manufactures (up from 1.6 percent in 1872 to 24.6 percent in 1913), machinery (up from 10.6 in 1872 to 27.7 percent in 1913), and vehicles (up from 14.2 percent in 1900 to 21.2 percent in 1913).[5] Of course, the United States remained a major exporter of primary products, increasing its share of the world's agricultural and raw materials markets. Germany's greatest gains were in manufactured exports, advancing very strongly in chemicals, metals and manufactures, and machinery. Like England, France lost ground in manufacturing, losing export market share in all but one category, vehicles. On the basis of this redistribution of manufactured product market shares, the dollar and the reichsmark should have experienced rising demand as international currencies, while sterling and the franc should have seen their roles diminish.

The literature on international currency gives particular emphasis to a nation's share of world markets in differentiated manufactured goods. Among the categories of manufactured products given in Table 3.3, machinery and vehicles are most likely to be characterized by product specialization and differentiation, if only by brand name. The "Machinery" category includes steam engines and turbines, farm equipment, construction, mining, and oil field machinery, machine tools, electrical appliances and measuring instruments, and communication equipment. The "Vehicles" class includes motor vehicles, trailers, ships and boats, locomotives, railroad equipment, and bicycles and motorcycles. As opposed to standardized, interchangeable commodities such as wheat or steel, these are differentiated products, and their manufacturers generally command some degree of market power. Hence, a country that gains global market share in these sectors should see a corresponding gain for its currency as an invoicing medium.

Table 3.3 shows that the U.S. share of world exports in machinery

---

[5] The data for 1872 on vehicles should be disregarded, given the minimal size of the market at that time.

Table 3.2. National export values, 1872, 1900, 1913 (in millions of dollars at contemporary prices)

| | Primary products | | Manufactured products | | | | | |
	I Food, drink, tobacco	II Raw materials	III Metals, manufactures	IV Machinery	V Vehicles	VI Chemicals	VII Textiles	VIII Other manufactures
United Kingdom								
1872	34	78	200	38	–	34	681	180
1900	68	214	204	97	44	63	545	180
1913	156	341	365	204	107	107	964	311
Germany								
1872	126	160	40	8	4	15	122	72
1900	139	173	157	56	15	88	227	251
1913	226	459	471	201	43	225	321	483
France								
1872	198	84	27	5	–	21	197	193
1900	138	140	35	12	9	31	169	259
1913	162	319	66	24	52	68	290	347

Other Western Europe[a]								
1872	121	190	40	8	1	16	61	35
1900	155	289	75	25	22	45	160	126
1913	299	542	167	57	36	74	303	180
United States								
1872	187	250	5	7	3	11	4	13
1900	568	542	139	72	15	35	27	55
1913	513	1,031	348	186	64	69	76	149
TOTAL								
1872	666	762	312	66	8	97	1,065	493
1900	1,068	1,358	610	262	105	262	1,128	871
1913	1,356	2,692	1,417	672	302	543	1,954	1,470

Sources: Charles P. Kindleberger, *The Terms of Trade: A European Case Study* (Cambridge: Technology Press of MIT, 1956), table 3–4a, pp. 58–59; Mary L. Eysenbach, *American Manufactured Exports, 1879–1914* (New York: Arno Press, 1976), table 3, pp. 40–41.
[a] Includes Italy, Belgium-Luxembourg, Sweden, and Switzerland within contemporary borders. Switzerland is not included in the 1872 figures.

Table 3.3. National share of world exports, 1872, 1900, 1913 (percent)

Product group and exporter	1872	1900	1913
I. Food, drink, tobacco			
United Kingdom	5.1	6.4	11.5
Germany	18.9	13.0	16.6
France	29.7	12.9	11.9
Other Europe	18.2	14.5	22.0
United States	28.1	53.2	37.8
II. Raw materials			
United Kingdom	10.2	15.7	12.7
Germany	20.1	12.7	17.0
France	11.0	10.3	11.8
Other Europe	25.0	21.3	20.1
United States	32.8	39.9	38.3
III. Metals, manufactures			
United Kingdom	64.1	33.4	25.8
Germany	12.8	25.7	33.2
France	8.7	5.7	4.6
Other Europe	12.8	12.3	11.8
United States	1.6	22.8	24.6
IV. Machinery			
United Kingdom	57.6	37.0	30.4
Germany	12.1	21.4	29.9
France	7.6	4.6	3.6
Other Europe	12.1	9.5	8.5
United States	10.6	27.5	27.7
V. Vehicles			
United Kingdom	—	41.9	35.4
Germany	50.0	14.3	14.2
France	—	8.6	17.2
Other Europe	12.5	21.0	11.9
United States	37.5	14.2	21.2
VI. Chemicals			
United Kingdom	35.0	24.0	19.7
Germany	15.5	33.6	41.4
France	21.6	11.8	12.5
Other Europe	16.5	17.2	13.6
United States	11.3	13.4	12.7
VII. Textiles			
United Kingdom	64.0	48.3	49.3
Germany	11.5	20.1	16.4
France	18.5	15.0	14.8
Other Europe	5.7	14.2	15.5
United States	0.4	2.4	3.9
VIII. Other manufactures			
United Kingdom	36.5	20.7	21.2
Germany	14.6	28.8	32.9
France	39.1	29.7	23.6
Other Europe	7.1	14.5	12.2
United States	2.6	6.3	10.1

Source: Data from Table 3.2.

grew by 161 percent over the period, to attain a 27.7 percent share of the world total in this category by 1913. Mary Eysenbach's data reveal the specific U.S. industries where growth was particularly strong—steam engines and turbines, farm equipment, special industrial machinery, and other commercial machinery and equipment.[6] In 1879, U.S. firms exported $225,000 worth of steam engines and turbines; in 1914 the figure was $5.8 million. Farm equipment exports valued at $2.9 million in 1879 rose to $32 million in 1914. Special industrial machinery exports were $3.6 million in 1879 and $39 million in 1914, while exports of commercial machinery and equipment rose from $1.9 to $30 million over the period. Equally important was the machinery group, which was, for the most part, characterized by a comparatively high level of industry concentration and, hence, oligopolistic market power. In 1909, the first year that data is available on concentration ratios, 16 percent of total output in the machinery group (excluding electrical machinery) was produced by oligopolistic industries (defined as six firms contributing 50 percent of industry output).[7] The electrical machinery group contained three industries in 1909, two of which were oligopolistic and accounted for 68 percent of product value for the group.

In the "Vehicles" group, the United States attained a world market share of 21.2 percent by 1913. Disregarding the 1872 data, when the worldwide production of these goods was in its infancy, we see that the United States experienced a 49 percent increase over its 1900 share. Growth was especially rapid in motor vehicles, locomotives, and railroad equipment. Motor vehicle exports led the product group in 1914, at $33 million.[8] Exports of locomotives rose from $567,000 in 1879 to $4 million in 1914, and railroad equipment sales rose from $249,000 to $11 million in the same period. Again, concentration characterized the vehicles product group, as two of the eight industries in this group were oligopolistic, and they accounted for 9 percent of the total production of the group: "Manufactured exports grew fastest in those industry groups made of industries with the highest number of the 100 largest firms. Moreover, these industry groups contained industries with the highest percentages of output controlled by oligopolistic firms. To put it simply, 'big business' dominated the industry groups with the largest percentages of manufactured exports."[9]

[6] Eysenbach, *American Manufactured Exports*, appendix table 8, pp. 271–75.
[7] Alfred D. Chandler, Jr., "The Structure of American Industry in the Twentieth Century: An Historical Overview," *Business History Review* 43 (Autumn 1969): 291–93; William H. Becker, *The Dynamics of Business-Government Relations: Industry and Exports, 1893–1921* (Chicago: University of Chicago Press, 1982), pp. 13–14.
[8] Eysenbach, *American Manufactured Exports*, appendix, table 8, pp. 271–75.
[9] Becker, *The Dynamics of Business-Government Relations*, p. 14.

For convenience, cumulative data on the relative composition of exports are summarized in Table 3.4. Here only three broad categories are reported: "Primary Products" (Classes I and II), "Manufactured Products"(Classes III through VIII), and "Specialized Manufactured Products" (Classes IV and V). The data consistently suggest a greater role for the dollar. America's share of world manufactured exports rose by 566 percent (from 2.1 percent to 14 percent) over the period, while England's share fell by 42 percent (from 55.6 percent to 32.4 percent). Germany gained too, but at the lesser rate of 117 percent (12.6 percent to 27.4 percent). As for differentiated products, the United States nearly doubled its market share to 25.7 percent, while England's share fell 38 percent from its 1872 level to 31.9 percent of the total. Germany increased its 1872 share of 16.2 percent of differentiated goods markets by 55 percent, attaining a 25.1 percent share in 1913.

A fourth influence on international currency use is the extent of trade with developing countries. Trade between developed and developing

Table 3.4. National share of world exports by product group, 1872, 1900, 1913 (percent)

Product group and exporter	1872	1900	1913
Primary products[a]			
United Kingdom	7.8	11.6	12.3
Germany	20.0	12.9	16.9
France	19.7	11.5	11.9
Other Europe	21.8	18.3	20.8
United States	30.6	45.8	38.1
Manufactured products[b]			
United Kingdom	55.6	35.0	32.4
Germany	12.6	24.5	27.4
France	21.8	17.4	13.3
Other Europe	6.1	14.0	12.8
United States	2.1	10.6	14.0
Specialized manufactured products[c]			
United Kingdom	51.4	38.4	31.9
Germany	16.2	19.3	25.1
France	6.8	5.7	7.8
Other Europe	12.2	12.8	9.5
United States	13.5	23.7	25.7

Sources: Data from Table 3.2
[a] Includes catgegories I and II (food, drink, tobacco, and raw materials).
[b] Includes categories III through VIII (metals and metals manufactures, machinery, vehicles, chemicals, textiles, and other manufactures).
[c] Includes categories IV and V (machinery and vehicles).

countries is typically invoiced in the developed country's currency, and the logic explaining this outcome relates to traders' relative exposures to exchange-rate risk. That is, because developed-country exporters of manufactured products are relatively more exposed to exchange-rate risk than are developing-country importers and exporters, trade between these regions is carried in the currency of the developed country. Hence, a rise in an exporting nation's relative share of trade with the developing world implies a greater international role for its currency.

Tables 3.5 and 3.6 report two factors that would indicate a rising potential use of the dollar, buttressing the potential implied by America's growing share of world exports. First, the U.S. share of developing-country markets rose between 1872 and 1913, whereas the shares of England and France fell. Second, the U.S. share of this trade rose more than that of any other major country, including Germany.

Table 3.5 groups exports by destination. Restrictions of the data cause some problems, for example, grouping all Western European countries in the "Industrial Countries" category. Nevertheless, general trends in the direction of exports are quite clear. In 1872, the United Kingdom held the dominant position as exporter to the developing world, with 53.4 percent of the total (Table 3.6). By 1913, however, England's share had fallen to 35.5 percent, implying a reduced role for sterling as a vehicle currency. France's share also fell, from 16 percent to 9.7 percent of the total, with a similar implication for the franc. In contrast, the U.S. share more than doubled, from 6.9 percent to 14.2 percent. Again, these data imply increased global use of the dollar. While Germany also increased its share of developing country markets, its gain of 4.3 percent represented a more modest 20 percent increase over its 1872 share. Simply put, the United States was the fastest growing exporter to the Third World.

The comparative data presented in Table 3.5 is somewhat vague in terms of the direction of U.S. exports, particularly in regard to the "All Others" category. Table 3.7 provides finer distinctions of the destination of U.S. exports. In absolute terms, the share of total U.S. exports going to developing countries rose from 14 percent in 1872 to 20.8 percent in 1913, and Latin America was by far the main recipient. Over the period, Latin America received 69 percent on average of all U.S. exports to developing countries. With the rise of trade with the Far East and, to a lesser degree, Australia and Oceania, some diversification took place. Yet by 1913, these markets still consumed only 16 and 10.5 percent, respectively, of U.S. developing country exports, while exports to Latin America accounted for 67.8 percent.

As for exports to industrial countries, England was the most important consumer of U.S. goods, but its share, expressed as a percentage of

Table 3.5. Destination of national exports, 1872, 1899, 1913 (in millions of dollars at contemporary prices)

	To industrial countries				To developing countries			World total
	United Kingdom	Continental Western Europe	North America	Total (including Japan)	Southern Dominions, India, and Pakistan	All Others	Total	
United Kingdom								
1872	—	511	200	711	155	380	536	1,246
1899	—	518	210	768	318	518	836	1,604
1913	—	639	259	969	671	916	1,587	2,556
Germany								
1872	—	—	—	336	—	—	208	544
1899	191	321	96	618	28	356	384	1,002
1913	343	729	184	1,285	60	1,060	1,120	2,405
France								
1872	—	—	64	565	31	130	161	726
1899	240	303	49	594	6	216	222	816
1913	283	555	86	927	12	420	432	1,359
Other Western Europe[a]								
1872	—	—	11	443	13	17	30	473
1899	172	479	57	712	15	184	199	911
1913	264	791	118	1,181	45	453	498	1,679

United States								
1872	265	128	29	423	—	—	69	492
1899	506	372	86	981	39	184	223	1,204
1913	591	793	403	1,850	71	563	634	2,484
Canada								
1872	—	—	—	—	—	—	—	—
1899	93	8	53	154	3	7	10	164
1913	160	73	151	385	10	37	47	432
Japan								
1872	—	—	—	—	—	—	—	—
1899	6	18	33	57	4	52	56	113
1913	16	53	95	164	19	132	151	315
TOTAL								
1872	—	—	—	2,478	—	—	1,003	3,481
1899	—	—	—	3,884	—	—	1,930	5,814
1913	—	—	—	6,761	—	—	4,469	11,230

Sources: Alfred Maizels, *Industrial Growth and World Trade* (Cambridge: Cambridge University Press, 1963), table A1, pp. 426–27; Charles P. Kindleberger, *The Terms of Trade: A European Case Study* (Cambridge: Technology Press of MIT, 1956), table 3–4c, pp. 62–63; U.S. Department of Commerce, *Historical Statistics of the United States, Colonial Times to 1970* (Washington, D.C.: GPO, 1975), pt. 2, table U317–334, pp. 903–4.

ª Includes Belgium-Luxembourg, Italy, Netherlands, Norway, Sweden, and Switzerland. Excludes goods consigned from the Netherlands. Switzerland and Norway are not included in the 1872 figures.

Table 3.6. National export share by area, 1872, 1899, 1913 (percent)

Exporter and Markets	1872	1899	1913
United Kingdom			
World[a]	35.8	27.6	22.8
Industrial Countries	28.6	19.8	14.3
Developing Countries	53.4	43.3	35.5
Germany			
World[a]	15.6	17.2	21.4
Industrial Countries	13.6	15.9	19.0
Developing Countries	20.7	19.9	25.0
France			
World[a]	20.9	14.0	12.1
Industrial Countries	22.8	15.3	13.7
Developing Countries	16.0	11.5	9.7
Other Western Europe[b]			
World[a]	13.5	15.6	14.9
Industrial Countries	17.8	18.3	17.3
Developing Countries	3.0	10.3	11.1
United States			
World[a]	14.1	21.0	22.1
Industrial Countries	17.0	25.3	27.4
Developing Countries	6.9	11.6	14.2
Canada			
World[a]	—	2.8	3.8
Industrial Countries	—	3.9	5.6
Developing Countries	—	0.5	1.0
Japan			
World[a]	—	3.2	2.8
Industrial Countries	—	1.4	2.4
Developing Countries	—	3.0	3.5

Source: Data from Table 3.2

[a] Includes the United Kingdom, Germany, France, the United States, Canada, Japan, Netherlands, Italy, Belgium-Luxembourg, Sweden, Switzerland and Norway.

[b] Includes Belgium-Luxembourg, Italy, Netherlands, Norway, Sweden, and Switzerland. Excludes goods consigned from the Netherlands. Switzerland and Norway are not included in the 1872 figures.

U.S. exports to developed countries, dropped by more than half between 1872 and 1913 (i.e., from 62.8 to 30.1 percent). Diversification of exports to other industrialized European markets and Canada was responsible for England's declining share. For example, Canada's share of U.S. exports to industrial countries rose sharply from 6.9 percent in 1872 to 21.3

Table 3.7. Destination of U.S. exports, 1872–1913 (in millions of dollars at contemporary prices)

| | To industrial countries | | | | | | | To developing countries | | | | | | | |
Year	United Kingdom	France	Germany	Other Europe	Canada	Japan	Total	Cuba	Mexico	Brazil	Other Latin America	China and other Asia	Australia and Oceania	Africa	Total
1872	265	31	41	56	29	1	422	14	6	6	34	3	4	2	69
1877	346	45	58	76	37	1	563	13	6	8	35	9	8	3	82
1882	408	50	54	88	37	3	640	12	15	9	40	16	13	6	111
1887	366	57	59	93	35	3	613	11	8	8	42	17	14	3	103
1892	499	99	106	147	43	3	897	18	14	14	50	17	16	5	134
1897	483	58	125	147	65	13	891	8	23	12	51	26	23	17	160
1902	549	72	173	214	110	21	1,139	27	40	10	55	48	29	33	242
1907	608	114	257	319	183	39	1,520	49	66	19	115	62	33	17	361
1913	597	146	332	404	415	58	1,952	71	54	43	180	82	54	29	513

Source: U.S. Department of Commerce, Historical Statistics of the United States, Colonial Times to 1970 (Washington, D.C.: GPO, 1975). pt. 2, table U317–334. pp. 903–4.

percent in 1913. Nevertheless, exports to Canada, as well as exports to every other destination in the developed and developing world, continued to be invoiced and financed in currencies other than the U.S. dollar.

The final international factor affecting the global use of national currencies involves the balance of payments, which is a relative measure by definition. When a nation's payments position develops to the point where current account surpluses are regular and persistent, a promotional effect accrues to the use of its currency. A surplus on current account implies offsetting capital outflows, which provide deficit countries with the liquidity to finance imports from the surplus nation. This promotes the internationalization of the surplus nation's currency, since the export of capital induces nonresidents to acquire balances denominated in the capital-exporting country's home currency, both as a means to service their long-term obligations and to pay for imports from the surplus nation. In short, current account surpluses typically mean that nonresidents must obtain financial instruments denominated in the surplus country's currency to make payments and settle trade.

Table 3.8 reports data on the evolving balance of payments position of the United States. Essentially, this period saw the U.S. change from running persistent current account deficits, financed by capital inflows and occasional gold outflows, to running persistent current account surpluses, financed by capital outflows and gold inflows. Although surpluses generally prevailed in merchandise trade from as early as 1875, it was not until after 1896 that the country finally reversed its overall payments position. The "American Century" that followed was largely defined by this surplus condition.

Two important international financial consequences came with the shift from deficit to surplus status. First, American investors began to extend long-term credit overseas to finance the growing discrepancy between the nation's exports of goods and services and its imports. Table 3.8 presents the turnaround in the payments situation and the subsequent rise in U.S. capital exports after 1896. Although the country was a consistent net capital importer from the 1870s to the mid-1890s, from the mid-1890s to 1905 it was a consistent net exporter, with the period 1898–1902 seeing an average yearly net export of more than $250 million. After 1905, the United States reverted to being a net capital importer, but at a level well below the levels reached in the 1870s and 1880s. In short, while the United States remained a net debtor until World War I, it lessened its dependence on foreign savings and developed into a large exporter of its own funds.[10] Second, the United States also began to accu-

---

[10] U.S. Department of Commerce, *Historical Statistics of the United States*, series U 40, p. 869.

mulate large amounts of monetary gold, as the portion of its surplus that was not financed through American overseas lending was covered by gold imports, or by the retention of domestically produced gold. Table 3.9 gives evidence of the sharp, yet steady, increases in the country's total gold stock and breaks down the sources of this accumulation.

To summarize, theoretical considerations indicate that several factors combine to advance the internationalization of a currency. The U.S. position, with respect to the necessary domestic factors, was analyzed in Chapter 1, and the major shortcoming was found to be in respect to the breadth, depth, and resiliency of its domestic financial markets. This chapter has considered international level factors: (1) a country's share of world exports, (2) the composition of its trade; that is, its share of manufactured and differentiated manufactured products, (3) its share of trade with developing countries, and (4) the position of enduring current account surpluses. In each of these areas, the relative position of the United States changed after 1872 in the direction presaging an expanding role for the dollar as global money. As shown below, however, the dollar did not serve the functions of money in the international realm, due to the absence of the domestic preconditions. If the logic is correct, the beneficiaries of international currency use should have found incentives arising from the advancing economic position of the nation to install the requisite domestic institutions.

International Currency Usage

Data on international currency use in the period is sketchy at best; yet, most estimates indicate the predominance of sterling, a rising role for the German mark, some reserve currency usage of the French franc, and the virtual absence of the U.S. dollar in global financial affairs. The dollar's parochialism was most exceptional, as usage lagged the advance in the nation's relative global position after the 1870s. This result gives testimony to the overriding importance of domestic prerequisites in shaping patterns of international currency use.

Sterling is estimated to have invoiced from 80 to 90 percent of world trade by the early nineteenth century.[11] For the second half of the century, sterling's vehicle currency status probably declined somewhat, but

For the specifics of American capital exports, see Cleona Lewis, *America's Stake in International Investments* (Washington, D.C.: Brookings Institution, 1938); and Douglass North, "International Capital Movements in Historical Perspective," in *U.S. Private and Government Investment Abroad*, ed. Raymond F. Mikesell (Eugene: University of Oregon Books, 1962).

[11] Charles Morgan-Webb, *The Rise and Fall of the Gold Standard* (New York: Macmillan, 1934), pp. 53–54.

Table 3.8. U.S. balance of international payments, 1872–1913 (in millions of dollars at contemporary prices)

Year	Current account		Capital account			
	Balance on goods and services	Unilateral transfers, net [to foreign countries (−)][a]	U.S. capital flows, net [outflow of funds (−)][b]	Foreign capital flows, net [outflow of funds (−)][c]	Changes in monetary gold stock [increase (−)]	Errors and omissions, net
1872	−246	4		242[d]	—	—
1873	−181	14		167	—	—
1874	−61	−11		82	−11	—
1875	−99	−14		87	27	—
1876	20	−11		2	−10	—
1877	102	−13		−57	−33	—
1878	218	−11		−162	−44	—
1879	202	−8		−162	−44	—
1880	114	−4		30	−140	—
1881	137	−5		−41	−91	—
1882	−55	−13		110	−42	—
1883	−12	−22		51	−17	—
1884	−59	−24		105	−23	—
1885	12	−27		34	−19	—
1886	−77	−28		137	−32	—
1887	−157	−28		231	−46	—
1888	−226	−30		287	−30	—
1889	−166	−44		202	−30	—
1890	−150	−45		194	1	—
1891	−90	−50		136	4	—

Year						
1892	−20	−54		41	33	
1893	−119	−44		146	17	—
1894	98	−54		−66	22	—
1895	−127	−55		137	44	—
1896	43	−49		40	−25	—
1897	132	−41		−23	−68	—
1898	444	−44		−279	−121	—
1899	427	−68		−229	−130	—
1900	507	−95	−143	−75	−91	−103
1901	438	−104	−212	−33	−61	−28
1902	258	−105	−105	−30	−71	53
1903	340	−115	−41	20	−71	−11
1904	279	−137	−109	59	−25	−67
1905	298	−133	−139	56	−71	−11
1906	296	−147	−46	114	−171	−46
1907	296	−177	−65	136	−154	−36
1908	427	−192	−135	89	−44	−145
1909	26	−187	−112	171	18	84
1910	46	−204	−90	345	−71	−26
1911	274	−224	−123	171	−90	−8
1912	257	−212	−209	232	−81	13
1913	374	−207	−165	252	−25	−229

Source: U.S. Department of Commerce, *Historical Statistics of the United States, Colonial Times to 1970* (Washington, D.C.: GPO, 1975), series U 168–192, pp. 866–68.

[a] Private and government.

[b] Private (direct investment and other long-term) and government.

[c] Long-term.

[d] U.S. and foreign capital flows, net.

Table 3.9. Changes in the U.S. gold stock, 1890–1913 (in millions of dollars)

Year	Total gold stock	U.S. production	Net foreign flow [inflow (+)]	Industrial consumption	Increase or decrease
1890	648	33	−4	15	15
1891	626	33	−34	15	−22
1892	582	33	−59	15	−44
1893	591	36	−7	13	9
1894	539	40	−81	10	−52
1895	503	47	−71	12	−36
1896	589	53	46	11	86
1897	638	57	—	11	49
1898	832	64	142	11	194
1899	897	71	6	13	65
1900	989	79	13	17	92
1901	1,050	79	−3	19	61
1902	1,121	80	8	20	71
1903	1,191	74	21	23	71
1904	1,217	80	−36	24	25
1905	1,288	88	3	23	71
1906	1,458	94	109	28	170
1907	1,605	90	88	33	147
1908	1,654	95	−31	34	49
1909	1,638	100	−89	15	−16
1910	1,709	96	—	30	71

Source: Wesley C. Mitchell, *Business Cycles* (Berkeley: University of California Press, 1913), tables 71 and 72, pp. 283–85.

estimates still range from 60 to 90 percent of world trade.[12] The French franc, however, was not one of the currencies that made headway against sterling as an invoicing medium. Although some French banks (e.g., the Comptoir d'Escompte de Paris) participated in trade finance from the 1860s onward, issuing franc-denominated bankers' acceptances, "they were lightweight in comparison with their British counterparts. The French banks were able to capture only a very small part of the international business in London."[13] Moreover, after the French franc was rendered inconvertible by the war with Germany in 1870, Paris was demoted from its previous position as a center of short-term international finance, and much of this business fled to London.[14] Paris never recov-

[12] The higher figure is from A. C. Whitaker, *Foreign Exchange* (New York: D. Appleton, 1920), p. 555; the lower is from Williams, "The Evolution of the Sterling System," p. 268.

[13] Hubert Bonin, "The Case of the French Banks," in *International Banking, 1870–1914,* ed. Rondo Cameron and V. I. Bovykin (New York: Oxford University Press), p. 77. See also Karl E. Born, *International Banking in the 19th and 20th Centuries* (New York: St. Martin's Press, 1983), pp. 77–78.

[14] Bagehot stresses how the internationalization of the London money market after the fall

ered its previous stature as a result of its failure to establish a free gold market. In 1907, *The Economist* found France's monetary uncertainty heartening: "So long as Paris is comparatively dead and nerveless, with a gold trap instead of a gold market, so long is the supremacy of London assured."[15]

In contrast to the franc, the German mark did make significant inroads as a vehicle currency. From the 1870s, German joint-stock banks began establishing foreign branches, through which they invoiced a growing portion of German trade in mark-denominated bankers' acceptances.[16] According to Richard Tilly:

By the eve of World War I the presence of German banks in most of the world's important commercial centers, in association with the rapid growth of German foreign trade, had made the mark an international currency. It had not become a challenge to the pound, but in certain areas it had become a "key currency"—for, example, in trade with Sweden, Denmark, Rumania, Italy, Austria-Hungary, and even for part of the German-American business. And in many other areas—in South America and Asia, for example—the mark bill had become a possible alternative, increasingly utilized.[17]

In the context of Germany's rising economic position, German financial firms emulated British international banks and discount houses in developing mark-denominated bills of exchange and networks of overseas branches and subsidiaries: "The methods and forms adopted in assisting German trade were those of the English banks and . . . had been used by these, not in the service of British trade alone, but to a great extent also in the service of the commerce of other countries—including that of Germany."[18] One of the main aims of the establishment of German overseas banks—typically offshoots of the big German joint-stock banks—was "the gradual displacement of sterling bills for mark bills."[19]

of Paris imposed new pressures on the Bank of England. Walter Bagehot, *Lombard Street* (Westport: Hyperion Press [1873] 1979).

[15] W. T. C. King, *History of the London Discount Market* (London: George Routledge, 1936), p. 279.

[16] P. Barrett Whale, *Joint Stock Banking in Germany: A Study of German Credit Banks Before and After the War* (London: Macmillan, 1930), pp. 83–85; Peter Hertner, "German Banks Abroad before 1914," in *Banks as Multinationals*, ed. Geoffrey Jones (London: Routledge, 1990), pp. 99–119.

[17] Richard Tilly, "International Aspects of the Development of German Banking," in *International Banking, 1870–1914*, p. 109.

[18] Whale, *Joint Stock Banking in Germany*, p. 83.

[19] Hertner, "German Banks Abroad before 1914," p. 101.

Indeed, the Deutsche Bank was founded in 1870 by a group of private bankers, for the express purpose of "capturing a share of the short-term credit and payments business that was 'needlessly' flowing into British hands."[20] Jacob Reisser's study remains the authoritative source on how German banks "devoted themselves energetically to the promotion of [their] industrial and commercial relations with overseas countries" after the 1870s.[21]

In contrast to the mark, which was increasingly utilized, the U.S. dollar remained insignificant as a vehicle currency, despite the nation's rising international position. Sterling continued to serve as the primary vehicle currency for American trade, as bankers' acceptances issued by English financial firms formed not only the basis of British trade with the United States, but with U.S. trade to other regions.[22] As Benjamin Beckhart put it:

> Before the Great War the elaborate and intricate machinery of the London discount market . . . was relied upon for the financing of the bulk of the foreign trade of the United States. Whether it was the importation of coffee from Brazil, shellac from India, nitrates from Chile, silk or rubber from the Far East, or the exportation of cotton, wheat, or tobacco, the financing required was conducted on the basis of the sterling letter of credit. Only a very small portion of the foreign trade was financed in Berlin and Amsterdam. London's position was undisputed . . . However important the position of New York in domestic trade finance, as a capital distributing center, and in settling domestic balances, its position was unimportant in financing foreign trade.[23]

As for the store of value function, it is widely known that, by the 1880s, foreign governments and central banks held a large portion of their reserves as sterling assets in the London money market, to be converted into gold upon demand. Peter Lindert's data, however, show a diminution in London's status as the only reserve center after 1899, as

---

[20] Tilly, "International Aspects of the Development of German Banking," p. 93. According to its charter, the object of the Deutsche Bank was the "transaction of all sorts of banking business, particularly the fostering and facilitating of commercial relations between Germany, the other European countries, and overseas markets." Cited in Jacob Reisser, *The Great German Banks and Their Concentration* (Washington, D.C.: GPO, 1911), p. 421.

[21] Reisser, *The Great German Banks*, p. 420.

[22] For a detailed study of American trade finance in the nineteenth century, see Edwin J. Perkins, *Financing Anglo-American Trade: The House of Brown, 1800–1880* (Cambridge: Harvard University Press, 1975).

[23] Beckhart, *The New York Money Market*, p. 253.

Paris and Berlin became rival reserve centers.[24] Table 3.10 reproduces these data. While sterling reserves still exceeded the combined value of reserves denominated in all other currencies at the end of the period, sterling had indeed declined in relative importance as a reserve currency. Looking only at official foreign-exchange holdings—the data on private holdings being far less complete—shows that sterling's share of total foreign exchange holdings fell to 37.8 percent by the end of 1913, down from its share of 42.6 percent at the end of 1899.

The franc realized the most dramatic increase as an official reserve currency, growing tenfold in absolute terms over the period. The franc's relative share of total foreign exchange assets more than doubled, growing from 11 percent in 1899 to 24.5 percent by 1913. These data, however, seriously overstate the importance of Paris as a reserve center, since, as Lindert notes, only one country, Russia, held substantial franc assets.[25] Russia's franc holdings were not based on the calculation that the franc was absolutely secure; instead, they were closely linked to Russian access to the French capital market. The Russian State Bank, in order to ensure continued access to long-term loans, kept large sums on deposit in the French banks that distributed Russian bonds to French investors. Without the connection between the deposits and long-term loans—and the special political relationship between France and Russia—it is unlikely that the Russian central bank would have preferred francs as the basis of its foreign currency reserves.[26] Excluding Russia's holdings, the franc's role as a reserve currency was actually in steep *decline*, with its share of total official holdings falling from 11 percent in 1899 to 4.7 percent in 1913.

In contrast, the German mark gained prominence as an official reserve currency, rising from 9.8 percent of total official reserves in 1899 to 12.2 percent by the later date. The mark's reserve currency position was probably more significant than that of the franc, since the mark was held in large quantities by more countries across a wider geographic area. In 1913, mark-denominated assets were held by official institutions in Russia ($53 million), Chile ($34.8 million), Italy ($17.8 million), Sweden ($15.4 million), Rumania ($10.5 million), Austria-Hungary ($8.3 million),

[24] Peter Lindert, *Key Currencies and Gold, 1900–1913*, Princeton Studies in International Finance, no. 24, International Finance Section, Princeton University (1969).

[25] In 1913, the Russian State Bank held $221.8 million in franc assets, representing over 80 percent of all reported foreign holdings of franc exchange ($275.1 million). Lindert, *Key Currencies and Gold*, pp. 18–19, 29–31.

[26] For the geopolitics of the French-Russian financial relationship, see Herbert Feis, *Europe: The World's Banker, 1870–1914* (New Haven: Yale University Press, 1930), pp. 118–56, 210–34.

Finland ($5.4 million), Norway ($3.1 million), and Japan ($2 million).[27] This diversification, second only to that of sterling, suggests that the mark was a more useful and reliable reserve asset than the franc— usefulness being a function of Germany's more important position in world trade and payments; reliability a function of Germany's more credible commitment to the gold standard (see below).

As for the U.S. dollar, the data show some reserve currency usage, but like the French franc, this represented special circumstances. At the end of 1913, Canadian joint-stock banks held $141.6 million in foreign exchange, mostly in U.S. dollars, but with some sterling assets as well.[28] One reason why only Canadian banks held dollar assets was that Canada's short-term money markets were even more underdeveloped than American markets. Lacking a liquid short-term money market for the placement and management of bank funds, Canadian banks substituted extensive dealings in the New York "call loan" market, where they held liquidity balances and operated an exchange business.[29] Moreover, Canadian banks came to rely on maintaining large external reserves in New York (and London) as a source of liquidity. Absent the special relationship between Canadian banks and the New York market, it is very unlikely that the dollar would have served any reserve currency role before 1913: "The importance of the dollar in world finance has been overstated by the figures on dollar holdings, which reflect the close ties between the Untied States and Canada."[30]

Although limitations in the data make it difficult to draw firm conclusions on patterns of international currency use before 1914, the broad trends appear sufficiently clear. The vehicle and reserve currency roles of sterling and the franc (excluding Russia's holdings) seem to have fallen between the 1870s and 1913, tracking the relative economic decline of these nations, while the mark advanced significantly and in association with Germany's rapid ascent on the world stage. For these three currencies, international usage followed changes in relative international economic position, confirming the importance of the supplementary international factors outlined in the literature on currency use. The U.S. dollar was the crucial exception. Even though the United States had become an equal of England and Germany in many areas of world economic position important to currency use, the dollar remained parochial, utilized as a reserve currency only by Canadian banks for peculiar reasons. This

[27] Lindert, *Key Currencies and Gold*, table 2, pp. 18–19.
[28] Ibid.
[29] Ian M. Drummond, "Banks and Banking in Canada and Australia," in *International Banking, 1870–1914*, pp. 192, 202.
[30] Lindert, *Key Currencies and Gold*, p. 17.

was due to the fact that relative positions in specific categories of world trade and payments are but the supplemental factors influencing currency use. The more fundamental considerations are domestic and concern national monetary and financial attributes. Regardless of a nation's position in the world economy, its money will not assume global prominence unless its currency is stable and unless its financial markets are deep, open, and liquid.

At the outset of this chapter I developed a political framework that ties the international and domestic considerations together. Recall the basic prediction: advances (or declines) in the international economic position of nations should be reflected in the political demands of social coalitions for (or against) currency internationalization. More specifically, in a large nation that is advancing rapidly in the world economy, constituents of the internationalist coalition should articulate strong political demands for the establishment of the domestic prerequisites of currency use. The converse should also hold true. A nation declining in relative economic importance should be less likely to commit (or to remain committed) to making the trade-offs necessary for globalizing the currency, due to gains in the nationalist coalition's political power.

Currency Politics in Europe

How closely do these arguments track currency politics in Europe? The cases are sufficiently diverse to get a rough gauge—two nations in relative economic decline (England and France) and one advancing globally (Germany)—and the findings, though tentative, are broadly consistent with the logic. In Germany, the beneficiaries of internationalizing the mark successfully advanced this agenda, while in France and England, pressure from economic nationalists for greater macroeconomic independence tracked declines in global economic position.

Sterling's long reign as international money gives testimony to the overriding importance of domestic factors to international currency use. Inasmuch as Britain's relative share of world merchandise exports was consistently lower than sterling usage, and fell throughout the period (Table 3.10), the importance of monetary confidence and money market structure as basic determinants of currency use is amply demonstrated. England's enduring commitment to monetary stability and the superior development of its financial markets meant sterling remained in high demand, even as England's relative position in the world declined. Nevertheless, with economic decline came domestic political pressure to secure greater freedom for domestic monetary policy under the gold stan-

Table 3.10. Growth and composition of foreign-exchange assets, 1900–1913 (in millions of dollars)

	End of 1899	End of 1913	Change	1913 index (1899 = 100)
Official institutions[a]	246.6	1124.7	878.1	456
known sterling	105.1	425.4	320.3	405
known francs	27.2	275.1	247.9	1,010
known marks	24.2	136.9	112.7	566
other currencies	9.4	55.3	45.9	590
unallocated[b]	80.7	232.0	151.2	287
Private institutions	157.6	497.8	340.2	316
known sterling	15.9	16.0	0.1	100
known francs	—	—	—	—
known marks	—	—	—	—
other currencies	62.0	156.7	94.7	253
unallocated[b]	79.7	325.1	245.4	408
All institutions	404.2	1,622.5	1,218.3	401
known sterling	121.0	441.4	320.4	365
known francs	27.2	275.1	247.9	1,010
known marks	24.2	136.9	112.7	566
other currencies	71.4	212.0	140.6	297
unallocated[b]	160.4	557.1	396.7	347

Source: Peter Lindert, *Key Currencies and Gold, 1900–1913*, Princeton Studies in International Finance no. 24, International Finance Section, Princeton University (1969), table 3, p. 22.
[a] Central banks and treasuries.
[b] Foreign asset figures not broken down by currency.

dard, a nationalistic agenda which posed threats to sterling's global position.

The linchpin of monetary stability in England was commitment to the gold standard, a commitment suspended only temporarily under exceptional circumstances (e.g., war).[31] The historiography of British policy confirms the unwavering official commitment to gold.[32] To the extent that there existed other goals of policy, these were accorded lower priority:

[31] For a treatment of the English gold standard as a "contingent rule," abandoned only temporarily in the face of severe adverse shocks (i.e., war), see Michael D. Bordo and Finn E. Kydland, "The Gold Standard as a Rule: An Essay in Exploration," *Explorations in Economic History* 32 (October 1994): 423–64.
[32] See, for example, John Dutton, "The Bank of England and the Rules of the Game Under the International Gold Standard: New Evidence," in *A Retrospective on the Classical Gold Standard*, ed. Michael D. Bordo and Anna J. Schwartz (Chicago: University of Chicago Press, 1984), pp. 173–95; John Pippenger, "Bank of England Operations, 1893–1913," in *A Retrospective on the Classical Gold Standard*, pp. 203–27; R. S. Sayers, *The Bank of England, 1891–1944* (Cambridge: Cambridge University Press, 1976).

"If the nation simultaneously experienced gold losses and a cyclical downturn, or gold losses and financial panic, there was no question that the authorities attached priority to the defense of the monetary standard, even if this implied an intensification of domestic difficulties."[33] Sterling's position as international currency demanded as much.

The London money market was also the world's most advanced. No other country had as deep and well-organized a money market. None had discount houses of such prominence, and none practiced discounting on a comparable scale. The business involved the operation of many bankers, brokers, and companies known as discount houses, organized especially for the purpose of buying and selling bankers' acceptances. The operations of banks, brokers, and discount houses created a very efficient payments system, characterized by prompt and extended distribution of bills.[34] In 1873, Walter Bagehot noted the advantages of London's financial sophistication: "This efficient and instantaneous ready organization gives us an enormous advantage in competition with less advanced countries—less advanced, that is, in this particular respect of credit. In a new trade English capital is instantly at the disposal of persons capable of understanding the new opportunities and making good use of them . . . All *sudden* trade comes to England."[35]

Put more succinctly, "London without its specialized discount market would be London without its greatness."[36] The Bank of England stood at the center of the discount market and its role was to accommodate extraordinary demands to exchange sterling bills for currency by rediscounting. The Bank's *global* position derived partly from the depth and complexity of London's payment system which, due to the economies involved, attracted foreigners to sterling for financing international transactions and for reserve purposes. More importantly, England's century-long commitment to the basic principles of the gold standard—that is, the tradition of honoring the pledge to convert sterling into gold to any amount, and to allow gold to exit and enter the country freely under any circumstances—worked to make the London market the safest and most predictable in the world. As a result, foreigners were drawn to London not only because of its broad and deep short-term credit markets, but also because the rules governing the issue

---

[33] Barry Eichengreen, "Gold Standard Since Alec Ford," in *Britain in the International Economy, 1870–1939*, ed. S. N. Broadberry and N. F. R. Crafts (Cambridge: Cambridge University Press, 1992), p. 75.
[34] King, *History of the London Discount Market*; Williams, "The Evolution of the Sterling System."
[35] Bagehot, *Lombard Street*, p. 87 (emphasis in original).
[36] King, *History of the London Discount Market*, p. 321.

of sterling made it an ideal international currency. London achieved and maintained its commanding international position both because the City had a competitive advantage in short-term global finance and because England developed the gold standard earlier, and committed to it more strongly, than any other potential challenger.

England's currency internationalists provided the political support for the legal and institutional structures of the English financial system.[37] The London banking community—a coalition of merchant banks, acceptance houses, discount houses, and, later, joint-stock banks—was indeed firmly wedded to the international financial status of London.[38] Under the gold standard, bankers perceived a high and stable valuation of sterling to be very much in the interests of the City of London as a global financial center. As banker Alexander Goshen put it in 1891, the credible commitment to gold made it "known that any obligations payable in England mean absolutely and safely so much gold."[39] The gold standard thus ensured sterling's place in the international financial system, and thereby garnered rents for the banking sector, which was its strongest supporter.[40] After 1844, the City reaped the international advantages of the country's domestic monetary arrangements, as London flourished as a worldwide financial center and sterling became the premier international currency.

While there is little evidence in the secondary literature that other expected beneficiaries of international currency status (e.g., exporting producers of manufactured products and importing merchants) *actively* lobbied for the gold standard and fixed exchange rates, tacit agreement was the order of politics, at least until relative industrial decline set in after about 1875. With the decline of Britain's industrial competitiveness and the loss of world market share in manufactured exports, the currency coalition lost a portion of its manufacturing component (e.g., iron and steel) to economic nationalism.[41] The loss of export markets and the rise of competition with imports led these previously pro-gold manufac-

---

[37] The argument and evidence is consistent with Randall Henning's views on the domestic politics of external monetary policy. C. Randall Henning, *Currencies and Politics in the United States, Germany, and Japan* (Washington, D.C.: Institute for International Economics, 1994), pp. 336–38.

[38] See, for example, Frank Longstreth, "The City, Industry, and the State," in *State and Economy in Contemporary Capitalism*, ed. Colin Crouch (New York: St. Martin's Press, 1979), pp. 157–90; and Frank W. Fetter, *Development of British Monetary Orthodoxy, 1797–1875* (Cambridge: Cambridge University Press, 1965).

[39] Cited in P. J. Cain and A. G. Hopkins, *British Imperialism: Innovation and Expansion, 1688–1914* (London: Longman Group, 1993), p. 149.

[40] King, *History of the London Discount Market*, pp. 264–82.

[41] See, for example, P. J. Cain and A. G. Hopkins, "The Political Economy of British Expansion Overseas, 1750–1914," *Economic History Review* 33 (November 1980): 463–90.

turers to shift their stance on monetary matters to the "nationalist" position held by uncompetitive, domestically bound producers and the nontradables sector. Still unable to sustain a concerted attack on the gold
standard itself, nationalists concentrated their political efforts on reducing the Bank of England's single-minded dependence on discount rate
policy as a stabilization tool. Their efforts produced the brief experiment
with "gold devices" in the 1880s and 1890s.[42] According to W. M. Scammell, "the dilemma of choice between domestic and external stability
was ever in the forefront of Bank thinking from about 1880 onwards and
the Bank sought to soften this dilemma by the timing and selection of its
actions."[43]

The gold devices, however, were never as important as discount rate
policy and were used only rarely after 1900.[44] In the main, the reason
why gold market operations failed to become a more prominent part of
English monetary policy was that they were antithetical to the idea of a
fixed currency price of gold. They also cast doubt on the soundness of
sterling and, by imposing obstacles in the path of market-driven gold
flows, threatened the free gold market. Deviating from the two central
principles of the gold standard was something the gold coalition, especially the City component, sought to prevent. The financial sector's international rents depended upon worldwide confidence in sterling, which,
in turn, was based on England's long history of adhering to gold standard orthodoxy. It was probably for this reason that manipulating the
gold market to insulate the domestic economy was kept to a minimum
in England.

Arthur Bloomfield's data supports the claim that England came closer
to complying with the rules of the game than any other European nation.[45] Using annual data, Bloomfield found that the Bank of England
reinforced the effects of gold flows on the domestic money supply in 16
of the 34 years between 1880 and 1913 (i.e., the bank played by the rules
47 percent of the time). The Reichsbank did so during only 10 of the 34
years (29 percent), and the Bank of France followed the rules in only 9

---

[42] Taken together, the gold devices increased domestic monetary autonomy by placing obstacles in the way of capital and gold flows. They were usually used as alternatives or
supplements to discount rate policy because they did not burden domestic industry and
commerce with higher borrowing costs.

[43] W. M. Scammell, "The Working of the Gold Standard," *Yorkshire Bulletin of Economic and
Social Research* (May 1965): 113.

[44] R. S. Sayers, "The Bank in the Gold Market, 1890–1914," in *Papers in English Monetary
History*, ed. T. S. Ashton and R. S. Sayers (London: Clarendon Press, 1953); Arthur I. Bloomfield, *Monetary Policy under the International Gold Standard* (New York: Federal Reserve Bank
of New York, 1959), pp. 52–55.

[45] Bloomfield, *Monetary Policy under the International Gold Standard.*

years (22 percent). Moreover, there is ample qualitative evidence that the Bank of England tended to use gold devices less frequently than its counterparts on the continent.[46] The bank even refused to hold any foreign exchange assets, a practice widespread among continental central banks because it offered greater flexibility in accommodating foreign drains without violating the rules of the gold standard.[47] According to Beckhart, the reason the bank refused to discount bills drawn in foreign currencies was that "its object [was] to have as much of the world's trade as possible financed by means of sterling. To discount foreign bills would defeat this object and encourage the financing of trade through some other center."[48]

While the identity of gold and sterling "seemed almost a law of nature," the French franc failed to attain such a standing.[49] Nominally, France maintained a bimetallic standard throughout the nineteenth century, but silver constituted the greater part of the coinage before 1850. The Bank of France usually cashed its notes in silver, and when gold coin was wanted for export in bulk, it generally commanded a premium.[50] In the early 1870s, when a glut of silver on world markets threatened to drive gold entirely from circulation, France and the other bimetallic countries of the Latin Monetary Union responded by suspending the free coinage of silver.[51] The French, however, did not adopt a full gold standard. Instead, from 1878 until 1914, they operated a "limping" gold standard, which gave monetary authorities greater flexibility in accommodating external pressures to domestic macroeconomic priorities. The convertibility of banknotes into gold was not guaranteed by law, but was left to the central bank's discretion: in effect, capital controls were imposed in order to maintain monetary sovereignty.[52]

[46] See, for example, A. Giovannini, "How Do Fixed-Exchange-Rate Regimes Work? Evidence from the Gold Standard, Bretton Woods and the EMS," in *Blueprints for Exchange Rate Management*, ed. M. Miller, B. Eichengreen, and R. Portes (San Diego: Academic Press, 1989), pp. 13–41.

[47] Lindert, *Key Currencies and Gold*; Bloomfield, *Monetary Policy under the International Gold Standard*, pp. 52–55.

[48] Benjamin H. Beckhart, *The Discount Policy of the Federal Reserve System* (New York: Henry Holt, 1924), p. 32.

[49] Leland B. Yeager, *International Monetary Relations: Theory, History, and Policy*, 2d ed. (New York: Harper and Row, 1976), p. 299.

[50] J. H. Clapham, *The Economic Development of France and Germany, 1815–1914* (Cambridge: Cambridge University Press), pp. 124–25; Yeager, *International Monetary Relations*, pp. 296–99.

[51] Giulio M. Gallarotti, "The Scramble for Gold: Monetary Regime Transformation in the 1870s," in *Monetary Regimes in Transition*, ed. Michael D. Bordo and Forrest Capie (Cambridge: Cambridge University Press, 1994), pp. 15–67; Charles A. Conant, *A History of Modern Banks of Issue* (New York: G. P. Putnam's Sons, 1915), pp. 60–65.

[52] Giovannini, "How Do Fixed-Exchange-Rate Regimes Work?"

Under the limping standard, the Bank of France could legally redeem its notes in either French gold coin or in five-franc silver pieces, at its own discretion. Having the right to make any payments in silver which it did not care to make in gold, the bank could protect its gold reserve from foreign drains. In practice, whenever the bank wished to limit gold exports, it refused to redeem its notes in gold at the mint par rate of exchange and developed the policy of making gold payments at a premium. In other words, instead of refusing to maintain the gold convertibility of the franc, the bank elected to charge a premium for gold—a mini-devaluation—to check external drains.[53]

The gold premium policy was utilized extensively before 1900, and constituted a "formidable barrier (when the exchange rate was 'unfavorable') to the outward movement of short-term funds, and rendered the French gold holdings insensitive to movements of discount rates in foreign money markets."[54] While the policy had the effect of discouraging gold exports, its main disadvantage was that it impaired the credibility of the French gold standard, and thereby limited the expansion of French international banking and the development of the franc as an international currency. Indeed, the occasional refusal of the Bank of France to redeem its notes in gold, except after the payment of a premium, meant a virtual abandonment of the gold standard. The uncertainty of being able to redeem the currency in gold at the legal parity made foreigners less eager to utilize franc exchange for international purposes, or to buy bills of exchange or securities issued in francs, meaning that, as long as the policy was in practice, Paris could never challenge London's position. As Hartley Withers expressed it, "anyone who has a credit in Paris has a credit of no international value, except in so far as he can make use of it, by means of exchange, to buy a credit in London, which is convertible into gold as a matter of course."[55] *The Economist* held a similar view: "The policy of isolation gives stability in discount rates, but it excludes French bankers from the large profits made by London in the work of international banking."[56] Put simply, "If Paris had maintained a free gold market, it would have experienced a far more considerable demand from foreign borrowers for short-time loans."[57]

[53] Harry D. White, *The French International Accounts, 1880–1913* (Cambridge: Harvard University Press, 1933), pp. 182–200.
[54] Ibid., pp. 185, 192–95. According to White, a premium on gold of 0.65 of 1 percent would nullify a 3 percent difference between discount rates in France and England.
[55] Hartley Withers, *The Meaning of Money*, 2d ed. (London: Smith, Elder, 1909), p. 87.
[56] *The Economist* (November 1909), pp. 1031–32. Cited in Ford, *The Gold Standard, 1880–1914*, p. 21.
[57] C. F. Dunbar, *The Theory and History of Banking*, 4th ed. (New York: G. P. Putnam's Sons, 1922), p. 191.

After 1900, the Bank of France began to lessen its dependence on the gold premium policy. To do so, it began to accumulate and hold a much larger gold reserve, so that even a substantial drain could be accommodated while keeping monetary policy steady.[58] By 1908, the Bank had amassed a gold reserve of $593 million, well over three times the reserve held by the Bank of England (See Figure 4.1). The Bank of England could maintain convertibility on a "thin film of gold" by adroit manipulation of interest rates; the French preference was to keep interest rates low and stable by amassing a reserve large enough to handle even severe foreign drains. The policy of stockpiling gold actually complemented the use of the gold devices in that both facilitated "interest rate smoothing."[59] As one governor of the Bank of France stated: "The extent of our reserves allows us to contemplate without emotion important variations of our metallic stock, and we only exceptionally have recourse to a measure [an advance in the discount rate] which is always painful for commerce and industry. The stability and moderation of the rate of discount are considered as precious advantages, which the French market owes to the organization and traditional conduct of the Bank of France."[60]

The result was that the Bank of France was able to keep its discount rate extraordinarily stable, in line with the nation's preference for domestic monetary independence. While the Bank of England changed its discount rate about six times per year on average between 1880 and 1913, it was not uncommon for the Bank of France to go for stretches of five years or more without a change from its traditional 3 percent rate. Moreover, the range of fluctuation was much narrower in France than England, as Table 3.11 illustrates. But the policy of insulation from market forces detracted from the internationalization of the Paris market and global use of the franc.

French short-term financial markets were also relatively underdeveloped. French finance was primarily a domestic business until the final third of the nineteenth century, when long-term foreign lending blossomed under the aegis of the state. However, other than its role in distributing foreign bonds to France's small investors—who were protected from the exchange risk of the limping standard by gold clauses in the loan contracts—French finance was decidedly parochial.[61] The market for

[58] Stefan Oppers, "Was the Worldwide Shift to Gold Inevitable? An Analysis of the End of Bimetallism," *Journal of Monetary Economics* (forthcoming, 1996).

[59] M. Goodfriend, "Central Banking Under the Gold Standard," Carnegie-Rochester Conference Series on Public Policy (1988), pp. 85–124.

[60] National Monetary Commission, *Interviews on the Banking and Currency Systems of England, Scotland, France, Germany, Switzerland, and Italy* (Washington, D.C.: GPO, 1910), p. 215.

[61] Paul Einzig, *The Fight for Financial Supremacy* (London: Macmillan, 1932), p. 66.

Table 3.11. Stability and range of official discount rates in France, Germany, and England, 1878–1909

	Number of discount rate changes	Average period of discount rate stability	Two longest periods of discount rate stability	Range of discount rates
Bank of France	29	12.83 months	82 months (May 25,1900–March 21, 1907) 65 months (February 22, 1883–February 16, 1888)	2%–4%
Reichsbank	110	3.38 months	25 months (January 18, 1883–March 10, 1885) 21 months (February 5, 1894–November 11, 1895)	3%–7.5%
Bank of England	183	2.02 months	30 months (February 22, 1894–August 10, 1896) 10 months (April 21, 1904–March 9, 1905)	2%–7%

Source: National Monetary Commission, *Statistics for Great Britain, Germany, and France, 1867–1909* (Washington, D.C.: GPO, 1910).

foreign short loans was limited, the international significance of the Paris money market small, and the use of the franc as a reserve currency largely confined to Russia for political reasons, as noted above. Indeed, Myers argues that the underdevelopment of the French money market was the major reason for the franc's lack of international standing.[62]

The political sources of French monetary institutions and policies were deeply ingrained in the structure of French society. Unlike England, France did not develop an alliance of finance, export industry, and commerce, in favor of gold standard orthodoxy. Although these groups shaped the country's financial institutions and policies, their specific situations in the global economy induced monetary outlooks that were quite different from those of their English counterparts.

The structure of French industry mitigated against the development of a strong pro-gold lobby among manufacturers. The country lacked the powerful export industries that had supported monetary internationalism in England. Staple French exports (other than wines and spirits)

[62] Margaret Myers, *Paris as Financial Center* (New York: Columbia University Press, 1936), pp. 1–5.

were mainly manufactured textile specialties of silk, wool or cotton, which tended to be produced in traditional, small workshops and sold in the high-income urban areas of the world.[63] These were not the inexpensive, standardized goods which British exporters excelled in, or the differentiated manufactured exports of Germany and the United States. Even the most modern sectors of French industry (iron and steel, for example) were not competitive on world markets. Overall, exports played a much smaller role in industrial activity than in England and, as a consequence, France did not possess a strong segment of the manufacturing class to stand behind international currency institutions. The relatively small foreign trading sector that did exist was overpowered by the farm sector in the politics of money and credit:

> France is primarily an agrarian nation, and to the peasant classes a low and non-fluctuating discount rate is the greatest desideratum. Further it must be remembered that the foreign trade of France is by no means as extensive as that of either England or Germany. It is much more essential to exporters and importers, in those nations, that the value of the currency remain constant in terms of foreign currencies than that the Bank rate remain stationary. In England and Germany, the importers and exporters constitute a large and important group, while in France they are few in number and do not possess the political influence of the agrarian group.[64]

France's small farmers had another reason for opposing gold standard orthodoxy. As investors in government bonds (Rentes), farmers objected to using the discount rate as a tool of international monetary policy because a policy of high discount rates, aimed at attracting or retaining gold, would negatively affect the value of their investments: "Nearly every peasant there owns a government bond, and raising the rate of discount causes a fall in the value of gilt edged securities; . . . a high rate of discount would produce some kind of national disaster; it is therefore, of much higher importance in France to support the price of Rentes than to foster the stability of the foreign exchanges, whose alterations act only on a limited part of the population."[65]

Without an externally oriented manufacturing sector to support it, the fate of the gold standard rested upon the position and influence of the French financial community. French finance, however, developed along

[63] John H. Clapham, *The Economic Development of France and Germany, 1815–1914* (Cambridge: Cambridge University Press, 1921), pp. 245–55; Tom Kemp, *Economic Forces in French History* (London: Dennis Dobson, 1971), pp. 243–45.
[64] Beckhart, *The Discount Policy of the Federal Reserve System*, p. 71.
[65] N. E. Weill, *Bankers' Magazine*, London (October 1901), p. 466. Cited in Beckhart, *The Discount Policy of the Federal Reserve System*, p. 71.

lines quite distinct from the trajectory in Britain and, consequently, there were few enthusiasts among its ranks for committing to a full gold standard. In England, merchant bankers had originally become involved in international banking through the finance of trade.[66] Long-term lending came later and was built upon the extensive, worldwide connections derived from trade financing.[67] With the emergence of the discount companies in the 1830s, the gradual shift in joint-stock banking toward international business, the decline in the domestic (inland) bill of exchange, and the growing number of foreign banks that opened offices in the City from the 1870s, the London money market became thoroughly internationalized.[68] In 1900, sterling was the world's premier trading and financial currency, with roughly nine bills being drawn on London by foreign countries for every one bill drawn in London on foreign countries.[69] Writing in 1906, W. R. Lawson remarked that "Lombard Street is no longer a purely English or even British institution; it belongs to all nations."[70] In short, the structure of the London market was international in outlook from an early date, and this gave its players a distinct interest in supporting institutions and policies that encouraged the international use of sterling.

This segment of the financial community was largely absent in France. While French financiers did participate in long-term foreign finance, the bread and butter of French banking was discounting *domestic* bills for local firms, merchants, and manufacturers—a business that benefited from low and nonfluctuating interest rates. Indeed, the Paris market for acceptances was only a fraction of the London market (one-eighth the

---

[66] S. D. Chapman, "The International Houses: The Continental Contribution to British Commerce, 1800–1860," *Journal of European Economic History* 6 (1977): 5–48; T. Balogh, *Studies in Financial Organization* (Cambridge: Cambridge University Press, 1947), p. 229; Karl E. Born, *International Banking in the 19th and 20th Centuries*, p. 163; Charles A. Kindleberger, *The Formation of Financial Centers*, Studies in International Finance, no. 36, International Finance Section, Princeton University (1974).

[67] Balogh, *Studies in Financial Organization*, pp. 232–36; E. C. Corti, *The Rise of the House of Rothschild* (New York: Cosmopolitan Books, 1928).

[68] On these trends see P. T. Cottrell, "International Factors in the Formation of Banking Systems: Great Britain," in *International Banking, 1870–1914*, pp. 25–47; King, *History of the London Discount Market*, pp. 264–82.

[69] Cottrell, "International Factors in the Formation of Banking Systems: Great Britain," p. 34.

[70] W. R. Lawson, cited in King, *History of the London Discount Market*, p. 282. The *discount* market, however, remained predominantly British, as foreign banks operating in London could not engage in the acceptance business. Foreign banks were legally "agencies" on the money market, therefore their bills were ineligible for rediscount at the Bank of England. According to Tilly, "Foreign banks operating in London suffered a competitive disadvantage relative to British banks in that the Bank of England refused to grant foreign banks access to its rediscount facilities." Tilly, "International Aspects of the Development of German Banking," p. 109.

size, according to one estimate).[71] Accordingly, "French bankers appeared timid compared with the specialized English bill brokers and discount houses" in respect to pursuing short-term international financial opportunities.[72] With little internationalization to give money market participants in Paris an interest in encouraging a stronger commitment to the gold standard, there were few calls from the financial sector for altering the existing state of affairs along British lines.[73]

In several respects, the German experience is most relevant to the American case, since Germany and the United States were the two countries advancing rapidly in the world economy in those areas suggesting greater international use of their currencies. By 1913, each had matched England's position as exporters (Table 3.1), and manufactured goods largely accounted for this redistribution of world export shares. Germany's greatest relative gains were in chemicals, metals, and machinery exports, while the areas of fastest export growth for the United States were metals, machinery, and vehicles (Table 3.2). In addition, both Germany and the United States advanced rapidly as exporters of differentiated manufactured products, coming to rival England by 1913 (Table 3.4). Finally, both Germany and the United States attained importance as exporters to the developing world in this period (Table 3.6). Although the U.S share of this trade rose more than that of any major exporter between 1872 and 1913, Germany started and finished with a larger absolute share. In short, the global positions of both nations evolved in directions associated with greater international use of their currencies, implying similar patterns of domestic politics.

Although their systemic situations were comparable, the nations differed dramatically in terms of the development of their domestic financial markets. First, Germany already possessed a well-developed discount market, second in size and stature only to London.[74] The general use of two- and three-name bills of exchange, and their acceptance by banks, was the basis of the Berlin discount market. According to Reisser's estimates, between 70 and 75 percent of the entire bill holdings of German joint-stock banks consisted of bankers' acceptances—the credit

[71] Bonin, "The Case of the French Banks," p. 77.

[72] Ibid.

[73] Beth Simmons also makes this point in regard to the origins of French monetary preferences during the interwar period. Beth A. Simmons, *Who Adjusts? Domestic Sources of Foreign Economic Policy during the Interwar Years* (Princeton: Princeton University Press, 1995), p. 167.

[74] For a comparison of the discount systems of England, Germany, France, and the United States, with special emphasis on the role of central banking, see Beckhart, *The Discount Policy of the Federal Reserve System*, pp. 30–129.

instrument with the lowest international transaction costs.[75] The U.S., in contrast, had no discount market to speak of, and its largest joint-stock banks were prohibited by law from accepting bills of exchange. Second, Germany possessed a central bank—the Reichsbank, founded in 1875—whose primary banking function was to provide liquidity, by rediscounting the bills of banks.[76] Thus, "the credit system rested on the assumed liquidity guarantee of the Reichsbank."[77] At no time did the Reichsbank refuse to rediscount eligible paper: "The Reichsbank has always been the last resort and a thoroughly reliable resort."[78] Finally, German bankers faced no legal restrictions on foreign branching of the sort that impaired the participation of American banks' in short-term international finance. In short, Germany's internationalists had to overcome fewer domestic obstacles to internationalize the mark.

With competitive exporters in tow, German banks aggressively seized the opportunities afforded by the nation's rapid ascent in the world economy, and extended their operations overseas.[79] From an early date, the great German banks appear to have recognized that the dominance of sterling as international currency represented foregone profits.[80] Beginning in the 1860s and 1870s, German bankers, international traders, and subsequently business journalists and politicians, sought to redress the system in which short-term trade finance and payments remained dependent on sterling. For German bankers, the problem was that Germany's overseas trading partners had a strong preference for taking and making payments in sterling bills on London, which excluded German banks from earning the commissions and fees (broadly, denomination rents) associated with invoicing trade. According to one contemporary

---

[75] Reisser, *The Great German Banks,* p. 279.

[76] According to Paul Mankiewitz of the Deutsche Bank, "The great strength of our financial system in Germany is the Reichsbank. Under that system the question of our own cash reserve is of secondary importance, as we can at all times convert our holdings of commercial paper into cash at the Reichsbank." National Monetary Commission, *Interviews on the Banking and Currency Systems,* p. 374.

[77] Knut Borchardt "Währung und Wirtschaft," in *Währung und Wirtschaft in Deutschland, 1876–1895,* ed. Deutsche Bundesbank (Frankfurt: 1976), p. 46. Cited in Tilly, "International Aspects of the Development of German Banking," p. 92.

[78] National Monetary Commission, *Renewal of the Reichsbank Charter* (Washington, D.C.: GPO, 1910), p. 246.

[79] The direct and indirect links between banks and industry in Germany are explored by Andrew Shonfield, *Modern Capitalism: The Changing Balance of Public and Private Power* (London: Oxford University Press, 1969); Alexander Gerschenkron, *Economic Backwardness in Historical Perspective* (Cambridge: Cambridge University Press, 1962); and Alfred Marshall, *Industry and Trade* (London: Macmillan, 1919). For a discussion of how the structure of bank-industry relations influences international monetary policy, see Henning, *Currencies and Politics.*

[80] Tilly, "International Aspects of the Development of German Banking," pp. 90–112.

account circulated in German banking circles, British banks earned about 500,000 marks per year in the late 1880s by financing Germany's trade with Chile alone.[81] Extrapolating to Germany's total trade yields a far higher amount of profits foregone to British bankers. According to Reisser, German bankers were familiar with estimates of the huge profits British banks earned by intermediating and invoicing German and world trade "merely because all acceptances by means of which these [commercial] exchanges were effected had to be liquidated in the British market."[82] Needless to say, German banks were interested in this potential business.

For Germany's industrial exporters, the practice of invoicing in sterling imposed "unusual hardships" in the form of higher costs and exchange risk: "The exporter has to draw on his foreign customer bills in a foreign currency for the latter's acceptance. Owing to the limited market for such notes, he finds it difficult to discount them, and has to bear the loss resulting from fluctuations in the rate of foreign exchange which may take place in the interval."[83] Like the big joint-stock banks, Germany's competitive industries were aware of the benefits to be derived from internationalizing the mark, in the context of rising exports. "More German exports stimulated the demand for means to pay for them, and institutions that could satisfy that demand could induce more exports. The role of the overseas banks was to provide credit and payment services to the local merchant communities. Their presence reduced the risks to home-country banks of the export credits they extended. Their presence also recruited both additional customers for German exporters and additional supplies of exports to Germany."[84]

To render German trade and payments independent of sterling, contemporaries saw the need for two developments: the "establishment of a unified German currency, the mark, on the basis of the gold standard; and the establishment of a network of foreign, and especially overseas, banks."[85] With domestic financial markets progressing toward the requisite characteristics of depth, breadth, and resilience, attention focused on institutionalizing the gold standard and foreign branching.

In 1873, Germany was able to adopt the gold standard with the help of a large gold indemnity paid by France for losing the Franco-Prussian

---

[81] Reisser, *The Great German Banks*, p. 538. See also Tilly, "International Aspects of the Development of German Banking," p. 106.

[82] Reisser cites the figure of 432 million marks ($87 million) as the aggregate commissions earned by British banks for invoicing world trade in sterling in 1898. Reisser, *The Great German Banks*, pp. 538–39.

[83] Reisser, *The Great German Banks*, p. 276.

[84] Tilly, "International Aspects of the Development of German Banking," p. 107.

[85] Ibid., p. 106.

War.[86] The gold mark became the new national monetary unit, and the free and unlimited coinage of silver was discontinued. Formally, the new German standard was not a limping standard of the French variety, but a full gold standard along textbook lines. In practice, however, the German commitment to gold took an intermediate position, though closer to English orthodoxy than French obstructionism. As in England, the official discount rate in Germany was the primary tool of international monetary policy, and the relative frequency and range of discount rate changes in Germany supports this view (Table 3.11).[87] Nevertheless, the Reichsbank employed techniques that were outside the norms of a true gold standard. Several of these were of the "gold device" variety and may have resulted from the need to insulate nationalists in the agricultural sector from gold standard discipline. For example, when the Reichsbank wanted to draw gold to Germany, it could offer a premium, or grant interest-free loans to importers.[88] To discourage gold drains, the Reichsbank also offered foreign coin for export that was as light as legally possible. In addition, the Reichsbank used "moral suasion" to limit demands for gold for export. According to Goshen, "a kind of moral pressure, a pressure from above, is put on, and every effort used to prevent the depletion of the stock of gold, pressure of a kind which no one in this country [England] would approve."[89]

Suasion was effective in stemming foreign drains because German bankers feared the loss of privileges with the central bank: "In theory Berlin has a gold standard, and the notes of the Imperial Bank are theoretically payable on demand in gold. . . . But anyone who wants to draw on the Imperial Bank's share to any great extent is likely to . . . be met with a most discouraging countenance when he next requires accommodation."[90] The fear of antagonizing the central bank was so potent that, on at least one occasion, German bankers did not wait for the word from the Reichsbank before they curtailed demands for gold. During the worldwide crisis of 1907, which began with an American panic, exchange rates advanced beyond the gold export point, but German banks

---

[86] Conant, *A History of Modern Banks of Issue*, pp. 197–200; Charles F. Dunbar, *The Theory and History of Banking*, 4th ed. (New York: G. P. Putnam's Sons, 1922), pp. 199–202; Gustav Stolper, *The German Economy, 1870–1940* (New York: Reynal and Hitchcock, 1940), pp. 31–37.

[87] National Monetary Commission, *Interviews on the Banking and Currency Systems*, p. 357.

[88] National Monetary Commission, *German Bank Inquiry of 1908* (Washington, D.C.: GPO, 1910), pp. 337, 426, 457–58, 556; National Monetary Commission, *The Reichsbank* (Washington, D.C.: GPO, 1910), pp. 236–38.

[89] G. J. Goschen, *Essays and Addresses on Economic Questions* (London: Edward Arnold, 1905), p. 119.

[90] Hartley Withers, *The Meaning of Money*, 2d ed. (London: Smith, Elder, 1909), p. 87.

did not seek gold for export. The currency internationalists in Germany immediately regretted this action, since it undermined international confidence in the mark:

> Our foremost object must be the maintenance of the exchange parities in order that our credit in the international market and the reputation of the German gold standard may not suffer, with the purpose of finally placing the latter beyond all doubt and on the same firm basis on which the English sovereign stands today. We may safely say that all businessmen agree in considering it detrimental and regrettable that no gold was sent abroad when exchange for a while in 1907 ruled above the gold export point; and that it may be well to emphasize the fact that the management of the Reichsbank reached the same conclusion. As we explained before, it must have been either mistaken patriotism or fear of antagonizing the Reichsbank which for so long a time kept our bankers from exporting gold, and which really created a depreciation, however short lived, of our monetary standard in the international money markets.[91]

Yet in contrast to France, German policymakers placed fewer obstructions and interfered less frequently in the gold market, with the effect that international bills drawn in marks came to have a definite gold value. Berlin's nascent development as an international banking center required as much. To the benefit of the German banking sector, bills denominated in marks became a reserve asset, not only for foreign central banks (see above), but also for private banks. The experience of the Warburg bank in Hamburg, which had a large acceptance business, confirms this view: "Foreign banks bought large quantities of German trade bills on a commission basis . . . and brisk trading developed through Rothschilds and other London friends in trade bills denominated in marks, considered such excellent investment for foreign banks that they came to be called 'Zuckerbrot' ('Sugarbread')."[92]

The mark, as noted, also became an important invoicing currency in trade with Europe, South America, and Asia, and much attention was devoted to extending German bank operations overseas to secure this business. Foreign branches not only handled foreign trade financing in marks, but also served informational functions useful to German exporters. Overseas branches furnished news on trade opportunities, provided credit information on potential buyers, handled collection items,

---

[91] National Monetary Commission, *Renewal of the Reichsbank Charter*, p. 31.
[92] Eduard Rosenbaum and H. J. Sherman, *M. M. Warburg & Co., 1798–1938* (London, 1979), p. 98.

and supplied data on tariff duties and trade practices.[93] Led by the Deutsche Bank, German banks actually began to extend their banking operations abroad *before* the currency was unified and placed on the gold standard in 1873, which caused predictable problems. Internationalizing the mark was "especially difficult at the beginning of the period, when the gold standard did not exist in Germany, for bills in terms of the multifarious German currencies were unknown and disliked in international business."[94] As a case in point, the Deutsche Bank's branches in Yokohama and Shanghai, established in 1872 "to buy bills drawn on Germany, so that the German exporter, who had calculated the selling price of his goods in marks, might be paid in marks," had to be closed in 1874, "mainly because of the depreciation of silver."[95] However, by the end of the 1870s, the German mark had become a gold standard currency, and German banks intensified their overseas branching drive. German banks, exporters, and importers benefited, as the mark advanced steadily as an international currency for German trade. German manufacturers and traders no longer had to invoice in a foreign currency, while the banks at the apex of the financial system captured some of the denomination rents previously earned by English banks:

> As a result of continuous efforts mark bills have gained a respected position in foreign markets alongside of sterling bills. . . . [T]he time may be said to have passed, at least in the majority of cases, when German exporters, in order to collect foreign claims, and foreign exporters, selling goods to Germans, had to settle in London. . . . Through the financing of the foreign business of our merchants, German bank acceptances have been introduced to foreign markets, with the result that the ofttimes considerable earnings of foreign concerns in this field have been turned into German channels.[96]

Summary

The economics literature identifies the essential (domestic) and supplementary (international) factors that contribute to the choice and usage of

---

[93] "The purpose of these [overseas] banks is as much to aid German commerce by carrying on a regular banking business in the countries in question as to further the large financial undertakings of the parent institutions (underwriting foreign loans)." Robert Franz, *The Statistical History of the German Banking System, 1888–1907* (Washington, D.C.: GPO, 1910), p. 101.

[94] Reisser, *The Great German Banks*, p. 422.

[95] Ibid., pp. 422–23. See also Hertner, "German Banks Abroad before 1914," p. 102.

[96] Reisser, *The Great German Banks*, pp. 431–32, 538.

national currencies for international purposes. In the previous chapter, I drew out the domestic political ramifications of international currency use, arguing that large money-center banks and exporters of manufactured products are especially keen on seeing the national currency developed for international use. In the theoretical portion of this chapter, I extrapolated a causal relationship running from change in the supplemental factors (relative position in world trade and payments) to change in the domestic factors (price stability and development of national financial markets). Change in a country's relative international economic position in directions presaging greater (or lesser) use of its currency, feeds back on domestic politics by affecting size and preference intensities of coalitions for (or against) globalizing the currency. When a country advances in world trade and payments to a position where the national currency has the potential to assume a global role, internationalists are expected to press for the necessary domestic institutions that underpin all international currencies. Conversely, when a nation experiences relative economic decline, nationalists should become more powerful in their resistance to the domestic institutions that underpin the global use of the currency.

The empirical portion of the chapter presents data on the relative economic positions of major states in the categories pertinent to international currency use. The findings show the United States and Germany advancing industrially and commercially in the decades before World War I, presaging a rising role for the dollar and the mark in international trade and financial affairs. In contrast, the positions of Britain and France slipped. Data on actual currency usage shows rising international use of the German mark, an exceptionally small role for the U.S. dollar, and slight declines in the global role of the pound sterling and the French franc. The parochialism of the U.S. dollar most clearly demonstrates the importance of the basic domestic determinants of international currency use.

While a brief sketch of currency politics in the European cases cannot do justice to the historical record, the tentative findings are encouraging. England, France, and Germany experienced patterns of domestic politics on international currency use that reflected changes in global economic position. In France, the country least likely to internationalize its currency by virtue of its declining relative position in the world system, economic nationalists dominated, and the nation resisted installing the domestic prerequisites for globalizing the franc. In England, where price-stabilizing institutions and exceptionally well-developed financial markets prevailed since at least the 1870s, pressures for policies conducive to greater national monetary flexibility arose as the nation's relative position slipped toward the end of the century. In Germany—the country most like the United States in terms of its international economic position—bankers, merchants, and industrial exporters moved to make the (relatively limited) changes needed to internationalize the mark, as the nation gained prominence in the world trade and payments systems. In the United States, as we shall see in the next chapter, the German pattern prevailed: money-center bankers and exporting manufacturers seized the opportunity provided by the panic of 1907 to effect the extensive changes required to internationalize the dollar.

4 /

The Rise of the U.S. Economy and
the Banking Reform Movement

International trends foreshadowed an expanded global role for the U.S. dollar after the 1870s, but the dollar remained a parochial currency. The barriers were domestic and institutional, not international and economic. The U.S. payments system lacked the characteristic traits of depth, breadth, and resilience, which constrained the supply of assets appropriate for international currency use. Moreover, these shortcomings were also the source of America's internal financial woes. The narrow and inelastic character of American money and banknote markets led to an unusually high incidence of financial panics and sharp seasonal fluctuations in interest rates. In this sense, there was a basic complementarity between the two problems of financial organization facing the United States: the constraints on dollar globalization also undermined the smooth operation of the payments. This complementarity is essential to understanding the demand for payments system reform.

Payments system reform involved the production of *joint benefits* in which the private output (internationalizing the currency) could not practicably be disassociated from the complementary collective output (payments system stability), forming a concurrence between the private and social costs of banking reform. In this chapter, I link the onset of advocacy for domestic institutional changes to change in the nation's international position. As demand for dollar-denominated financial services increased with the rapid ascent of the United States in the world economy, members of the international currency coalition were motivated to supply the political entrepreneurship for domestic reform. Standing to gain disproportionately from reform (due to the more excludable benefits of internationalizing the dollar), this subgroup had private incentives to absorb a disproportionate share of the overall costs of improving the institutional characteristics of the payments system. Moreover, preference intensities within this subgroup also varied as anticipated, with money-center bankers the most responsive to the changing international signals. Bankers saw how international change had created opportunities for the dollar and for New York City, and they designed and advocated new domestic institutions consistent with the external signals. In addition, bankers were clearly cognizant of the complementarity of the joint products, expressing repeatedly the immutable interdependence of internationalizing the currency and stabilizing the payments system.

International Sources of Financial Reform

By the end of the nineteenth century, the United States faced two serious problems of financial organization. Its payments system was structurally unstable. In addition, the United States was the only major industrial exporting country whose money had not taken on international functions, despite very favorable trends in the nation's global position. If the joint products interpretation is correct, and these two problems could not be resolved independently, advocacy for remaking American institutions should be closely associated with the new opportunities in short-term international finance that came with the country's advancing international position. As the internationalization of the dollar would confer concentrated benefits upon a narrow and specific category of social agents—currency internationalists—the advancing position of the United States should have given this constituency ever stronger incentives to install the necessary domestic institutions. In other words, we should observe disproportionate levels of political entrepreneurship on the part of these agents, and a greater intensity of their efforts over time, as the economy's position advanced. This much of the argument is supported by the evidence.

In terms of both problems of financial organization, price stability was not the issue. Price stability was neither the primary factor in limiting the internationalization of the dollar, nor the source of domestic financial instability—which is probably why the gold standard was treated so casually in debates leading up to the Federal Reserve Act. The gold standard attained de facto status in January 1879, and convertibility was

never suspended thereafter, despite the silver agitation and the legislation of 1878 (the Bland-Allison Act) and 1890 (the Sherman Silver Purchase Act). Confidence in the dollar was further enhanced by the vast
increases in the U.S. stock of monetary gold that came after 1896, with
increased gold production and inflows associated with current account
surpluses (Table 3.9). The treasury absorbed the bulk of this gold because the public brought gold to the treasury in exchange for "gold certificates," a paper currency which was preferred to specie as a matter of
convenience. Table 4.1 shows the dramatic rise in the treasury's gold
holdings after 1896, the amount of gold held for gold certificates, and the
rising share of gold in the national stock of money. As gold certificates
were simply warehouse receipts backed by treasury gold on a one-to-
one basis, specie held no special attraction for note holders. The simple
point is that the treasury's huge gold reserve after the mid-1890s was
more than adequate to ensure convertibility.

The treasury's gold resources soon came to dwarf those of any European central bank. Figure 4.1 displays the gold holdings of the major

Table 4.1. Holdings of the U.S. Treasury (millions of dollars)

	1 Gold in Treasury	2 Gold for certificates	3 Total gold stock	4 Total stock of money[a]	5 1/3 (%)	6 1/4 (%)	7 3/4 (%)
1896	177	43	589	1,904	30	9	31
1897	197	37	638	1,954	31	10	33
1898	281	36	838	2,178	34	13	38
1899	400	33	897	2,253	45	18	40
1900	481	201	989	2,449	49	20	40
1901	541	247	1,050	2,544	52	21	41
1902	618	306	1,121	2,651	55	23	42
1903	688	377	1,192	2,763	58	25	43
1904	696	466	1,217	2,839	57	25	43
1905	763	485	1,288	2,993	59	25	43
1906	895	527	1,458	3,226	61	28	45
1907	951	600	1,613	3,349	59	28	48
1908	1,035	783	1,656	3,399	63	30	49
1909	1,032	815	1,638	3,426	63	30	48
1910	1,104	803	1,710	3,509	65	31	49
1911	1,184	930	1,800	3,618	66	33	50
1912	1,254	943	1,880	3,719	67	34	51
1913	1,292	1,004	1,904	3,764	68	34	51

Source: U.S. Department of the Treasury, *Annual Report* (Washington, D.C.: GPO, selected
years).
[a] Includes gold, silver, United States notes (Greenbacks), Treasury notes, and National Bank
notes.

Figure 4.1. Gold holdings of the U.S. Treasury, the Bank of England, the Bank of France, and the Reichsbank, 1878–1913 (annual averages, in millions of dollars)

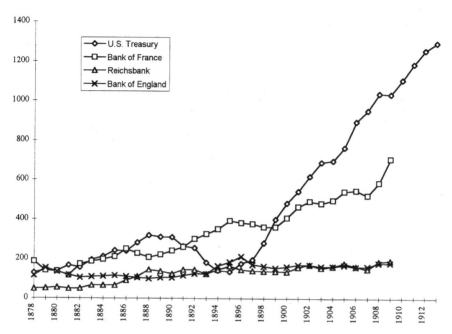

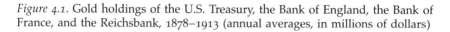

Source: A. Piatt Andrew, *Financial Diagrams* (Washington, D.C.: GPO, 1910), plate 24.

European central banks relative to those of the treasury. By 1899, the treasury held gold reserves larger than any central bank, even the Bank of France. By 1909, the sum nearly equaled the combined reserves of the three leading European central banks.

These figures suggest that the dollar was one of the world's most secure currencies by the end of the century. Moreover, the American gold standard was arguably *purer* than that of any other major country, including England, by virtue of the absence of a central bank capable of influencing gold flows and the adjustment process. As Margaret Myers put it, "this period furnishes an example of the *unregulated* gold standard at its simplest. . . . There were no complications of bimetallism . . . and the introduction of the telegraph and improvements in shipping had made the gold market almost instantly responsive to changes in the balance of payments."[1] On rare occasions, manipulation of gold flows did occur, either through the auspices of private bankers (e.g., the Morgan-

[1] Margaret G. Myers, *The New York Money Market: Origins and Development*, vol. 1 (New York: Columbia University Press, 1931), p. 339; emphasis added.

Belmont syndicate of 1895–96), or the U.S. Treasury (which used gold devices in 1906–7), but these were *ad hoc* measures cobbled together on a temporary basis. For example, when the bimetallism controversy produced speculative pressures that led to foreign gold outflows in 1895, the government contracted with the Morgan-Belmont syndicate to stem the drain and temporarily attract foreign gold.[2] In addition to purchasing 3.5 million ounces of gold from foreign countries and selling it to the government for bonds to build the specie reserve, the syndicate introduced a system of private exchange control to keep the dollar above its gold export point. The treasury's foreign exchange operations were no more systematic. On only one occasion did the treasury emulate the European central bank practice of subsidizing the interest costs of gold in transit, thus decreasing the gold import point and making it profitable for banks to import gold.[3] In the main, unregulated gold and capital flows, with consequent effects on prices and economic activity, formed the basis of American adjustment to temporary and fundamental payments disequilibria.[4] There is, in fact, a large literature on how uncontrolled free market demands for gold, stemming from seasonal changes in the U.S. current account, as well as American banking panics, caused severe problems in the operation of the international gold standard, and induced cooperation among European central banks.[5]

Again, the credibility of the U.S. commitment to gold and stable monetary policies was not in doubt, nor was this the source of the dollar's lack of international standing. The remaining problem was the thin, illiquid nature of the American money market, an area in which Great Britain and Germany maintained distinct advantages over the United States. The U.S. discount market was less developed than that of any other country, so much so, in fact, that Paul Warburg was probably correct in

[2] Peter M. Garber and Vittorio U. Grilli, "The Belmont-Morgan Syndicate as an Optimal Investment Banking Contract," *European Economic Review* 30 (June 1986): 649–77; Matthew Simon, "The Morgan-Belmont Syndicate of 1895 and Intervention in the Foreign-Exchange Market," *Business History Review* 42 (Winter 1968): 385–417; Vincent P. Carosso, *The Morgans: Private International Bankers, 1854–1913* (Cambridge: Harvard University Press, 1987), pp. 311–49.
[3] Richard H. Timberlake, Jr., "Mr. Shaw and His Critics: Monetary Policy in the Golden Era Revisited," *Quarterly Journal of Economics* 77 (February 1963): 40–54; A. Piatt Andrew, "The Treasury and the Banks under Secretary Shaw," *Quarterly Journal of Economics* 21 (August 1907).
[4] C. A. E. Goodhart, *The New York Money Market and the Finance of Trade, 1900–1913* (Cambridge: Harvard University Press, 1969).
[5] Marcello de Cecco, *Money and Empire: The International Gold Standard, 1890–1913* (London: Oxford University Press, 1974); Barry Eichengreen, *Golden Fetters: The Gold Standard and the Great Depression* (New York: Oxford University Press, 1992), pp. 29–66; and Giulio M. Gallarotti, *The Anatomy of an International Monetary Regime: The Classical Gold Standard* (Oxford: Oxford University Press, 1995), pp. 111–40.

his assessment that the U.S. was as financially backward as "Europe at the time of the Medicis."[6] The discount market in double-name paper was in decline, national banks were legally prevented from accepting bills of exchange, and the commercial paper market revolved around unsecured promissory notes. Moreover, the only market that New York joint-stock banks participated in extensively was the market for call loans secured by stock exchange collateral. In contrast, in England and Berlin, the double-name bill of exchange and bankers' acceptance remained the usual forms and these bills came to serve the functions of money, nationally and internationally. If the U.S. dollar was to serve widely as the means for international payments, not only in the trade of the United States, but also in the trade of the world at large, the U.S. discount market had to be broad and deep enough to absorb at all times a large volume of bills. Only then could currency internationalists reap the concentrated advantages of key currency status. The redistribution of denomination rents from English to American banks, and reduced costs and risk of foreign exchange to American exporters and importers, were at stake: "The acceptance of bills by reputable banks would make them prime short-term investments in the discount market and attract capital to trade finance at low rates of interest. The arrangement would eliminate the risk in converting to sterling and the commissions to British banks. Knowledgeable advocates of this policy predicted it would increase business for American banks, retain money for banking services which would otherwise flow to England, and increase America's international prestige."[7]

In addition, the United States was deficient by virtue of the absence of a central bank and foreign branch banking. Britain's (and later Germany's) internationalists had long recognized that solid domestic foundations sustained sterling as the primary means of international payments and London as the world's premier clearing center. Buttressing England's inviolate adherence to the gold standard and its articulated discount market for prime bankers' acceptances was the Bank of England, which served as a stabilizer, governor, and ultimate source of liquidity for the discount market. In turn, the vast web of British overseas banks linked trading markets throughout the world to the London money market, providing intermediation and informational services to exporters and importers. Combined, these institutions served as sterling's institutional backbone in world affairs. By the late 1890s, the

[6] Paul M. Warburg, "Defects and Needs of Our Banking System" [1907], in Paul M. Warburg, *The Federal Reserve System*, vol. 2 (New York: Macmillan, 1930), p. 9.
[7] Paul P. Abrahams, *The Foreign Expansion of American Finance and Its Relationship to the Foreign Economic Policies of the United States, 1907–1921* (New York: Arno Press, 1976), p. 10.

United States possessed only a credible commitment to the gold standard, and the absence of the other institutions precluded the entrance of American firms into international banking.[8] According to Vincent Carosso and Richard Sylla, there were "three great drawbacks to international banking" before the introduction of the Federal Reserve legislation:

> First, the sentiment against branch banking embodied in federal and state banking laws prohibited most American joint-stock banks from establishing branches abroad as well as at home. . . . Second, American joint-stock banks were either legally forbidden or (what amounted to the same thing) lacked specific authorization to accept drafts or bills of exchange. Since acceptances were the main instrument by which banks participated in the finance of international trade, the inability to accept bills and drafts placed American joint-stock banks at a competitive disadvantage relative to banks in other nations. . . . Third, the absence of a central bank and a discount market for acceptances and other short-term instruments such as was facilitated by the central banks of other countries . . . meant that the United States could not compete on the field where the contest of international short-term finance was played. The problem, it seems, was institutional rather than purely economic.[9]

The domestic financial machinery, in short, was ill suited to the nation's advancing position in the world economy. The use of bankers' acceptances as evidences of indebtedness behind loans and discounts was virtually nonexistent, there was no central bank to make a market for these bills in times of stress, and the large national banks with the resources needed to establish branches were legally prevented from doing so. These constraints provide the basis for a sufficient explanation for the rise of the reform effort. The claim is that the rise in America's global economic position gave internationalists within the United States incentives to effect these changes. As Samuel McRoberts, vice president of the National City Bank (Citibank today) expressed it, the "National Banking

[8] As of 1910, only five small state-chartered banks had established foreign branches, and only one of these institutions—the International Banking Corporation—was designed to finance American trade and business abroad. The others were New York trust companies that primarily sought to attract foreign investment into the United States. Clyde W. Phelps, *The Foreign Expansion of American Banks: American Branch Banking Abroad* (New York: Ronald Press, 1927), pp. 85–86, 147–54, 221; Mira Wilkins, "Banks over Borders: Some Evidence from Their pre-1914 History," in *Banks as Multinationals*, ed. Geoffrey Jones (London: Routledge, 1990), pp. 231–33.
[9] Vincent P. Carosso and Richard Sylla, "U.S. Banks in International Finance," in *International Banking, 1870–1914*, ed. Rondo Cameron and V. I. Bovykin (New York: Oxford University Press, 1991), pp. 52–53.

Act was enacted at a time when little thought was given to financing foreign commerce. It was drawn solely with an eye on internal needs; and a study of its text leads one to the conclusion that its author [Salmon P. Chase] not only failed to make any provision for foreign banking, but, unwittingly, prohibited it by the terms of the act."[10] To Frederick Kent, vice president of the Bankers Trust Company of New York, use of European currencies for invoicing American trade was increasingly anachronistic, due to trends in the nation's international accounts: "We pay Europe interest and commissions for the use of its money; and, while we have been content to do so in the past, the future will find a shifting of the load on to our own shoulders to a considerable extent. This will come about more and more as our floating capital finds less demand for use in our industries and in the development of our resources. Such a condition will, of course, be greatly retarded by our banking laws, but when the necessity becomes sufficiently great they will be changed to meet the emergency."[11]

Within American society, bankers and corporate exporters in New York derived incentives to alter domestic banking laws from the advancing position of the United States in the world economy. Yet of this coalition, bankers took the lead when it came to articulating the institutional specifics of reform. In 1904, for example, Comptroller of the Currency William B. Ridgely recommended that the largest national banks (those with a capital base of over $1 million) be specifically authorized to "accept bills drawn on them not to exceed four months after sight," and to establish "such offices, agencies, or branches as may be necessary to conduct business in foreign countries, in the island possessions of the United States, and in the Panama Canal zone."[12] The powers of acceptance and foreign branching were explicitly pitched as export-enhancing. But the reform ideas did not originate with the comptroller, or even with manufacturing exporters. Instead, "the measures proposed by Mr. Ridgely are intended, so far as present immediate objectives are concerned, to facilitate the plans of one or two large National banks in New York, and possibly in Chicago, which for some time have been largely engaged in the foreign exchange business, and which have recently been considering plans for engaging in a wider scale in international banking."[13]

---

[10] Samuel McRoberts, "The Extension of American Banking in Foreign Countries," *Annals of the American Academy of Political and Social Science* 36 (November 1910): 32.
[11] Frederick I. Kent, "Financing Our Foreign Trade," *Annals of the American Academy of Political and Social Science* 36 (November 1910): 29.
[12] U.S. Department of the Treasury, *Annual Report* (Washington, D.C.: GPO, 1904), pp. 507–8.
[13] *New York Times*, 18 December 1904, p. 1.

While exporters obliquely voiced support for amending the National Banking System so that U.S. banks could operate internationally to aid in the expansion of American exports, it was bankers who provided the intellectual firepower for the more far-reaching changes in the payments system. Interested in developing the domestic basis by which the American dollar would become as acceptable as the British pound in invoicing foreign transactions, the vision was nothing less than to transfer the banking capital of the world from London to New York. For this to happen, the institutions of the National Banking System had to be replaced, not modified.

On questions of banking reform, corporate exporters and importers generally deferred to the bankers, who, with their long experience in international finance, had superior understanding of the mechanics of international exchange. Moreover, since the well-being of the New York banks was closely tied to that of the large industrial corporations, who were their major clients, the latter probably assumed that bankers would design institutional reforms with corporate interests in mind. In fact, important commercial and industrial organizations, such as the New York Chamber of Commerce, the Manufacturers' Association of New York, and the New York Produce Exchange appointed leading international bankers to their banking and currency committees, and the reform proposals that emanated from these committees were thus largely the work of bankers.

A key case in point was the work of the currency committee of the New York Chamber of Commerce. In a speech before the chamber on 6 January 1906, Jacob Schiff of Kuhn, Loeb and Company denounced the National Banking System as "nothing less than a disgrace to any civilized country" and recommended that the chamber immediately take up the matter of banking reform.[14] The chamber's standing finance committee responded to Schiff's suggestion, and within a month, developed a plan. Its recommendations, however, were tentative and limited, and bankers were not at all pleased. According to Frank Vanderlip, president of National City Bank from 1909 to 1919: "No one was ever discourteous enough to suggest that the ignorance of Wall Street on the subject of currency was as dense as this document, coming from this representative body shows it to be."[15] Thereupon, the bankers quickly disposed of the plan and moved to replace the chamber's standing committee with a special committee composed primarily of New York bankers.

[14] New York Chamber of Commerce, *Annual Report* (New York: Chamber of Commerce, 1906–1907), p. 30.
[15] Frank A. Vanderlip to James Stillman, 2 February 1906, part B, series 1, box 1, Frank A. Vanderlip Papers, Rare Book and Manuscript Library, Columbia University.

Jacob Schiff, J. P. Morgan, Sr., and George Baker of First National Bank were to join Vanderlip on the new committee, but for various reasons, only Vanderlip could serve.[16] Nevertheless, the new committee was dominated by such bankers as Vanderlip, Charles Conant, treasurer of the Morton Trust Company of New York, and Dumont Clarke, president of the American Exchange Bank. Vanderlip was the principal author of the revised plan, which was reported to the full chamber in November of 1906. After listing the principal defects of the existing system, Vanderlip identified the actors who should be the main agents of reform: "No important financial measure will receive favorable consideration in Congress unless it has the endorsement of representative bankers. Such being the case, we are of the opinion that the bankers of New York City ought to take up the question and reach agreement upon some satisfactory measure."[17]

Vanderlip's committee then provided an outline of such a measure. In line with the bankers' international objectives, the committee advocated "the creation of a central bank of issue." This central bank was to have a capital of not less than $50 million, to carry a large reserve of gold, to act as the custodian of the country's gold, to redeem all kinds of paper, and to act as the government's fiscal agent, thereby relieving the treasury of its quasi-central banking powers.

Vanderlip, however, was not the leading light in the New York reform movement. If one banker among this group deserves credit as the "father" of the Federal Reserve System, it is Paul Warburg. In 1902, Warburg emigrated from Germany to join Kuhn, Loeb and Company in New York, and almost immediately he assumed intellectual leadership of the reform movement.[18] In the 1920s, before the Federal Reserve fell into disrepute for its failure to prevent the collapse of the banking system and subsequent depression of the early 1930s, the paternity of the Federal Reserve Act was heatedly debated. The mother of the Federal Reserve Act must have been very immoral, Warburg quipped, because so many men claimed to be the father.[19] The dispute was the source of several books by contemporary participants in the reform process: Carter Glass challenged Charles Seymour, Warburg responded to Henry Parker

[16] James Livingston, *Origins of the Federal Reserve System: Money, Class, and Corporate Capitalism, 1890–1913* (Ithaca: Cornell University Press, 1986), pp. 159–64.

[17] New York Chamber of Commerce, *The Currency: Report of the Special Committee of the Chamber of Commerce of the State of New York* (New York: 1906), p. 6.

[18] For biographical information, see Ron Chernow, *Warburgs: The Twentieth-Century Odyssey of a Remarkable Jewish Family* (New York: Random House, 1993).

[19] Paul Warburg to Carter Glass, 22 December 1926, box 24, Carter Glass Papers (no. 2913), Manuscripts Division, Special Collections Department, University of Virginia Library.

Willis, and Laurence Laughlin looked critically at Warburg.[20] Although others may lay claim to specific portions of the act, its fundamental financial provisions came almost exclusively from Warburg. In a *New York Times* editorial, economist Edwin Seligman of Columbia University portrayed Warburg's idea of a discount market supported by a central bank as the fundamental basis of the law; all else was of secondary importance: "One man, and one man only is responsible—Paul M. Warburg. We speak of the English Law of 1844 as Peel's Bank Act because Peel carried it through Parliament. But every tyro knows that the real actor, as Peel himself acknowledged, was Samuel Jones Loyd, soon thereafter raised to the peerage of Lord Overstone. What Overstone was in England, Warburg has been in this country."[21]

Warburg, who was rewarded for his work by an appointment to the Federal Reserve Board in 1914, had extensive experience in European banking methods and brought this knowledge to bear in the campaign for institutional change. His most basic contributions were in recognizing the new possibilities posed by America's advancing international position and in originating and promulgating the fundamental features of what was to become the Federal Reserve Act in response to these forces.

Contributions of Paul Warburg

According to historian Robert West, Warburg was "the single most powerful force in shaping the direction of American banking reform" from the early 1900s through 1913.[22] Warburg strongly advocated the development of an American discount market based on European-styled acceptances, supported by a central reserve-holding agency that would stand ready to absorb the surplus stock of eligible acceptances from the market. In a series of speeches and publications sponsored by New York's financial and mercantile community, Warburg contrasted American practices with European methods and built a strong case for developing these institutions on both international and domestic grounds.[23] After the panic of 1907, his suggestions were taken up by a wider audience, but

[20] Carter Glass, *An Adventure in Constructive Finance* (New York: Doubleday, Page, 1927); Charles Seymour, *The Intimate Papers of Colonel House* (Boston: Houghton Mifflin, 1926); Henry Parker Willis, *The Federal Reserve System: Legislation, Organization, and Operation* (New York: Ronald Press, 1923); Paul M. Warburg, *The Federal Reserve System: Its Origin and Growth*, 2 vols. (New York: Macmillan, 1930); Laurence J. Laughlin, *The Federal Reserve Act: Its Origins and Problems* (New York: Macmillan, 1933).

[21] *New York Times*, 29 January 1927.

[22] Robert C. West, *Banking Reform and the Federal Reserve, 1863–1923* (Ithaca: Cornell University Press, 1974), p. 54.

[23] Many of Warburg's writings and speeches are collected in Warburg, *The Federal Reserve System*.

the global benefits were always at the forefront of internationalists' attentions. Most of his recommendations were incorporated as main features of the Federal Reserve System, which allowed national banks to accept bills of exchange arising out of foreign trade, and which provided for their purchase by the regional Federal Reserve banks.

Warburg identified two European innovations as the key differences with American banking—the importance of the bill of exchange in financial intercourse against American promissory notes, and central banking against America's decentralized system of thousands of note-issuing banks. He stressed that the two components worked hand in hand: "Without such paper, the government banks of Europe could not accomplish their work; and vice versa, the role which this paper generally plays in Europe's financial household is dependent on the existence of central banks. The two cannot be separated."[24]

In terms of banking methods, Warburg documented how bills of exchange that were accepted (guaranteed) by well-known joint-stock or merchant banks served as the basis of discount markets in Europe, but had only a small position in the American system, due to restrictive legislation and banking custom. The addition of the banker's endorsement turned commercial paper into bankers' acceptances, which dramatically improved their security, negotiability, and liquidity:

> Through the addition of the banker's signature the question of the maker's credit is eliminated and the note, instead of being a mere evidence of an advance, is transformed into a standard investment, the purchase and sale of which will be governed only by the question of interest. This investment commands the broadest possible market. . . . From being a scarcely salable promissory note, the ownership of which entails a more or less pronounced commercial risk, the paper has been transformed . . . into a standard investment, the equivalent of which in cash can be easily secured at any time.[25]

Warburg articulated how the low transaction costs associated with bankers' acceptances were particularly important in international exchange, by virtue of the difficulty in securing foreign credit information. For this reason, bankers' bills were chiefly employed as a basis for international short loans, as well as for holding foreign exchange reserves. Lawrence Jacobs of the National City Bank made the same point in regard to sterling acceptances: "Obviously the guaranty of a banker of high standing adds an important element of security to bills of exchange

---

[24] Paul M. Warburg, "The Discount System in Europe," [1910] in Warburg, *The Federal Reserve System*, 2: 186.
[25] Warburg, "The Discount System in Europe," p. 186.

as a basis for the lending or investment of bank funds. It is an additional assurance to the foreign exporter that he can discount his bills at a low rate so that he can afford to make a favorable price to the English buyer. It makes them all the more satisfactory investments for foreign banking institutions."[26]

The United States, by reason of the absence of such bills, was excluded from participating in financing international commerce. To Warburg, America's problem was not simply that national banks were forbidden from accepting bills of exchange arising out of foreign trade, thus guaranteeing their payment at maturity. As important was the fact that acceptances, supported by shipping and insurance documentation, were not used to any significant extent, even within the United States. Instead, borrowing at a bank was accomplished by the borrower giving the bank his promissory note for the term of the loan. Warburg claimed that promissory notes, lacking the endorsement of a reputable bank, could not feed an interbank discount market, as they held no uniformity as to quality and security. The quality of each note depended solely upon the credit of the maker, and since this information was necessarily limited to those who were well acquainted with the borrower, this paper did not circulate widely. For Warburg, this meant "that every dollar invested by a bank in American commercial paper, that is every dollar invested to satisfy the most legitimate requirements of business, leads, without fail, to a locking up of cash in unsalable assets."[27]

Although interbank rediscounting was rare in the United States, Warburg was exaggerating on this point. Commercial paper houses on the East coast had dealt in two- and three-name paper since as early as the 1840s, and, by 1913, these houses had branches or representatives in all the large cities of the United States which bought and sold commercial paper for banks (see the Introduction).[28] While promissory notes were bought, endorsed, and sold by bill brokers and commercial paper houses within the United States, Warburg was correct in arguing that this multiple-name paper did not serve as the basis of an *international* discount market, as it had no standing overseas. European bankers and central bankers rarely, if ever, invested in American commercial paper, because it was far more difficult for them to judge its quality and/or the reputa-

---

[26] Lawrence M. Jacobs, "Bank Acceptances," in National Monetary Commission, *Miscellaneous Articles* (Washington, D.C.: GPO, 1910), p. 38.

[27] Paul M. Warburg, "American and European Banking Methods and Bank Legislation Compared" [1908], in Warburg, *The Federal Reserve System*, 2: 43.

[28] I am indebted to Lance Davis for referring me to Albert Greef's *The Commercial Paper House in the United States* (Cambridge: Harvard University Press, 1938), for information on the operation of the American commercial paper market.

tions of the local commercial paper houses that gave it their seals of approval:

> New York is in a class by itself. Without bank-accepted bills it can have no discount market. Without a discount market, funds cannot move to it as they do between financial centers of Europe, because there are no bank-accepted bills in which foreign banks can invest. Our commercial paper is not suitable. Foreign banks will not purchase it because they are not acquainted with, or sure of the rating of, miscellaneous mercantile establishments, and because such paper could not be readily disposed of in case it became necessary or profitable to withdraw funds from New York for remittance elsewhere.[29]

The instrument of short-term international finance was the bankers' acceptance, which had not developed in the United States. The consequence was that the American commercial paper market was unusually isolated from the discount markets of Europe. Borrowing Warburg's metaphor of an acceptance-based discount market as a "reservoir of credit," the vice-president of New York's National Bank of Commerce wrote: "A broad discount market in this country would become the reservoir of credit with which similar reservoirs abroad would become connected. Without such a reservoir here we can have no really effective connection with the world's money market and would be subject to the erratic movements of interest and exchange rates which are always the feature of isolated markets."[30]

Warburg's central point was incontrovertible: The first need, prompted by international considerations, was to redirect the paper market toward liquid and highly marketable bankers' acceptances on the worldwide standard. That is, in order to integrate the domestic market with those across the Atlantic and to make dollar assets as attractive as sterling assets for all international purposes, the United States had to develop the kind of negotiable instrument that had long been the basis of short-term international exchange—the bankers' acceptance.[31]

For Warburg, the creation of American bankers' acceptances was a

[29] Jacobs, "Bank Acceptances," p. 9.

[30] John E. Rovensky, *The Acceptance as the Basis of the American Discount Market* (New York: National Bank of Commerce, 1919), p. 3.

[31] According to Eugene Agger, "One of the purposes of the Federal Reserve Act was to create an open discount market to which foreign as well as domestic bankers would be attracted. If, however, there be only or primarily single-name paper [promissory notes] available in the market, it is contended that the foreigner would not be persuaded to come into it on a scale sufficiently large to guarantee the fulfillment of its purpose." Eugene E. Agger, "The Commercial Paper Debate," *Journal of Political Economy* 22 (1914): 672.

prerequisite for establishing an international discount market in New York. A broad discount market, in turn, offered several benefits. Some of these advantages were of a private character, destined to benefit certain internationalists; yet, Warburg consistently couched the makeover in terms of the broad public interest—a claim that has merit due to the complementary nature of the reforms. Money-center bankers would clearly benefit, due to the enhanced demand for banking services in New York that would accompany the rise of the dollar as an invoicing and reserve currency. Warburg's many references to "foregone profits" and "tribute" paid to London resulting from the "dependence" on sterling acceptances, shows cognizance of the denomination rents associated with issuing an international money.[32] Casting the situation in terms of both rents and prestige, Warburg wrote: "It is impossible to estimate how large a sum America pays every year to Europe by way of commissions for accepting such documentary bills, and other bills with which we shall now deal, but the figure runs into the millions. The annual tribute to Europe resulting from our primitive financial system is not merely a waste of money, but reflects upon the dignity of a nation of the political and economic importance of the United States."[33] Although Warburg did not cite specific figures on the "annual tribute to Europe," National City Bank estimated that English bankers earned about $150 million per year in commissions by intermediating the American export trade alone before 1914.[34] Such figures do indeed suggest strong private motivations for bankers to absorb the costs of reform.

In addition to noting the gains to money-center bankers, Warburg very persuasively itemized the broad social welfare benefits attendant with the proposed changes. He frequently stressed how establishing a discount market in acceptances would allow New York's banks to discontinue the practice of investing the nation's reserves in stock exchange call loans, and would deflect a substantial portion of these funds into bills of exchange representing the foreign trade of the United States. A discount market allows banks to invest in the most liquid and safe form of paper and, in turn, to sell this, should it become necessary for them to increase their cash resources. But in the United States, where a functioning discount market did not exist prior to 1914, the call loan market was used for this purpose. Call loans were the only assets that offered a mod-

---

[32] See, for example, Warburg, "The Discount System in Europe," pp. 187–88; and Paul M. Warburg, "Circulating Credits and Bank Acceptances" [1911], in Warburg, *The Federal Reserve System*, 2: 227–28.

[33] Warburg, "The Discount System in Europe," pp. 187–88.

[34] National City Bank, *Foreign Exchange and International Banking*, National City Bank Education Series (New York: National City Bank, 1920), p. 5.

icum of liquidity—at least in normal times—to the New York banks that accumulated the bulk of the country surplus funds through the correspondent system. The consequence was that the money and capital markets became intertwined, causing a great deal of volatility in both:

> Every American bank, since it cannot count on reselling the notes which it buys, must necessarily limit the amount which it can properly invest in American paper, and as a consequence almost all the call money is invested in demand loans on the stock exchange. The result of this is that the overflow of money of the entire country, from the Atlantic to the Pacific, is thrown into the stock exchange, making stock-exchange money easy and stimulating speculation when trade is relaxing, while on the other hand, as soon as demand for money for commerce and industry increases, the funds to provide for the needs of the whole country are called from the stock exchange, causing a disturbance there. . . . The usual consequence is our annual money panic, and a resulting violent collapse of prices of securities. . . . Our much-maligned stock exchange is the scapegoat of the entire nation.[35]

If New York banks could safely invest in the bills of firms doing business in foreign countries—if they could buy acceptances drawn against foreign shipments—Warburg projected that the stock market would be divorced from the money market, and the violent fluctuations in the value of capital and in interest rates would be a thing of the past. That is, Warburg acknowledged that building the discount market involved *joint benefits*: "It would be a great national achievement in itself to bring about . . . the creation of an important worldwide discount market, which in turn would have, as a consequence, the turning into a broad bill market of the many millions that now flood and overflood Wall Street."[36] Elsewhere, Warburg emphasized the public benefit of increased banking stability as the most important gain:

> Bills will be drawn on American banks and bankers, instead of on London, Paris, or Berlin, and instead of being financed by others we may gradually become the "financiers" of others. Not only will this increase our trade, but most important of all, once we establish the modern banking bill in the United States, its use will grow and our own banks will reap

---

[35] Warburg, "The Defects and Needs of Our Banking System" [1907], in Warburg, *The Federal Reserve System,* 2: 13. See also Warburg, "American and European Banking Methods and Bank Legislation Compared," pp. 48–49.
[36] Paul M. Warburg, "Statement Before the Subcommittee of the Committee on Banking and Currency of the House of Representatives" [7 January 1913], in Warburg, *The Federal Reserve System,* 1: 559.

the tremendous advantage of being able to invest their deposit money in assets upon which they can realize at home and abroad. As the use of this modern paper increases, so will the financial safety of the banks and the business community.[37]

For Senator Nelson W. Aldrich of Rhode Island, who became the reformers' most ardent advocate in Congress, a dollar discount market in New York also recommended itself on both private and public grounds:

[New York bankers] probably were obliged to loan on call on stock-exchange collateral. There would be nothing else that they could do. . . . Banks do not dare now buy bills drawn against foreign shipments of the character which I have described, first because they have no knowledge of the responsibility of the parties making the drafts [as a result of the absence of acceptances], and second, because of the fear that at the time when they might need the money there would be no demand or market for paper of that class [as a result of the absence of a central bank]. To cure the banks of a bad habit we propose a plan by which instead of depositing their money at 2 percent in Wall Street to be used for speculative purposes they can safely invest it at, say, 3 to 4 percent in standard notes or bills of exchange representing the industries or the products of the United States. . . . There is not a particle of reason why prime sterling bills should forever remain the highest form of credit. . . . We ought to make a documentary bill drawn by a producer here . . . in the United States, drawn in dollars and cents, equal in currency and value to any drawn in pounds, shillings, and pence.[38]

Other diffuse society-wide benefits of constructing a modern discount market involved the equalization of interest rates between New York and Europe and greater economy in the use of gold to settle payments imbalances. All else equal, with a discount market in New York, overseas bankers and investors would be able to buy dollar drafts and remit funds to New York, should discount rates be higher there than in foreign markets, and this action would tend to bring interests rates internationally into equilibrium. As Warburg put it: "The discount system plays a most important role as an equalizer between nations. Money flows where it can earn the best return, provided it can be invested there with safety and with a confident expectation that the investment can easily be

[37] Paul M. Warburg, "A United Reserve Bank of the United States" [1910], in Warburg, *The Federal Reserve System*, 2: 132.
[38] Nelson W. Aldrich, "Address before the Annual Convention of the American Bankers Association" (New Orleans, 21 November 1911), Nelson W. Aldrich Papers, Manuscript Division, Library of Congress, reel no. 56, p. 1333.

resold and the proceeds of the sale easily collected."[39] But as things stood, the United States had no paper to offer which Europe could buy, leaving gold flows to settle payments imbalances:

> Between the indebtedness of one nation to another and the actual settlement in gold there lies as a buffer the borrowing power of the banking communities of the respective countries. Nations that are financially well-organized will find that for a moderate inducement money will flow to them freely for the purchase of securities, or for the purpose of short-time investment. This buffer is strong in England, as it is weak in the United States. We have no modern and readily salable paper which in critical times we can offer to foreign markets, and while the European banks work on fluctuations within fractions of 1 percent, our primitive methods often mean that before the tide can be turned we must suffer fluctuations of interest rates of 100 percent and a fall in the value of securities to bankruptcy prices.[40]

Albert Strauss, a partner in J. P. Morgan and Company, expressed it this way: "The bankers of European money centers are constantly scanning the possibilities of one another's markets. But they cannot operate directly in the New York market, because we have not created a commercial instrument responsive to their demand."[41] Hence, a public benefit of creating a discount market for dollar bills of exchange was that the United States would be able to access foreign financial markets without recourse to gold shipments induced by panic-level prices for securities, premia on gold, or short-term interest rates of 100 percent or more—all of which were distressing features of the 1907 crisis.[42] With a broad acceptance market giving dollar-denominated bills liquidity, European

[39] Warburg, "The Discount System in Europe," p. 197. Warburg skirts over the various levels of freedom with which gold could be exported from London, Berlin, and Paris, and the differences in the size of these discount markets—factors which help explain persistent differences in interest rates between these centers. Other New York bankers noted how these differences prevented an "exact equality" in interest rates among the financial centers. See, for example, Jacobs, "Bank Acceptances," p. 7–8; and Albert Strauss, "Gold Movements and the Foreign Exchanges," in *The Currency Problem and the Present Financial Situation*, ed. Edwin R. Seligman (New York: Columbia University Press, 1908), pp. 69–70.
[40] Paul M. Warburg, "A Central Bank System and the United States of America" [1908], in Warburg, *The Federal Reserve System*, 2: 98–99. See also Warburg, "The Discount System in Europe," pp. 197–98.
[41] Strauss, "Gold Movements and the Foreign Exchanges," p. 79.
[42] Ellis W. Tallman and Jon R. Moen, "Lessons from the Panic of 1907," *Federal Reserve Bank of Atlanta Economic Review* 75 (May/June 1990): 2–12; Oliver M. Sprague, "The American Crisis of 1907," *Economic Journal* (September 1908): 353–72; Charles A. E. Goodhart, *The New York Money Market and the Finance of Trade, 1900–1913* (Cambridge: Harvard University Press, 1969), pp. 107–21.

banks and central banks would invest in American bills as readily as they did in each other's short-term paper, should interest rates offer the proper incentives. Moderate fluctuations in interest rates would cause foreign investors to buy American paper in the same orderly fashion as they purchased acceptances in London or Berlin.

The development of the discount market was only part of the necessary reorganization, as Warburg was fully aware. Even though bills of exchange carrying the endorsement of reputable banking firms represented the most marketable form of short-term credit, there were still times at which even this paper could not be resold by banks. Depositors everywhere—but nowhere more frequently than in United States— showed a penchant for losing confidence in banks.[43] When a run on a single institution spreads for lack of stabilizing expectations throughout the banking system, accepted bills of exchange are no more liquid than any other asset. As Warburg recounted, the very existence of the discount markets of Europe rested upon the liquidity guarantee inspired by the central bank rediscount window. It was Warburg who most cogently expressed the close interrelationship between a discount market and a central bank. He argued that an international discount market could not develop in New York unless foreign and domestic purchasers of acceptances had sufficient confidence that they could liquidate these assets at any time and under any conditions. Warburg incessantly referred to the institution that provided this liquidity confidence in European systems— the central bank—and argued for the necessity of establishing one on American shores:

> In order to make our paper part and parcel of the means of the world's international exchange, it needs, however, as a preliminary condition, to become the foundation on which our own financial edifice is erected. It must always have a ready home market, where it can be rediscounted at any moment. This is insured in nearly every country of the world claiming a modern financial organization, by the existence of some kind of central bank, ready at all times to rediscount the legitimate paper of the general banks. Not only England, France and Germany have adopted such a system, but all the minor European states as well—and even reactionary Russia—have gradually accepted it.[44]

[43] Ellis W. Tallman, "Some Unanswered Questions about Bank Panics," *Federal Reserve Bank of Atlanta Economic Review* 73 (November/December 1988): 2–21.
[44] Warburg, "Defects and Needs of Our Banking System," pp. 12–13. See also Charles A. Conant, *The Development of Central Banks in Europe*, unpublished National Monetary Commission proof [1910], Nelson W. Aldrich Papers, Manuscript Division, Library of Congress, microfilm reel no. 56, pp. 487–612.

Warburg's reference to the "preliminary condition" for internationalizing the dollar reflects the dual and inseparable functions of the Federal Reserve Act: increasing the liquidity of the payments system through a system of rediscounting reserve banks was also necessary to make the dollar attractive as an international currency. The multiple products interpretation of American banking reform seems particularly clear in another passage from Warburg's writings:

> American commercial paper will not be considered a quick asset and will not take the place of the stock-exchange call loan unless the purchasers— both local and foreign—know that there will be a possibility of rediscounting a safe proportion of their holdings, if need be, with a central institution. While as a matter of fact the actual rediscounting by central institutions may be unimportant in normal times, the existence of such institutions creates the ultimate basis of confidence without which a discount market cannot be developed. No law can create a discount market without a central reserve; without the latter our paper would remain provincial and local and a "lock-up" as heretofore.[45]

With numerous examples drawn from European financial history, Warburg showed how central banks stood as the cornerstones of their respective discount markets, ready at all times to absorb the surplus stock of eligible acceptances in the market. "To insure the safety of such a discount system . . . to render it possible and effective, a central reservoir for all the cash of the nation is necessary." Vanderlip readily concurred:

> It is impossible to have such a discount market here without a central bank fully qualified to meet the responsibility that a central bank should bear; that is to say, in the last resort to rediscount commercial paper. We are willing to invest in commercial paper under that condition. If we know that when we need partially to liquidate our portfolio, and the market will not repurchase commercial paper, we can go to the central bank and have the paper rediscounted, we can then afford to buy it. It is the ability to go ultimately to the central bank for discounts that will create the discount market.[46]

Furthermore, central banking would also create in the United States the institutions of discretionary control, which allowed European mone-

---

[45] Warburg, *The Federal Reserve System*, 1: 560.
[46] Frank A. Vanderlip, "The Rediscount Functions of the Regional Banks," *Proceedings of the American Academy of Political Science* 4 (October 1913): 141.

tary authorities to insure gold convertibility in the face of temporary foreign drains. Warburg stressed the development of the two most successful European tactics: central bank discount policy, and the accumulation of foreign bills of exchange that could be liquidated abroad to draw gold or as a means of warding off destabilizing gold exports.[47] In the event of temporary worldwide pressures, the formation of an American central bank would, according to Warburg, also allow the United States to join the cooperative efforts of the leading European central banks in bringing order to the international system.[48] Indeed, one of the chief reasons for constructing a central banking system was that it would create "a central institution able to deal with other nations, in case exceptional measures become advisable, and with which other nations, even in times of the worst panic, can negotiate to furnish or obtain large loans of gold, as has frequently been the case between France and England."[49]

In summary, Warburg created for his peers in New York a comprehensive plan for banking reform steeped in the international opportunities that accompanied America's rapidly advancing international position. His main contribution was in seeing that the National Banking System was an inadequate foundation from which to base the country's future in international banking. Even if the Civil War laws were amended to allow large money-center banks to accept bills stemming from foreign trade and to set up foreign branches, the dollar could not develop as an international currency unless bankers' acceptances replaced call loans as the banks' primary asset, unless this paper had an extensive discount market at home, and unless a central bank was established to give both foreign and domestic purchasers sufficient confidence in the liquidity of dollar drafts. If these institutions were installed, the United States could attain "that place among nations which should be hers by destiny, and she will weather in safety and dignity the storms, from within and without, that may be in store for her. A modern financial system will enable banks fully and safely to finance the future growth of the country and,

---

[47] Warburg, "A Central Bank System and the United States of America," pp. 97–98; Warburg, "Circulating Credits and Bank Acceptances," p. 225; Paul M. Warburg, "A United Reserve Bank of the United States" [1910], in Warburg, *The Federal Reserve System*, 2: 133. See also Charles A. Conant, "A Central Bank of Issue," *Wall Street Journal* (27, 29 October; 2, 6 November 1909).

[48] J. Lawrence Broz, "The Domestic Politics of International Monetary Order: The Gold Standard," in *Contested Social Orders and International Politics,* ed. David Skidmore (Vanderbilt University Press, forthcoming); Eichengreen, *Golden Fetters*; Gallarotti, *The Anatomy of an International Monetary Regime.*

[49] Warburg, "A Central Bank System and the United States of America," p. 100.

vice versa, a healthy growth of the country is bound to bring prosperity to the banks."[50]

The Broader International Currency Coalition

While Warburg and other money-center bankers developed the specifics of financial reform, other members of the coalition came to see the advantages of invoicing trade in the home currency. The nation's commercial position was changing and the new trade conditions affected producers' institutional outlook. The National Banking System was established at a time when the country's foreign trade was small and, in the main, complementary with the trade of the major European countries. As primarily an agricultural nation, the United States did not compete with Europe for industrial markets, which made it perfectly acceptable to all parties to use British services in financing trade.[51] From the late-1870s, America's export business underwent both a major secular expansion, as well as a shift from an agricultural to a manufacturing basis. The growing volume of exports combined with the change in exports, from food and raw materials to manufactured products, to create complex and diverse problems for American exporters, which compelled them to demand improved foreign banking facilities from their local bankers. As the banks that served the large exporting corporations were primarily New York banks, it is not surprising that these firms played the leading role in designing the domestic banking reforms that would allow the development of dollar-based trade financing.

As American exporters began to compete directly with British and German industrial products in world markets, especially in the markets of Latin America and the Orient, the system of financing American trade through London banks was called into question. U.S. manufacturers felt that they were at a distinct disadvantage vis-à-vis their European competitors, as a result of the lack of dollar financing facilities and a network of American banks in overseas markets. As expected, exporters voiced two main complaints, reflecting the risks and costs of invoicing trade in sterling through British banks (see Chapter 2). On the one hand, in using sterling bills, American exporters assumed exchange risks, which disad-

[50] Warburg, "Circulating Credits and Bank Acceptances," p. 233.
[51] Phelps, *The Foreign Expansion of American Banks*, pp. 69–70, 86–91; Frank M. Tamagna and Parker B. Willis, "United States Banking Organization Abroad," *Federal Reserve Bulletin* 42 (December 1956): 1284–99; A. W. Lahee, *Our Competitors and Markets* (New York: Henry Holt, 1924).

vantaged them with respect to British exporters, who did not have to deal in foreign exchange. Although sterling fluctuated only within a narrow range (i.e., between the gold points), if "American exporters, in making out their prices in sterling, calculated at too low a rate for the future conversion of sterling into dollars, their prices would increase compared to British prices. If they did not calculate at a sufficiently low rate, they would get the business, but lose money on the transaction through a loss in exchange."[52] According to Jacobs:

> When we come to bill our goods in sterling, it is at once seen that our exporters are obliged to take a risk of exchange, which is a serious handicap when competing with British exporters. Our exporters who are to receive payment for their goods in sterling must previously decide on what rate of exchange will make the transaction profitable. If, in an effort to safeguard themselves against a loss of exchange, they calculate on too low a rate for the ultimate conversion of sterling into dollars, their prices become unfavorable compared to those made by British exporters and they lose the business. If they do not calculate on a sufficiently low rate they get the business but lose money on the transaction through a loss of exchange.[53]

In addition to the risks of exchange, American exporters were exposed to higher costs of trade finance. Because acceptances could not be drawn on American banks in dollars, traders had to pay double commissions in financing foreign shipments—one to the domestic bank that drew the bill and the other to a London bank that accepted it—while British traders paid only a single commission.[54] By eliminating the need for an English correspondent, American exporters expected to reduce the total cost of financing, thereby making their products more competitive: "In this way the American exporter can draw in dollars instead of in a foreign currency, a direct operation taking place instead of the triangular transaction necessitated when he draws in foreign money, with a consequent reduction in the expense of commissions . . . [he] can thus quote the lowest possible price to his foreign prospect."[55] New York bankers, in turn, hoped to capture the profits that previously had gone to English banks in financing American trade.

[52] Paul P. Abrahams, *The Foreign Expansion of American Finance and Its Relationship to the Foreign Economic Policies of the United States, 1907–1921* (New York: Arno Press, 1976), pp. 5–6.

[53] Jacobs, "Bank Acceptances," pp. 14–15.

[54] Phelps, *The Foreign Expansion of American Banks*, pp. 56–57. See also E. B. Filsinger, *Exporting to Latin America* (New York: D. Appleton, 1919), p. 218.

[55] Phelps, *The Foreign Expansion of American Banks*, p. 58.

These dual benefits were also understood by importers, who advocated developing the dollar as an international invoicing currency. For a merchant importing raw materials from Latin America, arranging a sterling acceptance imposed higher costs and greater exchange risk than conducting the same operation in dollar drafts: "It is expensive for the importer, for not only must he pay his bank a commission for arranging the credit, but there is included in this commission a charge made by the London bank for its acceptance. Further than that the importer must take a material risk of exchange. At the time a credit is opened the cost of remitting, say £10,000 to take up the bills in London, might be only $48,600, or at the rate of $4.86, whereas by the time the bills actually mature exchange may have risen and cost him $4.87, or $48,700."[56]

American exporters raised a series of other complaints about invoicing in foreign currencies. One common accusation was that British and German overseas banks were passing sensitive information (e.g., prices, client lists, etc.) about their operations to competing British and German firms, a problem that could be eliminated if American banks financed their trade. According to Edwin Kemmerer, "The fact that invoices, bills of lading and other documents passed through the hands of foreign banks and of South American or Oriental branches of foreign banks gave to our foreign competitors 'inside' information concerning our foreign business—information that was often used to their advantage in competition with our own citizens."[57] Another complaint was that European banks "tied" their commercial credits to the purchase of European goods, either formally or informally, to the disadvantage of American exporters.[58] U.S. manufacturers hoped that by developing dollar-based trade financing, they could overcome this disadvantage and secure more foreign business. American traders also sought the valuable information services British and German foreign branch banks provided for home-country exporters and pressured American banks to set up their own networks of foreign branches to level the playing field.[59] European manufacturers received "accurate and timely information upon economic and political conditions, upon the demand and supply of certain goods in the various foreign markets, and upon the credit standings of prospective clients" conveyed through the home offices of Europe's overseas

---

[56] Jacobs, "Bank Acceptances," p. 13.

[57] Cited in Phelps, *The Foreign Expansion of American Banks*, p. 48. See also Burton I. Kaufman, "The Organizational Dimension of United States Economic Foreign Policy, 1900–1920," *Business History Review 46* (Spring 1972).

[58] Phelps, *The Foreign Expansion of American Banks*, p. 70–77.

[59] Phelps, *The Foreign Expansion of American Banks*, pp. 50–56; Robert S. Mayer, *The Influence of Frank A. Vanderlip and the National City Bank on American Commerce and Foreign Policy, 1910–1920* (New York: Garland, 1987), chaps. 3–4.

banks.[60] American exporters believed that English banks did not supply these services as reliably, as accurately, or as immediately for their correspondents in the United States.

In short, as the export sector of the American economy reached an impressive scale and shifted from agricultural to manufactured products, using London bank acceptances to settle foreign accounts became increasingly costly. As a result, large corporate exporters and importers headquartered in New York turned to their local banks for the financial services needed in connection with foreign trade. The most pervasive request was for American banks to establish foreign branches in the countries where corporations had significant markets, and National City Bank, perhaps more than any other bank, received the bulk of this pressure.[61]

National City Bank was intimately connected with the leaders of American industry, especially businesses with foreign interests. Vanderlip sat on the boards of at least forty large exporting corporations and many corporate leaders were, in turn, directors of the National City Bank. William Rockefeller of Standard Oil, Cyrus H. McCormick, president of International Harvester, J. Ogdan Armour of Armour and Company, Joseph P. Grace of W. R. Grace and Company, and Henry R. Frick of the International Metal Corporation all held posts on the bank's board of directors.[62] As early as 1903, Vanderlip expressed eagerness to provide the bank's corporate customers with the foreign banking services they were seeking:

> Let us suppose that we have an organization of great financial strength, having in it the right elements of our own commercial and manufacturing life, and projected for the purpose of energetically and intelligently representing broadly our exporting interests in the world's markets. Suppose such an organization should establish exhibit rooms in various centers of trade throughout the world, having there expert salesmen and engineers equipped for the work of representing these products—men equipped with the technical training, with knowledge of the language, and with good understanding of both domestic and foreign conditions. Suppose

[60] Phelps, *The Foreign Expansion of American Banks*, p. 50.
[61] National City Bank received pressure to establish foreign branches from U.S. firms with foreign direct investments, especially in Latin America. These firms wanted the bank to provide the services that had previously been supplied by British banks—financing inventories, providing local credit, transferring money, and alerting the firms to profitable opportunities. Harold van B. Cleveland and Thomas F. Huertas, *Citibank, 1812–1970* (Cambridge: Harvard University Press, 1985), pp. 76–78.
[62] Mayer, *The Influence of Frank A. Vanderlip and the National City Bank on American Commerce and Foreign Policy*, p. 45.

such an organization should stand behind purchaser and producer, guaranteeing on the one hand the delivery of goods absolutely according to sample, on the other hand, guaranteeing the credit of the purchaser. If such an organization were equipped with men of trained intelligence, keen observers of commercial conditions, who would be quick to see an opportunity and devise methods of grasping it, and if that organization had behind it the cooperation of great manufacturing interests, I believe wonders could be accomplished.[63]

In terms of the bank's own interests, Vanderlip related the competitive advantages of following exporters overseas:

In casting about to see what directions we could offer special services to our commercial accounts, my mind has been particularly occupied with those accounts having to do with importing and exporting because it seemed to me that in that field there was room for special service that was not being performed. . . . The interest in the South American field is to me surprisingly general, and if I read the signs at all right, it indicates that we are facing a very large development in our South American trade relations. . . . [James A. Farrell, the president of U.S. Steel] says that if we will do that [establish branches in Sao Paulo and Rio de Janeiro] the steel company will cooperate in every way with us, will keep deposits with us, will give us access to all their credit files, and help us in every way that a cooperative spirit could indicate. . . . He said he felt sure that the International Harvester Company, Armour & Co., and Swift & Co. would at once furnish considerable business, and it is important to get these firms and others doing a large business tied up to us.[64]

As the growing importance of manufactured products in the country's foreign trade rendered traditional methods of financing in sterling bills problematic for American industrialists, traders pressured their New York bankers to establish better international banking facilities. The interests of New York banks and the interests of exporters thus moved in tandem with the relative economic advance of the United States, and a coalition formed among the major beneficiaries of international currency status. W. C. Moyer, the president of the Mechanics and Traders Bank of New York, described the mutually advantageous relationship in this way:

[63] Frank A. Vanderlip, *Business and Education* (New York: Duffield, 1909), pp. 292–93.
[64] Frank A. Vanderlip to James Stillman (5 June 1914), part B, series 1, box 5, Frank A. Vanderlip Papers, Rare Book and Manuscript Library, Columbia University.

No foreign bank can handle our foreign business satisfactorily in a distant land. Our banks, through foreign branches and agencies, must be able to follow trade through all its wanderings from factory to market. If a bank does less than this, it will satisfy neither its customers nor its stockholders. Hence, in order that the nation's commercial community and banking world may continue to reap the legitimate fruits of their growth, the banking system must be extended beyond the country's boundaries. . . . If the foreign commerce of the country be then encouraged . . . the nation's commercial elements will respond and with that response will come an increase in volume of the banks' transactions and corresponding profits. . . . In summing up you will agree with me that the development of our banks is intimately associated with the commercial future of the country and that with our rapidly growing wealth the best method of utilizing the country's surplus funds, so that they may serve as a valuable lever with which to move the world's commerce to and from our shores, is one of the most important economic questions of the day.[65]

While industrial exporters and importing merchants understood the narrow advantages of internationalizing the dollar, and pressed their resident banks to provide improved international financial services, bankers in the nation's central money market took the lead in articulating the content of banking reform in light of the changed international circumstances. Seeking to wrest from England and Germany a share of the rents that accrue to leading banks in nations whose currencies serve international functions, bankers defined a course of action that consistently attacked the narrow, thin, and illiquid nature of the American money market. Warburg in particular saw how the relative underdevelopment of the financial system kept the dollar from international usage, and so precluded New York banks from earning the rents associated with key currency status. He also understood that the very same structures contributed to payments system instability, the broader societal problem. Hence, Warburg proposed a set of fundamental changes that addressed both objectives simultaneously: First, create a new class of commercial paper—the ninety-day acceptance guaranteed like the European acceptance by a reputable bank—by legalizing accepting. Second, build an open discount market for American paper by shifting banks away from the practice of investing in call loans to purchasing acceptances for their secondary, or earning, reserves. Third, establish a central bank rediscount window to give domestic and foreign participants in the discount

[65] W. L. Moyer, "How Foreign Commerce Benefits the American Banker," in *Practical Problems in Banking and Currency*, ed. Walter H. Hull (New York: Macmillan, 1907), pp. 17–18, 22.

market confidence that dollar bills were as liquid as sterling bills, even in times of severe crisis. When combined with the country's commitment to gold and its free gold market—under which gold was permitted to enter and exit the country without interference—these institutions would allow the dollar, and New York City, to attain an international position commensurate with the nation's new standing in the global system. By widening, deepening, and adding resiliency to domestic financial markets, the program would also contribute to domestic financial stability.

Analytically, internationalizing the dollar and stabilizing the payments system were two sides to the same coin: inseparable and complementary outputs generating excludable private benefits, as well as nonexcludable social welfare gains. They were inseparable, because supplying the private output could not be divorced from the associated collective output: making the dollar fit for international functions meant "modernizing" the domestic financial system. They were complementary in consumption, because they enhanced one another's services: greater financial market liquidity would augment usage of the dollar internationally and enhance banking stability within the nation. The important point is that inseparability and complementarity are important in joint product situations, as they have a privatizing effect. Failure to contribute to the provision of the collective output also means that the private good is not then available.

Inseparability and complementarity lie behind the intellectual entrepreneurship of the New York bankers. As the share of private benefits increased with the advance of the United States in the world economy, collective action to update the domestic financial system became more likely. By the beginning of the century, international circumstances presaged an important global role for the dollar, and thereby provided the domestic beneficiaries with private incentives to install the necessary domestic prerequisites. As Warburg put it, "Our [New York bankers'] ambitions are great, and it hurts our pride that, while we have become powerful, and are leaders in many respects, we are an object of contempt and of ridicule when it comes to our monetary system. We cannot become a center of international finance on a par with European countries, unless we reorganize. If New York has to make some sacrifice in order to achieve this aim, she is willing to do her share, just as every part of the country will have to contribute."[66] Bringing the reforms to fruition, in other words, required majoritarian political consensus, and New York was willing to pay the lion's share of the costs to attain it.

[66] Warburg, "Circulating Credits and Bank Acceptances," pp. 32–33.

5 /

Collective Action for
Banking Reform

Bankers and other currency internationalists initially engaged the cause of payments system reform by developing a comprehensive institutional agenda that concurrently advanced the international role of the dollar and domestic financial stability. Yet much more collective political activity was needed to bring the proposed reforms to fruition. One obstacle involved incentives to free-ride *within* the coalition. Mancur Olson's familiar logic is that all political action is a public good, meaning that each individual member of the currency coalition had incentives to contribute less to the political effort than he would if only he were to benefit.[1] Another obstacle was existing political institutions, which defined the form and scope of collective action needed to make the program politically viable. In this chapter I examine the interaction of these constraints and their impact on the Federal Reserve legislation. A short analytical discussion introduces the topic. Subsequent sections track specific phases of the legislative process, beginning with agenda-setting and bill-formation in the specialized banking committees of Congress, and ending with the final vote on the floor of Congress. The argument is that lobbying strategy (collective action) is endogenous to the rules of a given political jurisdiction.

The international benefits of the reform measures proposed by New York bankers were concentrated and exclusive to members of the key currency coalition. Yet while the advantages of internationalizing the

---

[1] Mancur Olson, *The Logic of Collective Action* (Cambridge: Harvard University Press, 1965).

dollar would be consumed by these domestic actors and not others (i.e., they were private incentives from the viewpoint of society as a whole), individual agents within the coalition could benefit even if they were not among those who lobbied for the reforms. Hence, a second-order collective action problem arose. Segments of society may have had private motives to demand institutional change, but from the standpoint of intra-coalitional relations, the policy was a public good. With the exception of firm-specific subsidies, all policies generate nonexcludable goods, despite the fact that they have distributional consequences (that is, some actors cannot consume them). Hence, it was in the interest of each member to withhold resources from the reform effort, or to contribute less than he would if only he were to benefit.

In the case of the internationalizing coalition, the resolution of the intra-coalitional free-rider problem is partly explained by the logic of "privileged groups." A group or coalition is privileged when the per capita benefits going to one or several members are large enough to justify this subgroup providing the public good single-handedly, even if others free-ride. In this sense, the financial actors of New York privileged the overall coalition, because the benefits of maximizing future opportunities as an international financial center were sufficiently valued to outweigh the cost of lobbying for its creation. As argued in Chapter 2, money-center banks will have the strongest preference for internationalizing a currency. When the home currency serves as a vehicle currency, these banks capture international rents in the form of commissions, fees, and interest associated with financing world trade and payments. By the 1900s, Wall Street banks expected to earn in the vicinity of $150 million annually from invoicing U.S. exports in dollar-denominated acceptances. Moreover, as nonresident banks and central banks came to utilize dollar assets as a store of value (i.e., as a reserve currency), substantial inflows of short-term funds would enter the New York money market, further increasing the return to bankers. Overall, the expected increase in the demand for Wall Street's banking services that would derive from the international use of the dollar gave a small number of geographically concentrated banks large per-capita incentives to supply the coalitional public good of lobbying for banking reform.

This explanation is partial, since the costs of lobbying are intrinsically tied to the political institutions that maintain authoritative jurisdiction over policy.[2] Lobbying strategies are chosen in the context of given politi-

---

[2] For an introduction to the literature on political institutions and collective action, see Mathew D. McCubbins and Terry Sullivan, eds., *Congress: Structure and Policy* (Cambridge: Cambridge University Press, 1988); and Kenneth A. Shepsle and Barry R. Weingast, "Posi-

cal institutions. If the jurisdiction is relatively closed and nonmajoritarian, government policy typically reacts to small, well-organized lobbyists, and those interested in having their policies enacted need not organize a large mass movement. If the institution is open and majoritarian, aggregating the preferences of large numbers of people, groups wanting to have their interests represented must do so through large mass movements and mass organizations.[3] In short, institutions strongly influence patterns of collective political activity.

In the United States, lawmaking is an articulated and sequential process, involving several jurisdictions that vary according to the number of supporters needed to obtain allocative decisions. The overall Congress delegates responsibility for agenda-setting and bill-formation to specialized committees, which are relatively nonmajoritarian settings particularly responsive to small groups of lobbyists from the affected industries. From the committee level, lawmaking becomes ever more majoritarian as the policy moves toward the floor vote. At each successive stage, greater support must be culled from a more diverse set of sophisticated and unsophisticated actors (i.e., interested groups and voters). Since the costs of collective action are positively related to the size of a coalition, free-rider problems become more severe. As is commonplace in majoritarian settings, coalition building requires dispersing benefits more widely through compromise with other interests. As the size and diversity of the coalition expand, however, so do the costs of organizing, monitoring, and enforcing collective activity among the beneficiaries. These were the broad constraints facing proponents of payments system reform early in this century. How were they overcome?

In the abstract, several solutions are possible and can stand independently or work in conjunction with one another. First, if the coalition is privileged by the existence of a dominant actor(s) that sees sufficient value in the benefits of the policy, the rising costs can be internalized. Second, selective incentives might be employed to discriminate between contributors and noncontributors. Third, existing organizations established for other purposes might be converted to transform free-riders into "forced" riders.

In the following pages, I apply this simple logic about the relationship between political institutions and collective action strategies to the politics of American banking reform. As we shall see, the first legislative

---

tive Theories of Congressional Institutions," *Legislative Studies Quarterly* 19 (May 1994): 149–79.

[3] James E. Alt and Michael Gilligan, "The Political Economy of Trading States," *Journal of Political Philosophy* 2 (1994): 165–92.

sequence gave jurisdiction on payments reform measures to specialized congressional committees, and here we observe narrow pressure from bankers' lobbies. As the process moved through its majoritarian stages, however, the need to build massed-based support altered patterns of collective action. Attentive groups responded in ways that are largely consistent with the logic of the framework: Bankers compromised with organized rivals, which spread the benefits more widely, but raised the organizational and enforcement costs of collective action. To deal with these problems, existing organizations (i.e., the clearinghouse associations) were employed to coordinate the effort and enforce compliance among the wider set of beneficiaries. A mass organization was also founded (i.e., the National Citizens' League for the Promotion of Sound Banking) for the propose of mobilizing a very broad mass movement. Predictably, this organization was beset with free-rider problems, but New York bankers continued to absorb the lion's share of the lobbying costs: the expected benefits of payments reform were valued enough by bankers to outweigh the costs of maintaining even a very large coalition. Buttressing the privileged nature of the coalition was the fact that the legislation was modified so that only the nation's largest banks would benefit from its foreign banking provisions. These clauses ensured that a substantial share of the benefits remained excludable.

Congress, Committees, and Payments Reform

The most important existing political rule, as defined by nearly a century of judicial interpretations concerning the constitutional locus of banking and monetary authority, was that Congress was vested with the power to determine the organizational and regulatory aspects of the national payments system. While the Constitution gave Congress the express power only to "coin money" and "regulate the value thereof," a series of Supreme Court rulings in the nineteenth century supported Alexander Hamilton's application of the doctrine of implied powers, which enabled Congress to regulate national banking, to expedite the accomplishment of other enumerated powers.[4] This meant that the ultimate requisite for payments reform was that a majority of legislators coalesce around a reform plank that, at minimum, did not damage their electoral chances and, at maximum, strengthened their positions. Since constituencies vary

---

[4] Richard Sylla, "On the Constitutional and Legislative Position of Central Banks," mimeo. prepared for the Seventeenth SEANZA Central Banking Course (November 1988); James W. Hurst, *A Legal History of Money in the United States, 1774–1970* (Lincoln: University of Nebraska Press, 1973).

from one congressional district to another and legislators respond most readily to active constituencies within their districts, a broad, cross-sectoral coalition was a necessary precondition for positive congressional action on payments reform. Recognizing this in 1906, Frank Vanderlip wrote, "New York banks, of course, should be the leaders of such a movement, but it will be necessary to have the support of other sections of the country."[5]

Before the issue entered this stage of the congressional process, however, it encountered another set of political arrangements—the committee system—which affected political strategies in important ways. Even by this time, standing committees had begun to attain the kind of agenda-setting and bill-formation powers they are known for today.[6] Their jurisdictions were becoming fixed, and their work was increasingly technical and specialized—committees held special jurisdiction over particular areas.[7] The banking and currency committees of the House and Senate, for example, were repositories of policy expertise, incubators of policy, and gatekeepers of payments system policy for the overall legislature.[8]

For my purposes, the committee structure of Congress is relevant because it affected the political strategies of attentive social actors in discrete and observable ways. Recall the general point that political rules and norms determine the jurisdictions in which national policy is made, and that the requirements of these jurisdictions for taking decisive action determine the size and scope of successful political coalitions. The committee system places the power to define the content of a bill in the hands of a small group of congressmen, not the run of congressmen. Support from large segments of the population is therefore not necessary for committees to act. This encourages extensive political involvement by small groups of intent social actors.[9] Satisfying as many domestic actors as possible is less important to committees than satisfying powerful, organized, resource-rich interest groups.[10] Instead, the strength of groups will be the determining factor in committee outcomes. In committee, po-

[5] Frank A. Vanderlip to Charles A. Gaskell, 13 July 1906, part F, series 1, box 1, Frank A. Vanderlip Papers, Rare Book and Manuscript Library, Columbia University.
[6] Woodrow Wilson, *Congressional Government* [1884] (Baltimore: Johns Hopkins Press, 1981).
[7] Nelson W. Polsby, "The Institutionalization of the House of Representatives," *American Political Science Review* 62 (March 1968): 144–68.
[8] For a theory of the origins of committee power more generally, see Kenneth A. Shepsle, "The Institutional Foundations of Committee Power," *American Political Science Review* 81 (March 1987): 85–104.
[9] David R. Mayhew, *Congress: The Electoral Connection* (New Haven: Yale University Press 1974); John D. Huber, "Restrictive Legislative Procedures in France and the United States," *American Political Science Review* 86 (September 1992): 674–87.
[10] For a discussion in the context of trade policy, see Alt and Gilligan, "The Political Economy of Trading States," 165–92.

litical action involves resource-intensive lobbying and related direct per-
suasion of interest groups, and successful collective action does not
require bargaining away benefits to obtain mass support. Successful coalitions are typically small in size (involving relatively few individuals)
and scope (involving few economic sectors).

Consider the situation in late 1907, after the panic had struck. The
panic exhibited phenomena characteristic of a "public bad." Runs upon
banks and trust companies were followed by a general hoarding of
money, restriction of payments by banks nationwide, a premium on currency, credit contraction, unusually heavy bankruptcies, a spike in unemployment, and a sharp downturn in economic activity.[11] The fact that
the United States, with its vast gold reserves and modern industrial
economy, was the only major country to suffer such a complete breakdown of its credit system was also important, because society came to
see that a panic need not follow the end of a business cycle. That other
countries had gone through the worldwide crisis without panic proved
that financial stability was a function of the organization of the payments
system. In short, by causing generalized hardship, the panic focused attention on the payments system. As H. Parker Willis put it, "It is probably true that without the impetus furnished by the panic of 1907 it
would have been impossible to overcome the inertia in Congress."[12]

Bear in mind, however, that previous panics, such as the arguably
more severe panic of 1893 (see Table 5.1), had produced a similar window of opportunity; yet no major changes followed. Oliver Sprague recognized a pattern: while each major panic of the National Banking era
had heightened public awareness of the institutional problem, once the
financial system stabilized and the urgency of the crisis faded from
memory, attention turned to other matters (e.g., tariff reform) and banking reform was taken off the legislative agenda.[13] Thus, while the panic
had the effect that Peter Gourevitch attributes to economic crises more
generally—that of opening "the system of relationships, making politics
and policy more fluid"—it is not at all clear that major changes would
necessarily follow.[14] The opening could easily have been lost to public
apathy, unless some political entrepreneur(s) played a leadership role,

---

[11] For details on the panic's economic impact, see Milton Friedman and Anna J. Schwartz, *A Monetary History of the United States* (Princeton: Princeton University Press, 1963), pp. 156–58; and Wesley C. Mitchell, *Business Cycles* (Berkeley: University of California Press, 1911), pp. 512–30.
[12] H. Parker Willis, *The Federal Reserve System* (New York: Ronald Press, 1923), p. 43.
[13] O. M. W. Sprague, *History of Crises under the National Banking System* (Washington, D.C.: GPO, 1910).
[14] Peter Gourevitch, *Politics in Hard Times: Comparative Responses to International Economic Crises* (Ithaca: Cornell University Press, 1986), p. 22.

Table 5.1. Economic consequences of U.S. banking panics

	1873–74	1893–94	1907–08
Bank failures[a]	14	86	31
Capital of failed banks ($ millions)	4.07	13.7	7.3
Commercial failures	11,013	29,127	27,415
Liabilities of failed firms ($ millions)	383.7	519.7	419.7
Loan contraction[b] (percent)	—	6.5	3.1
Decline in bank clearings (percent)	—	15.9	8.8
Decline in per capita GNP (percent change in 1970 dollars)	—	10.2	10.7

Sources: A. Piatt Andrew, *Statistics for the United States, 1867–1909* (Washington, D.C.: Government Printing Office, 1910), tables 2, 12, 17; U.S. Comptroller of the Currency, *Annual Report* (Washington, D.C.: Government Printing Office, 1914), p. 542; U.S. Department of Commerce, *Historical Statistics of the United States, Colonial Times to 1970* (Washington, D.C.: Government Printing Office, 1975), series F 1–5, p. 224.
[a] National banks only. Excludes national banks that were returned to solvency within the period.
[b] Loans, discounts, and overdrafts of all banks (national, state, savings, private, and trust companies).

exerting constant pressure for change and building political support for a specific set of reforms.

Any number of public or private actors could have assumed the mantle of leadership, but the historical record is rich with evidence that only bankers mobilized on the issue, and then focused their efforts on the banking committees. As one participant expressed it, "bankers had directed the discussion, bankers had financed it, and bankers had kept it alive."[15] In contrast, neither presidents, nor cabinet officials, nor even party leaders were lifted out of lethargy by the panic. President Theodore Roosevelt had not acquired enough interest in the issue to study it intently, let alone to lead a resolution through domestic politics: "There is need of a change. Unfortunately, however, many of the proposed changes must be ruled from consideration because they are complicated, are not easy of comprehension, and tend to disturb existing rights and interests. . . . I do not press any especial plan."[16] Though he vaguely urged "better safeguards against commercial crises and financial panics" in the later years of his administration, Roosevelt did not lead when it came to reorganizing the payments system."[17]

[15] Willis, *The Federal Reserve System*, p. 33.
[16] James D. Richardson, *A Compilation of the Messages and Papers of Presidents*, vol. 10 (Washington, D.C.: National Bureau of Literature, 1911), p. 7461.
[17] Gabriel Kolko, *Triumph of Conservatism* (New York: Free Press, 1963), p. 151.

President Taft did hardly more. As his biographer notes, Taft's addresses and correspondence are "singularly bare of references to currency revision."[18] While Woodrow Wilson's contributions were more significant, his involvement came only after the basic agenda had been laid out, and after broad sections of societal support had been mobilized. Wilson's role was limited to resolving remaining points of conflict, the most important of which was the "control" issue—whether bankers or government appointees would staff and manage the new central banking system—and, in this way, facilitated the movement of the bill through Congress.[19] Yet there is little evidence that Wilson demonstrated much independent initiative. According to Arthur Link, the president was thoroughly reactive to political pressures: "Wilson was strangely surprised and of course profoundly disturbed by the dimensions of the [societal] struggle. . . . If he had any genuine convictions on the basic issues, we do not know them. Probably he was undecided, even unconcerned."[20]

Treasury officials, presumably better equipped than presidents to assess the financial situation, made only vague and fleeting suggestions for change, and did not use the department's resources to promote reform. Secretary Leslie Shaw presented a bare-bones plan in 1906, which centered on strengthening the treasury's ability to intervene in the national and international money markets in order to prevent panics, both at home and globally.[21] There is no evidence, however, that Shaw put the weight of his office behind the plan. Moreover, Shaw's successor, George Cortelyou, promptly dropped the idea of a treasury-based initiative and did not offer an alternative: "The present head of the department," he wrote humbly, "has not assumed the obligation [of managing financial markets] willingly and would be glad to be relieved of it at least in part by suitable legislation." But Cortelyou was even less concrete about institutional change. "A more desirable monetary framework," he wrote, would "adapt the movement of currency more nearly automatically to the requirements of business . . . and would greatly diminish the responsibility which must weigh heavily upon any occupant of [this] office. . . . What particular form this proposed legislation should take must be left

---

[18] Henry F. Pringle, *The Life and Times of William Howard Taft*, vol. 2 (New York: Farrar and Rinehart, 1939), p. 717.
[19] Ray S. Baker, *Woodrow Wilson: Life and Letters*, vol. 3 (New York: Scribner's Sons, 1931), pp. 131–98.
[20] Arthur S. Link, *Woodrow Wilson and the Progressive Era, 1910–1917* (New York: Harper and Row, 1954), pp. 47–48.
[21] U.S. Department of the Treasury, *Annual Report* (Washington, D.C.: GPO, 1906).

to the action of Congress. I have no pride of opinion as to the method, but I have the deepest concern that the result shall be adequately beneficial."[22]

In contrast to executive officials, bank lobbies were quick to seize the opening provided by the panic, and pressed their reform ideas upon congressional banking committees. The banking sector, however, was divided.[23] One lobby was composed of midwestern urban bankers, and its primary objective was to enhance the position of interior money centers such as Chicago and St. Louis vis-à-vis New York, by altering the rules governing the issuance of currency. The other was the New York-based coalition, whose more comprehensive internationalizing plan has already been described. For the midwestern city banks, the goal was to replace the National Banking System's government bond-secured note issue system with a currency issued against commercial bank assets ("asset currency" or "real bills"). This offered advantages, because the main business of interior city banks was to serve wholesalers and retailers engaged in the expanding volume of domestic commerce. According to the *Commercial and Financial Chronicle*, "The Chicago banking concerns . . . are banks in the truest and best sense of the word. It cannot be charged that their business is with Wall Street or with the stock market. They cater to the needs of the mercantile community and . . . their energies are devoted to satisfying the ever-expanding needs of the West."[24] Asset currency was appealing in this respect because of the unusually heavy demand for hand-to-hand currency in less modern agricultural regions, where the use of bank deposits and checks for transaction purposes was still very limited.[25] As their business consisted primarily of purchasing short-term paper arising out of current domestic transactions and providing the rural west with its currency needs, legalizing asset currency was seen as a way of promoting the special interests of the large interior city banks. As one midwestern city banker summed it up: "It is important for banks to have liberal note issue privileges, both be-

[22] Ibid.
[23] Robert H. Wiebe, *Businessmen and Reform: A Study of the Progressive Movement* (Cambridge: Harvard University Press, 1962); Robert H. Wiebe, "Business Disunity and the Progressive Movement, 1901–1914," *Mississippi Valley Historical Review* 44 (March 1958): 664–85; Richard T. McCulley, *The Origins of the Federal Reserve Act of 1913: Banks and Politics during the Progressive Era, 1897–1913* (Ph.D. dissertation, University of Texas at Austin, 1980); and F. Cyril James, *The Growth of Chicago Banks*, 2 vols. (New York: Harper and Brothers, 1938).
[24] Cited in James, *The Growth of Chicago Banks*, 2: 787–88. See also McCulley, *The Origins of the Federal Reserve Act*, pp. 152–56.
[25] Barry Eichengreen, "Currency and Credit in the Gilded Age," in *Technique, Spirit and Form in the Making of Modern Economies*, ed. Gary Saxonhouse and Gavin Wright (New York: JAI Press, 1984), pp. 87–89; McCulley, *The Origins of the Federal Reserve Act*, p. 112.

cause these banks need to use their credit in this way as a source of profit, and because their constituencies want just this kind of accommodation."[26]

Midwestern bankers generated at least twenty-two reform plans along these lines between 1880 and 1907.[27] The most important—the Baltimore Plan of 1894, the Indianapolis Plan of 1898, and the Fowler Plan of 1902—emanated from powerful Chicago bankers such as James B. Forgan, president of the First National Bank of Chicago; George Reynolds, president of the Continental Bank of Chicago; and James H. Eckels, president of the Commercial National Bank of Chicago.[28] The American Bankers Association (ABA) became the vehicle for the midwestern reform movement, as Chicago bankers dominated its executive positions.[29]

New York bankers were decidedly cold to asset currency. For one thing, New York banks were primarily banks of deposit, rather than note issue. Since the Civil War, note issuing by eastern city banks had declined steadily as the move to deposit banking progressed. In 1900, for example, the clearinghouse banks of New York City issued an average of only $24 million in national bank notes, but held net deposit liabilities of over $852 million; by 1909, the figures were $50.2 million in notes against $1,305 million in deposits.[30] The largest bank in the nation, National City Bank, was particularly averse to bank notes, issuing only $3.9 million, while holding over $252 million in deposits in the latter year.[31] Reforming the note issue mechanism along asset currency lines offered few advantages to big eastern banks.

Secondly, New York banks held large quantities of U.S. government bonds, not as backing for notes, but as direct investments or as security for government deposits. The value of these bonds would be adversely affected if the artificial market created by the National Banking System's bond-secured currency provisions were eliminated. In 1900, for example,

[26] *Bankers' Magazine* 58 (February 1899): 207.
[27] F. M. Taylor, "The Objects and Methods of Currency Reform in the United States," *Quarterly Journal of Economics* 12 (1898): 307–42. For a discussion, see Lawrence R. Stark, "Bankers and Reformers on the Eve of Progressivism: American Politics and Banking, 1880–1908" (Ph.D. dissertation, Washington State University, 1978).
[28] For representative statements of the Chicago bankers' reform demands, see James B. Forgan, "The Money Supply of the United States," in *Practical Problems in Banking and Currency*, ed. Walter H. Hull (New York: Macmillan, 1907), pp. 307–14; and James H. Eckels, "Reform of the Currency," *Practical Problems in Banking and Currency*, pp. 422–32.
[29] Wiebe, *Businessmen and Reform*, pp. 24–25; Fritz Redlich, *The Molding of American Banking*, vol. 2 (New York: Johnson Reprint Company, 1968), p. 211.
[30] A. Piatt Andrew, *Statistics for the United States, 1867–1909* (Washington, D.C.: GPO, 1910), pp. 108, 118.
[31] Harold van B. Cleveland and Thomas F. Huertas, *Citibank, 1812–1970* (Cambridge: Harvard University Press, 1985), pp. 319–23.

the ten largest New York banks held over $390 million in government bonds, or about 39 percent of the total national debt.[32] Shifting the backing for bank notes from U.S. bonds to commercial paper would undoubtedly reduce the demand for U.S. bonds, and so would work to reduce the value of this large component of the eastern banks' portfolios. The differences between New York and midwestern preferences dominated politics at the committee level. Sensing an opportunity amid the diffuse public clamor for legislative action, the two competing banking factions pressed the banking committees with renewed vigor. Midwestern interests were apparently in the stronger position. Since at least 1894, this faction had been well organized around the asset currency scheme and had obtained the support of Charles Fowler, chairman of the House Banking and Currency Committee.[33] New York bankers, however, launched the first legislative salvo. Sensing the political advantages of their midwestern competitors, Wall Street was determined at this point only to prevent the passage of any unfavorable Chicago-oriented legislation.[34] Their internationalizing campaign was temporarily put on the back burner. The immediate aim was to put forth a proposal that would meet the popular demand for anti-panic legislation without involving changes that would create long-term disadvantages with competing midwestern financial centers. After consulting with J. P. Morgan and other New York financiers, Nelson Aldrich, chairman of the Senate Banking Committee, introduced a bill in January 1908.[35]

Aldrich had close familial and financial ties to the New York banking community, which presumably explains his interest and preferences in banking matters.[36] According to Willis, Aldrich was "considered the mouthpiece of what was even then coming to be known as the 'Money Trust.'"[37] Vanderlip, for one, considered him "on the whole the best informed and most dominant man in Congress on financial measures."[38] Yet Aldrich's bill was not a thorough-going reform plan. It was a simple "emergency currency" bill that did not disturb the fundamental struc-

---

[32] McCulley, *The Origins of the Federal Reserve Act*, p. 113.

[33] James Livingston, *Origins of the Federal Reserve System: Money, Class, and Corporate Capitalism, 1890–1913* (Ithaca: Cornell University Press, 1986), pp. 150–51; James, *The Growth of Chicago Banks*, 2: 677.

[34] McCulley, *The Origins of the Federal Reserve Act*, p. 247.

[35] George E. Roberts to Frank A. Vanderlip, 21 December 1907, part A, series 1, Frank A. Vanderlip Papers, Rare Book and Manuscript Library, Columbia University. See also Eugene N. White, *The Regulation and Reform of the American Banking System, 1900–1929* (Princeton: Princeton University Press, 1983), pp. 88–89.

[36] Nathaniel W. Stephenson, *Nelson W. Aldrich: A Leader in American Politics* (New York: Scribner's Sons, 1930).

[37] Willis, *The Federal Reserve System*, p. 44.

[38] Frank A. Vanderlip, *From Farm Boy to Financier* (New York: D. Appleton, 1935), p. 210.

ture of the banking system. As Aldrich noted when his committee reported the bill, even though a small group of "thoughtful students" advocated "a central bank of issue . . . its adoption at this time, or in the near future, is out of the question." Moreover, his committee was "unanimous" in its opposition "to granting the sole power to issue notes" to the banks, as Chicago bankers contemplated. For a reform bill to stand any chance of political success, it had to be "some simple method of remedy and prevention that was merely an extension or supplement to the existing system and that could be provided through the use of existing machinery."[39] Aldrich astutely recognized that only incremental changes were possible in light of the impasse between the dominant organized banking factions.

Modeled along the lines of existing clearinghouse arrangements, the Aldrich bill proposed a system of currency associations organized by banks themselves on a voluntary basis. These associations were to issue emergency currency, backed by bonds deposited by the banks, to meet the demand for cash during a liquidity crisis. Its most controversial element was that bonds other than Federal obligations were to be eligible as security for the emergency currency—state and municipal bonds, as well as first mortgage railroad bonds, were to be acceptable as collateral.[40]

Much of this was familiar to the nation's bankers, as the clearinghouse associations had since 1857 issued emergency currency in a similar manner. As Charles Steele of J. P. Morgan and Company explained, "the intention of the framers of the Aldrich bill was to avoid another panic by practically legalizing clearinghouse certificates so as to give them currency all over the country."[41] But if the proponents of the Aldrich bill expected to unite interior bankers around such a modification of a well-known practice, they were sorely disappointed. It was not the idea of national currency associations or emergency currency that inflamed banker opposition in the midwest, but the type of bonds that would be eligible as security for the emergency currency. Western bankers complained that the big New York banks supported the plan because they held most of the railroad and local government bonds upon which the emergency currency would be based. Banks outside New York did not make a habit of extending loans on railroad or municipal securities, but rather held the bulk of their assets in short-term commercial paper. They were outraged at the bond feature of Aldrich's bill, for the reason that it excluded them from the benefits. Forgan sarcastically referred to the Al-

[39] U.S. Congress, Senate, *Congressional Record*, 60th Cong., 1st sess., 10 February 1908: 1756–57.

[40] J. Laurence Laughlin, *Banking Progress* (New York: Scribner's Sons, 1920), pp. 55–57.

[41] Livingston, *Origins of the Federal Reserve System*, p. 182.

drich bill as "an act to provide an artificial market for municipal and railroad bonds."[42] On the advice of George Perkins and J. P. Morgan, Aldrich removed railroad bonds as collateral, since this patently favored eastern banks.[43] With this concession, the bill passed the Senate and was referred in the House to the Committee on Banking and Currency on March 30, 1908.

The House committee, however, rejected even the watered-down Aldrich bill. A stronghold of the asset currency plan by virtue of Fowler's ties to such leading Chicago bankers as Forgan, Eckels, and Reynolds, the committee stood steadfast against any bond-secured currency measure.[44] The impasse was broken when Edward Vreeland, Republican congressman from upstate New York, brokered a compromise bill that went some distance toward midwestern demands. The Vreeland substitute accepted assets currency, but only as an emergency currency. That is, instead of government or railroad bonds, emergency currency was to be issued against short-term commercial paper.[45] In conference committee, the debate over the type of security eligible for the issuance of additional bank notes—negotiable securities of the Aldrich bill or short-term commercial paper of the Vreeland bill—was ultimately resolved by combining features of both bills. Commercial paper was eligible, but only under severe restrictions. As for long-term bonds, the conference bill not only stipulated Federal and municipal bonds, but also gave the currency associations the power to accept "as the basis for additional securities *any* securities" held by a national bank.[46] This compromise satisfied most Chicago and New York bankers, and the Aldrich-Vreeland bill passed both Houses in late May of 1908.

New York and Chicago bankers considered the emergency currency bill a stop-gap measure. Both groups remained committed to overhauling the banking system, but each had a contrasting vision of the necessary changes. Throughout the hearings, bankers expressed their long-term institutional objectives, with Chicago behind some version of assets currency and New York advocating a European discount market and

[42] U.S. Congress, House Committee on Banking and Currency, *Hearings and Arguments on Proposed Currency Legislation*, 60th Cong., 1st sess., 1908. See also Stanley Markowitz, "The Aldrich-Vreeland Bill: Its Significance in the Struggle for Currency Reform" (master's thesis, University of Maryland, 1965); James, *The Growth of Chicago Banks*, pp. 775–79; and Stephenson, *Nelson W. Aldrich*, pp. 324–31.

[43] Kolko, *The Triumph of Conservatism*, p. 157.

[44] James, *The Growth of Chicago Banks*, pp. 746–47, 775–79; McCulley, *The Origins of the Federal Reserve Act*, pp. 175–76, 249.

[45] U. S. Congress, House, *Congressional Record*, 60th Cong., 1st sess., 11 May 1908: 6109.

[46] U. S. Congress, Senate, *Conference Report on Amendment to H. 21871 to Amend National Banking Laws*, 60th Cong., 1st sess., 27 May 1908, S. Doc. 522: 2–3.

central banking system.[47] This pressure led the conference committee to include provisions in the Aldrich-Vreeland bill for the establishment of a bipartisan congressional commission "to inquire into and report to Congress, at the earliest possible date practicable, what changes are necessary or desirable in the monetary system . . . or in the laws relating to banking and currency."[48] The creation of this commission, known as the "National Monetary Commission," turned out to be more significant than the rather limited financial features of the 1908 law.[49]

The National Monetary Commission

By delegating bill formation responsibility to the National Monetary Commission, Congress circumvented the committee system deadlocked by the conflict between rival banking factions.[50] Roosevelt captured the significance of this event when he noted that the entire banking issue, on which "I am not sure of my ground, would now rest with the Commission."[51] The impact of the change of venue was that it created a closed, small group environment more conducive to collective action. It allowed contending New York and Chicago factions to hammer out their differences before engaging the congressional committees. In the past, bankers had focused on getting the committee in which they held special influence to produce a completely one-sided bill, which tended to polarize and stalemate reform. The epigram of a west coast observer summed up the situation: "[The] bankers are still divided, while the public and politicians look on, and smilingly say, 'Who shall decide when doctors disagree?'"[52] The commission, in contrast, offered a very closed setting within which compromise could be hashed out free from the glare of publicity. For Aldrich, who, in accordance with established procedure, was named chairman of the commission, "everything shall be done in the most quiet manner possible, and without much public announce-

---

[47] See the representative statements of Charles Conant and James Forgan, U.S. Congress, *Hearings and Arguments on Proposed Currency Legislation*.
[48] U.S. Congress, *Conference Report on Amendment to H. 21871*, p. 6.
[49] Emergency currency provided by the Aldrich-Vreeland Act was issued only once, at the beginning of World War I. Friedman and Schwartz, *A Monetary History of the United States*, p. 172; Alexander D. Noyes, *The War Period of American Finance* (New York: G. P. Putnam's Sons, 1926), pp. 77–82.
[50] Markowitz, "The Aldrich-Vreeland Bill," p. 117; Noyes, *The War Period of American Finance*, p. 35.
[51] Kolko, *Triumph of Conservatism*, p. 158.
[52] Wiebe, "Business Disunity and the Progressive Movement," p. 667.

ment."[53] The commission, in effect, functioned to remove the issue from public discourse and, by so doing, made it possible for the most interested actors to coalesce around a unifying institutional program. If organized lobbies could develop a compromise reform package, the committees and the overall Congress would be faced with a unity among major bankers which had been entirely lacking. A united front would mean that legislators would no longer have to make the unpleasant choice of antagonizing one active and powerful banking constituency for the benefit of another, a situation that promised few electoral benefits and potentially large costs. With the most interested actors in consensus, the banking committees could take the commission's plan as a baseline, hammer out remaining points of conflict, and bring forth a bill that was acceptable to the most active constituencies.

As an investigative body with the express mandate to study both domestic and foreign financial structures, the commission was highly dependent on banking experts for information, analysis, and recommendations. Since none of the eighteen politicians on the commission had practical banking experience or formal financial training, and only a few had legislative experience in such matters, private actors were relied upon to organize the investigations and to recommend institutional changes.[54] Indeed, two prominent bankers, representing the east-west banker schism, were given *ex officio* positions with the commission. Upon J. P. Morgan's recommendation, Aldrich appointed Henry Davison (former president of the First National Bank of New York, Morgan partner, and founder of the Bankers' Trust Company) to serve as New York's spokesman.[55] To represent the midwest, Aldrich recruited George Reynolds, president of Chicago's First National Bank and head of the American Bankers Association. Lastly, Harvard economist A. Piatt Andrew—a known advocate of central banking—was hired as the commission's special assistant, thus giving academia a place in the discussions. The small-group aspect of the commission is noted by Aldrich's biographer: "these three and Aldrich were at the heart of the matter."[56]

Over the course of its four years in existence, the commission relied most heavily upon New York bankers for policy advice. This derived

---

[53] Nelson W. Aldrich to Theodore Burton, 12 June 1908, Nelson W. Aldrich Papers, Manuscript Division, Library of Congress.

[54] N. A. Weston, "The Studies of the National Monetary Commission," *Annals of the American Academy of Political and Social Science* 99 (January 1922): 18.

[55] Stephenson, *Nelson W. Aldrich*, pp. 334–35; Thomas W. Lamont, *Henry P. Davison* (New York: 1933), pp. 88–115.

[56] Stephenson, *Nelson W. Aldrich*, p. 335.

primarily from two factors. First, the important comparative element of the commission's research agenda gave pride of place to individuals with backgrounds in, and well-established connections to, foreign banking systems. New Yorkers bankers, along with a handful of economists, held a virtual monopoly on information concerning the organizational features of foreign financial systems. Morgan and Schiff, in fact, organized the commission's 1908 European tour, arranging interviews with prominent foreign bankers and central bankers.[57] More broadly, the very mandate to conduct foreign investigations, as stipulated in section 18 of the Aldrich-Vreeland Act, worked to the advantage of the advocates of discount markets and central banking, since these were the core structural differences between the United States and Europe.[58] Second, Aldrich's association with Wall Street bankers predisposed him to lean toward these actors for technical analysis and advice. Indeed, by March 1909, Aldrich had enlarged the inner circle of banking experts to include Paul Warburg, Frank Vanderlip, and Benjamin Strong.[59]

The foreign orientation and the preponderance of New York bankers among its formal and informal staff led Aldrich to a complete *volte-face*. On the eve of the commission's European trip, Aldrich believed that all that was necessary in the way of banking legislation was to improve and perfect the Aldrich-Vreeland mechanism.[60] Interviews with Bank of England officials and pressure from New York bankers led Aldrich to undergo a change of heart. The arguments that were most effective in converting Aldrich to the bankers' reform plan involved international factors.[61] The global advance of New York's commercial and financial position had already induced Aldrich to expand his traditional role as defender of domestic business by developing a greater interest in international trade and finance. In England, Aldrich learned the important role that banking structures play in supporting international trading and financial relationships. Under the further guidance of Warburg, Vanderlip, and Strong, Aldrich became an ardent supporter of central banking and associated internationalist structures. In a speech to New England bankers and businessmen in 1910, Aldrich proclaimed:

[57] Vincent P. Carosso, *The Morgans: Private International Bankers, 1854–1913* (Cambridge: Harvard University Press, 1987), p. 548.
[58] A. Piatt Andrew, "The Problem before the National Monetary Commission," *Annals of the American Academy of Political and Social Science* 36 (November 1910); Weston, "The Studies of the National Monetary Commission," p. 21.
[59] Vanderlip, *From Farm Boy to Financier*, pp. 213–16; Livingston, *Origins of the Federal Reserve System*, p. 189.
[60] *New York Times*, 1 August 1908, p. 7.
[61] Stephenson, *Nelson W. Aldrich*, pp. 337–38.

From Mexico to Cape Horn there are great nations that ought to be aligned with us. You cannot imagine the possibilities of trade in the Orient and in reawakened China. But we cannot trade successfully with them until the United States by virtue of its great resources becomes the financial center of the world. . . . It is a disgrace to this country, with its vast resources, that we are obliged to pay our bills in sterling drafts or in drafts drawn payable in marks or francs in London or Berlin or Paris. The time will come—and it ought to come soon, gentlemen—when the United States will take the place to which she is entitled as the leading financial power in the world. (Great applause.) It will come soon if you will assist the Monetary Commission in the adoption of right and wise legislation.[62]

In the course of its work, the commission published twenty-three volumes, with the preponderance of attention given to foreign financial systems.[63] This work stands as one of the best statistical guides to pre-World War I monetary and banking structures. In addition to its academic value, the monographs also served a political purpose. The goal was to develop for sophisticated groups a consistent logic for central banking and associated institutions that had been proven by European experience. As Andrew remarked, the commission's publications furnished "an unparalleled opportunity for those who are interested in American financial problems to make a comparative study of conditions and experiences here and abroad. The public and Congress are equipped today as they never have been before in the case of any other great problem, with the expert knowledge which the whole world has to offer."[64] With scarcely a negative word to be found on central banking and discount markets, it would have been difficult for anyone, who made the effort to plow through the 15,000 pages of material, to conclude anything other than that the United States needed to move in the same direction.[65]

With the commission's publications serving as the preliminary propaganda, Aldrich and the inner circle of banking experts assembled at J. P. Morgan's duck hunting club in Georgia in November 1910 to prepare a bill.[66] Extraordinary measures were taken to ensure the conference re-

---

[62] *New York Times*, 5 March 1910, p. 1.
[63] Of the more than 15,000 pages, over 9,000 dealt with banking and monetary institutions in foreign countries. For a complete listing of the commission's publications and conferences, see J. Laurence Laughlin, *The Federal Reserve Act: Its Origins and Problems* (New York: Macmillan, 1933), pp. 279–88.
[64] Andrew, "The Problem before the National Monetary Commission," p. 5.
[65] Weston, "The Studies of the National Monetary Commission," p. 21.
[66] Stephenson, *Nelson W. Aldrich*, pp. 373–79; Vanderlip, *From Farm Boy to Financier*, pp. 210–19; Lamont, *Henry P. Davison*, pp. 96–102; McCulley, *The Origins of the Federal Reserve Act*, pp. 365–405.

mained secret because, as Vanderlip put it, "if it were to be exposed publicly that our particular group had gotten together and written a banking bill, that bill would have no chance whatever of passage by Congress."[67] Public perceptions of Wall Street were increasingly hostile, and the group—which in addition to Vanderlip, included Warburg, Davison, Charles D. Norton (president of Morgan's First National Bank of New York), Andrew, and Aldrich—was well aware of the political liability that it operated under. The conspiratorial aspects of the "Jekyl Island Conclave," however, should not be pressed too far. Although the group had as its objective to prepare a bill that was consistent with the increasingly international needs of the nation's largest money-center banks and their exporting and importing clientele, it was nonetheless fully conscious of the need to win the approval of other bankers, especially Chicago bankers, as well as to gain at least the passive acquiescence of less interested societal elements. The bill, which Aldrich and the inner circle of bankers produced, was thus carefully tailored to satisfy the interests of other active banking constituencies and to overcome latent popular prejudices against radical change. Even though the commission's proposal—the "Aldrich Plan"—was formulated in isolation by a small cadre of metropolitan bankers, the voice of other groups was at all times present. The majoritarian constraint imposed by the structure of political institutions thus modified the content of the measure bankers had developed.

Recognizing that the support of politically active Chicago bankers was crucial, Aldrich and his entourage of bankers included a modified form of assets currency in what was primarily a central banking bill. Instead of granting individual banks the unrestrained authority to issue currency directly on the basis of their commercial assets, the plan called for a central banking institution with branches, which bankers would own and operate, and which would regulate the issuance of asset currency. The rediscount function was to be handled by the branches. Acceptances, notes, and bills of exchange that were endorsed by a member bank were eligible for rediscount if they represented agricultural, industrial, or commercial transactions, but not if they were drawn on stocks, bonds, or other investment securities.[68] Indeed, even before the conference at Jekyl Island began, Aldrich had made overtures along these lines to Reynolds, Forgan, and other midwestern city bankers on the Currency Committee of the ABA. Aldrich let it be known that the bill would in-

---

[67] Vanderlip, *From Farm Boy to Financier*, p. 214.
[68] For details, see Robert C. West, *Banking Reform and the Federal Reserve, 1863–1923* (Ithaca: Cornell University Press, 1974), chap. 4.

clude asset currency, as well as a central bank, in recognition of the strong commercial aspect of midwestern urban banking.[69] This formed an alliance which Reynolds made public in his 1909 ABA presidential address, when he announced that an "ideal" reform package would include a note-issuing central bank that would accept commercial paper as collateral.[70]

To the thousands of small country bankers, the central bank's structure of policy control was far more important than whether it would issue bond- or asset-based currency. Their core concern was that a central bank would come under the influence of Wall Street, which would mean being oriented toward internationalist's concerns (external balance and exchange rate stability) over domestic macroeconomic goals. This was made clear in a survey conducted by Warburg through the *Banking Law Journal* in late 1909.[71] The poll, which produced over 5,000 responses from state and national banks throughout the country, asked the slanted question: "Do you favor a central bank, if not controlled by Wall Street or any Monopolistic element?" About 60 percent of the respondents were in the affirmative, 33 percent in the negative and 7 percent undecided.[72] Written responses from those who opposed a central bank (about 200 such responses were published in the *Journal*) revealed that small bank opposition was based upon the conviction that a central bank could not be designed in such a way as to prevent the domination of the New York "money trust." This information actually buoyed Warburg, because he felt it would not be difficult to prove that it was possible to create a central bank free from Wall Street control.[73]

At Jekyl Island, the reformers attempted to design a central banking system with a governance structure that would assuage the fears of small bankers and others with few international business interests. The Aldrich Plan, which became the model for the Federal Reserve Act, proposed a central institution called the National Reserve Association (NRA), with a capital stock of $300 million which would be subscribed and owned by national banks. The head office was to be in Washington, D.C., and this office would oversee fifteen branches operating in the fifteen districts into which the country was to be divided. Each of the fif-

[69] White, *The Regulation and Reform of the American Banking System*, p. 91.

[70] Wiebe, *Businessmen and Reform*, pp. 75–76. For Forgan's retreat from unrestricted assets currency and the political importance of his conversion to the Aldrich compromise, see James, *The Growth of Chicago Banks*, pp. 794, 799.

[71] "The Central Bank Question," *Banking Law Journal* 20 (October 1909): 941–79.

[72] For discussion and analysis of these data, see White, *The Regulation and Reform of the American Banking System*, pp. 91–94.

[73] Paul M. Warburg to Nelson W. Aldrich, 24 December 1909, Nelson W. Aldrich Papers.

teen districts was further divided into local associations of at least ten banks. The branches were to have the authority to rediscount notes and bills of exchange endorsed by member banks on agricultural, industrial, or commercial transactions of not more than twenty-eight days' maturity, thus giving local banking interests a say in policy. To sever the relationship between banking and the stock market, bills drawn to carry stocks, bonds, or other investment securities were ineligible for discount, except under certain restrictive conditions.[74]

As for its international functions and purposes, the Aldrich Plan clearly reflected the demands of internationalists. To allow leading American banks to engage in the business of financing international trade, the plan authorized national banks to accept bills having not more than ninety days to run, the traditional duration of foreign trade bills. To facilitate the expansion of a discount market for bankers' acceptances, the association was empowered to purchase acceptances "of banks and houses of unquestioned financial responsibility," thereby ensuring the liquidity of the paper. While the initiative for rediscounting resided at the district level, the governing board in Washington would set the discount rate for all fifteen branches. This was meant to ensure that the association would stand on equal footing with European central banks, for whom the ability to set the discount rate was the most important tool for influencing gold and capital flows. To further the prospects of international monetary coordination, the association was also empowered to deal at home and abroad in gold coin and bullion, and to make loans and borrow gold upon acceptable security. In addition, it was to have the authority to open and maintain banking accounts in foreign countries, and to establish agencies in foreign countries for the purpose of purchasing, selling, and collecting foreign bills of exchange. Finally, national banks were authorized to establish foreign branches, so as to conduct business in foreign countries on equal terms with English banks. In endorsing the plan, New York banker Isidor Straus summed up its international benefits:

> From the moment this plan goes into operation, the United States will loom up as the world's chief trade center. Heretofore, the foreign banker has held—and rightly, too—that a time bill on the United States or on New York locked up his money until maturity; whereas a time bill on London was practically cash. From the moment this plan is adopted that condition is eliminated. New York can never be an exchange center until

---

[74] U.S. Congress, Senate, *Suggested Plan for Monetary Legislation Submitted to the National Monetary Commission by Hon. Nelson W. Aldrich*, 61st Cong., 3d sess., 1911, S. Doc. 784.

we have facilities such as [this] plan provides. Thereafter, New York will not only equal but supplant London as the exchange center of the world.[75]

With the main elements of the proposal in place, Aldrich and his advisors focused on devising an organizational structure for the system that would convince rural bankers and other nationalists that the Reserve Association would not fall under the domination of Wall Street. One rather transparent tactic was to deny that the proposal was for the creation of a central bank at all, and to insist, instead, that it represented a modification of existing practices. Aldrich, for example, frequently stated that the "organization proposed is not a central bank, but a *cooperative union* of all banks of the country for definite purposes and with very limited and clearly defined functions. It is, in effect, and extension, an *evolution of the clearinghouse plan modified* to meet the needs and requirements of an entire people."[76] Reformers hoped that the opponents would find the plan more palatable if it were couched in familiar terms: "By giving it the name of 'Reserve Association of America,' [the originators of the Aldrich Plan] tried to avoid the idea of a central bank. This was a method of organization worked out largely by Senator Aldrich himself. It was intended to meet the idea then quite common that the control of the institution might be held by a small group of men in Wall Street."[77] However, the contention that the NRA was anything other than a central bank did not go unchallenged. Representative Richard Hobson of Alabama, for example, in citing a report from a small banker in his district, found no difference between the NRA and European central banks, adding that "there is no reasonable excuse for not terming it a central bank."[78] Nevertheless, the obfuscation was pursued throughout the debates leading up to the Federal Reserve legislation.

In addition to deceptive language, the Jekyl Island conferees offered several substantive safeguards to assuage the fear that the association would fall under the control of an "individual or combination of individuals in Wall Street or elsewhere, for selfish or sinister purposes."[79] First, an election procedure was devised to limit the influence of larger banks at all levels of the organization. In selecting directors of the local associa-

---

[75] *New York Times*, 18 October 1911, p. 14.

[76] Nelson W. Aldrich before the Annual Convention of the American Bankers' Association, New Orleans (21 November 1911), in Paul M. Warburg, *The Federal Reserve System*, vol. 1 (New York: Macmillan, 1930), p. 573 (emphasis in original).

[77] Laughlin, *The Federal Reserve Act*, p. 32.

[78] Richard H. Timberlake, Jr., *The Origins of Central Banking in the United States* (Cambridge: Harvard University Press, 1978), p. 190.

[79] Nelson W. Aldrich before the Annual Convention of the American Bankers' Association, New Orleans (21 November 1911), in Warburg, *The Federal Reserve System*, 1: 574.

tions, small bankers were to be in the majority, since three-fifths of the directors were to be chosen according to a one-bank, one-vote electoral rule. To insure that large banks did not defeat the purpose of this restriction by organizing a number of small banks, whose votes would allow it to control the local association, the plan stipulated that, when any person, partnership or corporation owned 40 percent or more of the stock in each of two or more banks, that owner as a unit was to have only one vote. Only in the selection of the other two-fifths of the directors would large banks have the advantage, since the voting rule here stipulated that each bank was to have a number of votes proportionate with its holdings of the association's stock.

The election of directors of the district branches was also weighted toward small banks, but to a somewhat lesser degree. Here, each local association was required to elect a voting representative, all of whom together would elect half of the branch directors on the basis of one vote per representative. In the election of one-third more, each representative was to cast votes in proportion to the shares held by all banks belonging to that local association. The directors elected in this manner would then choose the remaining one-sixth of the directorate, but these directors could not be bankers. As a sop to nonfinancial interests, these directors had to fairly represent the agricultural, commercial, industrial, and other interests of the district. Nevertheless, as with the local associations, the unit system of voting, and the comparatively small number of directors chosen on a voting basis proportioned to stock ownership, gave preponderance to banks.

The selection of the board of directors of the central association in Washington was calculated to make it impossible for any combination of interests to gain control and to secure a fair representation of nonbanking interests. The board of the central bank would consist of forty-five directors of four different classes. One class of fifteen would be representatives of the branches, each branch electing one director. Another class of fifteen would be representatives of agricultural, trade, and other commercial interests, with the boards of each branch choosing one such member. A third class of nine directors was to be selected by the branches, but here voting was weighted to reflect the financial size of each district: each branch would cast a number of votes equal to the number of shares in the National Reserve Association held by all member banks. However, to ease the fear that New York would dominate this class, it was determined that no more than one director could come from any one district. For a similar purpose, the plan also required every director of all three classes to reside in the district from which he was elected. A fourth class of six directors provided the executive branch of the federal government with representation on the board. The secretary of the treasury, the secretary of commerce and labor, and the comptroller of the currency would fill three slots.[80] In addition, a governor and two deputy governors would be selected by the president of the United States, but only from a list submitted by the other directors. The president, however, had the authority to remove the governor for cause.

By including a small element of governmental influence in the system—cabinet officials and presidential appointees had but six of forty-five votes in the directorate—the planners hoped to diffuse the charge that large urban banks would monopolize the system to the detriment of small banks, their farmer/small business clientele, and nationally bound economic interests more generally. Since the institution would have powers of redistribution by way of its power to (1) fix discount rates, (2) manage exchange rates and gold shipments, (3) discriminate in rediscounts and direct loans, and (4) act as fiscal agent for the Federal government, it was only fitting to give the government some say in its administration.[81] As Aldrich put it, "I believe that the participation of these officials in the management of the institution to the limited extent prescribed is necessary to secure proper recognition of the vital interest which the public has in the management of the Association."[82] The fact that the reformers did not give the government real control reflected their concern that policy would be influenced by partisan or electoral cycle considerations. The planners feared that greater government influence would mean that "every election would be a referendum on the value of the dollar."[83] Moreover, since only member banks, rather than the government or the general public, would contribute to the capital and hold the stock of the reserve association, planners saw it fitting to vest bankers with policymaking authority. Indeed, Aldrich was bluntly candid in arguing that the shareholders who were to own the new bank should control it.[84] For these reasons, the Jekyl Island group placed authority over the administration of the NRA almost exclusively in the hands of bankers. The modest level of government oversight, however, became the Aldrich plan's most controversial element.

In addition to its administrative features and electoral rules, the Aldrich Plan contained two other provisions meant to convince opponents

---

[80] To further appease farmer and agricultural bank interests, the secretary of agriculture was added in the revised plan that was introduced to Congress on 8 January 1912.

[81] Edwin W. Kemmerer, "Some Public Aspects of the Aldrich Plan," *Journal of Political Economy* (December 1911): 819–30.

[82] Nelson W. Aldrich before the Annual Convention of the American Bankers' Association, New Orleans (21 November 1911), in Warburg, *The Federal Reserve System*, 1: 574.

[83] McCulley, *The Origins of the Federal Reserve Act*, p. 377.

[84] Stephenson, *Nelson W. Aldrich*, p. 394.

that a central bank would not operate solely to Wall Street's benefit. First, profits from stock ownership were limited to a 5 percent dividend, with any remaining capital gains divided equally between the association's surplus fund and the U.S. Treasury. Warburg and Aldrich believed that this provision removed any incentive for large banks to convert the central bank into a money-making vehicle. Aldrich repeatedly claimed that the intention was to "place beyond dispute" the question of Wall Street domination of the system.[85] Secondly, Aldrich insisted that the association maintain a uniform rate of discount throughout the United States, because this "was the only way to anticipate and refute the charge that great financial centers would, without this provision, inevitably influence the new bank so as to establish rates in different regions favorable to their operations, unfavorable in some cases to the locality."[86]

In short, the Aldrich Plan was designed to both overcome discord within the national banking community and to win over other, as yet latent, constituencies. To New York internationalists, the plan offered the institutions necessary for the country to attain a position in global banking affairs: a discount market for acceptances, foreign branching, and a central rediscounting agency of last resort legally empowered to coordinate policy with other central banks. To large midwestern city banks, the plan offered a step in the direction of assets currency, but within a central banking framework. To rural banks, elaborate checks on big-bank influence offered a system that would add stability to domestic finance and prevent policymakers from discriminating against banks, regardless of their size, location, and type of business. To nonfinancial groups, the plan offered managerial positions at both the branch and the national levels of the association, although the power to choose these directors rested with bankers. In addition, governmental representation offered a balance to banker control. Executive influence, however, was token rather than real, due to the planners' belief that elected officials would inevitably be forced, by constituent and electoral cycle pressures, to sacrifice sound money on the altar of full employment and steady domestic economic growth.

Soon after the plan was made public in January 1911, it became clear that further revisions were needed to gain the acquiescence of the overall banking community. In the modified bill that the commission finally submitted to Congress, state banks and trust companies, which previously had been excluded from joining the system, were allowed to subscribe to

---

[85] U.S. Congress, *Suggested Plan for Monetary Legislation Submitted to the National Monetary Commission*, 12–13
[86] Stephenson, *Nelson W. Aldrich*, p. 379.

the capital stock of the NRA and enjoy the advantages of membership.[87] This concession brought the allegiance of state-chartered national banks and thus "measurably advanced the prospect of reform."[88] In addition, to win the endorsement of the Currency Committee of the ABA, which Forgan ran as the mouthpiece for Chicago bankers, Aldrich had to further restrict the power of governmental actors on the association's board of directors.[89] To Forgan, the inclusion of even a modicum of government involvement was objectionable, primarily because previous government (treasury) attempts to manage the money market had benefited Wall Street.[90] The revised bill thus stipulated that the president select only the governor, rather than the governor and the two deputy governors, and that the power to remove the officers rest with the board of directors, rather than the president. Although this concession brought the full support of midwestern city bankers, it further weakened the plan's chances in Congress (as Aldrich, Vanderlip, Warburg, and Andrew suspected it might) by exposing it to the attack that without effective governmental supervision to counterbalance banker influence, Wall Street would dominate the councils of the central bank.

By late 1911, a fragile consensus among all classes of bankers had been created in support of the Aldrich Plan, without sacrificing any of its international features. Aldrich himself was instrumental in drumming up banker support, touring the country, and advocating the benefits of the plan before representative groups of local bankers and their customers. For example, on 25–26 October 1911, Aldrich spoke in Indianapolis before the Indiana Bankers' Association; on 11 November in Chicago before the Western Economic Association; on 14 November, in Kansas City before the Trans-Mississippi Commercial Congress; and on 21 November, in New Orleans before the American Bankers' Association.[91] His success can be judged by the endorsements the plan received from organized banking groups: all but one participant at the 1911 ABA annual convention in New Orleans approved the revised version of the plan, and twenty-nine of forty-six state banking associations also formally voiced their approval.[92] In a letter to Aldrich, the president of the ABA noted that bankers were practically united in acceptance of the National Reserve Association plan, and that such differences that remained were

---

[87] McCulley, *The Origins of the Federal Reserve Act*, pp. 394–96.
[88] *Commercial and Financial Chronicle*, 13 May 1911, p. 1297.
[89] Stephenson, *Nelson W. Aldrich*, pp. 390–92.
[90] McCulley, *The Origins of the Federal Reserve Act*, chap. 4.
[91] *New York Times*, 20 October 1911, p. 6.
[92] American Bankers' Association, *Proceedings of the Annual Convention* (1911), pp. 385–86; Wiebe, *Businessmen and Reform*, p.77.

over the details, not the principles.[93] With more consensus among bankers than had been attained in regard to any previous plan, reformers were poised to enter the next phase of the political campaign: exciting mass support for the measure.

The National Citizens' League

By the time the Monetary Commission formalized a plan, the general public was becoming apathetic to the issue. In late 1911, this indifference seemed the most important obstacle to reform, as Congress would not attempt such revolutionary changes unless public sentiment was crystallized so emphatically that delay would be costly to legislators. As Warburg remembered the situation, "it was certain beyond doubt, that unless public opinion could be educated and mobilized, any sound banking reform plan was doomed to fail."[94] By now, however, the bank coalition built through compromise had become very large and diverse, extending far beyond the confines of New York City. The organizational and financial costs of cultivating wider support were significant, and the coalition needed to ensure that individual members would contribute to the effort. I argue that most of these collective action costs were absorbed by New York bankers, who were to capture the bulk of the reform's international benefits. However, bankers also made use of an existing organization—the clearinghouse—to control free-riding within the coalition.

With the banking community largely behind the Aldrich Plan, the lobby turned its attentions to generating wider societal support. Warburg personally took charge of organizing business support for the Aldrich Plan. He felt that if all the commercial organizations of the country could be persuaded to commit to a central bank plan, it would greatly facilitate the final work of the Monetary Commission.[95] In this regard, he utilized his connections with three important commercial organizations—the New York Produce Exchange, the New York Merchants Association, and the New York Chamber of Commerce—to secure timely endorsements of the Aldrich Plan.[96] In addition, Warburg arranged for the three organizations to submit joint resolutions at the annual convention of the National Board of Trade, a gathering of commercial interests from all over the country. On 18 January 1911, just one day after the Aldrich

[93] F. O. Watts to Nelson W. Aldrich, 2 October 1911, Nelson W. Aldrich Papers.
[94] Warburg, *The Federal Reserve System*, 1: 68.
[95] Paul M. Warburg to A. Piatt Andrew, 3 January 1910, Nelson W. Aldrich Papers.
[96] McCulley, *The Origins of the Federal Reserve Act*, p. 391.

Plan was unveiled, the National Board of Trade passed a resolution (drafted by Warburg) in support of a "central banking organization" following the principles of the Aldrich Plan.[97] Another resolution, also inspired by Warburg, proposed the establishment of a national organization of businessmen to "carry on an active campaign of education and propaganda for monetary reform, on the principles . . . outlined in Senator Aldrich's plan."[98] The result was the formation of the National Citizens' League for the Promotion of Sound Banking on 17 April 1911, an organization that became the locus of the New York-led effort to generate popular support for the Aldrich Plan.

Although the National Citizens' League appeared to spring spontaneously from the business interests of the country, it was from the outset "practically a bankers' affair."[99] With Warburg at the helm, New York bankers established the league, formed its primary base of financial support, and designed its political strategy.[100] As with the Jekyl Island conclave, great pains were taken to keep New York's role in the league quiet. Warburg recognized that "it would have been fatal to launch such an enterprise from New York; in order for it to succeed it would have to originate in the West" and be nominally directed by men other than bankers.[101] To avoid the stigma of Wall Street domination, Warburg arranged for the league's national headquarters to be in Chicago, and selected leading midwestern businessmen and economists to its staff and to the league's forty-five state branches. John V. Farwell of Chicago was selected as president and J. Laurence Laughlin was recruited to be the active head of the league's propaganda efforts. New York bankers, such as Warburg, Vanderlip, and Davison were not formally associated with the league. To the average citizen and voter, the National Citizens' League must have appeared to be exactly what its name implied: "An organized phalanx of public opinion which was impartially interested in the development of legislation that would provide the United States with a sound financial system."[102]

The league's political strategy was designed by George F. Parker, a New York corporate lawyer and public relations expert. In a confidential memorandum prepared for Aldrich on the basis of discussions with

[97] The report and resolutions of the National Board of Trade are reprinted in Warburg, *The Federal Reserve System*, 1: 567–71. See also pp. 61–66.
[98] Warburg, *The Federal Reserve System*, 1: p. 569.
[99] *New York Times*, 6 July 1911, p. 4.
[100] Laughlin, *The Federal Reserve Act*, pp. 59–61.
[101] Warburg, *The Federal Reserve System*, 1: 68.
[102] James, *The Growth of Chicago Banks*, p. 802.

Warburg and Davison, Parker specified the target audience and outlined the basics of the publicity campaign.

The most difficult task, Parker noted, was to reach the average voter, who did not have sufficient knowledge or interest upon which to found a definite opinion on the issue—depositors of all classes, farmers, the mass of business and professional people. To reach many of these actors, Parker recommended addresses, pamphlets, official documents, and neighborly, personal appeals; a newspaper blitz would reach nearly everyone else.[103] The first order of business, however, was to publish a Currency Primer, which would set forth, simply and in brief scope, existing conditions and the changes proposed. Next in importance was the preparation of a textbook for speakers and writers, untechnical in character, and avoiding, as far as possible, economic terminology.

In other words, while the final object of the campaign was the vote of members of Congress, the strategy was to "educate the constituency, especially those most intelligent and influential, so that they will urge directly their opinions on their Representatives and Senators."[104] The majority rule constraint in Congress clearly influenced political strategy, as Parker's grass roots strategy was followed almost to the letter. The majority rule constraint in Congress clearly influenced political strategy.

The cultivation of a grass-roots movement in support of the Aldrich Plan was destined to be a costly affair, and the problem was how to get coalition members to bear their share of the expenses. In a letter to James Stillman, Vanderlip wrote: "The education of the United States is a large job—larger than can be undertaken by any half-dozen men, even though the popular imagination endows these half-dozen men with controlling the railroads and a great part of the industrial life of the nation. You and I know that they do not actually exert such a control and *they cannot distribute in any equitable way the expenses of such a campaign.*"[105] A clearer statement of the free-rider problem is hard to find. The actual solution was equally consistent with the logic of collective action: coalition members utilized preexisting organizations to coordinate, monitor, and enforce the joint effort.

Most banks were members of clearinghouse associations, because of the important services the organizations offered in settling payments be-

---

[103] George F. Parker to Nelson W. Aldrich, 25 November 1911, Nelson W. Aldrich Papers. See also George F. Parker to Nelson W. Aldrich, 10 November 1911, Nelson W. Aldrich Papers.
[104] Laughlin, *The Federal Reserve Act*, p. 70.
[105] Frank A. Vanderlip to James Stillman, 28 July 1911, part B, series 1, Frank A. Vanderlip Papers (emphasis added).

tween banks. For our purposes, the important point is that these banker organizations were already well established, which lowered the start-up costs of collective action (i.e., the costs of coordinating the fundraising drive among bankers). James Cannon described this additional role of the clearinghouses: "A Clearinghouse, therefore, may be defined as a device to simplify and facilitate the daily exchanges of items and settlements of balances among the [member] banks and *a medium for united action upon all questions affecting their mutual welfare.*"[106] Existing scholarship details how clearinghouses facilitated collective action in containing banking panics—holding reserves, examining member banks, and issuing emergency currency.[107] Little attention, however, has been given to the role of clearinghouses in facilitating joint political action. As the clearing and collection services were highly valued by clearinghouse members, the threat of withholding these services was a potent enforcement mechanism—a negative selective incentive.[108] That is, the clearinghouse could be employed to monitor and police individual contributions to the political lobbying effort, imposing sanctions on members in the event of nonpayment (free-riding). Thus, the existence of clearinghouses lowered the organizational costs of collective action in the political domain and provided mechanisms necessary to ensure that members did not free-ride on the efforts of others.

In the league's estimation, $500,000 would be needed to carry out the program of public education. A quota of $300,000 was assigned to the New York clearinghouse, $100,000 to the Chicago clearinghouse, and the balance apportioned among other major clearinghouses. These amounts presumably approximated the share of benefits which banks in each region hoped to receive. In a process emulated by other clearinghouses, A. Barton Hepburn, president of the New York clearinghouse, formed a special committee to look after the banks' contributions. This committee based each bank's cash contribution on its size, measured by capital and surplus. The specific formula was 32 cents per $1000 of capital and surplus.[109] Although clearinghouse officials asserted publicly that "no assessment has been levied upon the banks, and no pressure has been used to make any of them contribute," the possibility of being discriminated against in terms of access to clearinghouse services acted as a

[106] James G. Cannon, *Clearinghouses* (Washington, D.C.: GPO, 1910), p. 10 (emphasis added).
[107] Gary Gorton and Donald J. Mullineaux, "The Joint Production of Confidence: Endogenous Regulation and Nineteenth-Century Commercial Bank Clearinghouses," *Journal of Money, Credit, and Banking* 19 (November 1987): 457–68.
[108] Olson, *The Logic of Collective Action.*
[109] *New York Times,* 7 December 1911, p. 7.

strong inducement for banks to meet their allotments.[110] The daily settlement of accounts between banks was a necessary part of every bank's business, and the privilege was granted only to those banks that followed clearinghouse rules and directives. Indeed, despite some early resistance, there was little free-riding. The league's archives show only one instance of nonpayment: "In Cincinnati, there is one small bank that has refused to contribute its share of the ten thousand dollars approved by the clearinghouse, which delays action there somewhat, although there is no doubt of the ultimate payment of money."[111]

With the funds in hand, the league published and distributed 15,000 copies of its "currency primer," *Banking Reform*, written by Laughlin and his former student, H. Parker Willis.[112] It established a fortnightly journal, also named *Banking Reform*, with a circulation of 25,000 which, in the main, went to newspaper editors. It published about 950,000 free pamphlets of pro-Aldrich Plan statements and speeches, and provided newspapers all over the country with "literally millions of columns" of copy.[113] In many cases newspapers, even entire newspaper chains, published the league's prewritten galleys with no editing whatsoever.[114] The league also supplied speakers for gatherings of various interest-group organizations nationwide and sponsored mass letter-writing campaigns to Congress. In all its efforts, the league stressed the widespread public benefits of stabilizing the banking system, while giving special attention to the NRA's supposed freedom from Wall Street domination. The groups most concerned with this issue (e.g., small bankers, agrarians, and small businesses dealing in nontradable goods) received sustained and careful attention.[115]

In the final analysis, the league probably accomplished its task of creating popular acceptance of the need for banking reform along the lines of the Aldrich Plan. According to Warburg, "Through its efforts, supporting those of Senator Aldrich, the majority of the business and banking communities, as well as a large portion of the press of the country, were converted to the thought that the principles of the Aldrich Plan

---

[110] *New York Times*, 30 November 1911, p. 1.

[111] National Citizens' League, Organizational Report, 15 June 1912, James Laurence Laughlin Papers, Manuscript Division, Library of Congress.

[112] J. Laurence Laughlin, *Banking Reform* (Chicago: National Citizens' League, 1912).

[113] A. D. Welton, "The Educational Campaign for Banking Reform," *Annals of the American Academy of Political and Social Science* 99 (January 1922): 36.

[114] For examples of the league's newspaper copy and its correspondence with editors, see the National Citizens' League Files, James Laurence Laughlin Papers.

[115] For examples of the delicate handling accorded these interests, see the chapters in Laughlin, *Banking Reform*, entitled "The Farmer and the Bank," "Small Banks and the National Reserve Association," and "The Small Merchant."

should be embodied in legislation."[116] The Aldrich Plan, however, never made progress in Congress, as the bill died in committee shortly after it was introduced in January 1912. Its crippling political defect was that it placed policy control too much in the hands of bankers, which became *the* national issue with the onset of the "Money Trust" investigations. In addition, when the Democrats won the presidency and the Senate in the election of 1912, a reform measure, that bore the name of the politician most closely associated with Wall Street, had little chance in Congress. Nevertheless, the bill that was finally passed as the Federal Reserve Act in December 1913, while bearing the imprimatur of the Democrats in terms of the policy control issue, very closely followed the Aldrich Plan blueprint for payments system reform. This undoubtedly reflected the league's work in building wide nonpartisan and cross-sectoral support for a banking system modeled upon European practices. In speaking of the Federal Reserve bill, which he cosponsored, Carter Glass stated tersely: "No League, no bill."[117]

Demise of the Aldrich Plan

Even before the National Monetary Commission reported the Aldrich Plan to Congress, the unmaking of popular support was underway. A critical event was Vanderlip's formation of the National City Company in July 1911, a banking holding company with controlling interests in banks and trust companies throughout the country.[118] National City Bank was already the largest bank in the country and, by forming the National City Company, it established the largest bank-holding affiliate. The size and scope of the firm drew the attention of the anti-monopoly forces and aroused immediate suspicions that the "National City Bank interest would in some way dominate the directorate of the National Reserve Association."[119]

Anxiety over the National City Company was strong in banking and business circles throughout the west, but centered "specifically in Chicago."[120] The incident threatened to divide the fragile coalition of New York and Chicago banks, and thereby to undermine the National Citizens' League. The league's national president informed Warburg of Chicago bankers' concern with National City Bank's strategy, which was

---

[116] Warburg, *The Federal Reserve System*, 1: 76.
[117] Welton, "The Educational Campaign for Banking Reform," p. 36.
  McCulley, *The Origins of the Federal Reserve Act*, pp. 400–403. For a list of the company's holdings, see Cleveland and Huertas, *Citibank*, p. 64.
[119] *New York Times*, 25 August 1911.
[120] *Wall Street Journal*, 18 August 1911.

interpreted as a program to own stocks in many national banks, and in that way control the National Reserve Association.[121] To Laughlin, the action "could not have come out at a more unfortunate time, for my success" in organizing western support for the Aldrich measure. "These things are very difficult to handle, and little appreciated at their value in New York."[122] Warburg gave assurances that control of the National Reserve Association was as remote to the managers of National City Bank as the Northpole, but the fear of Wall Street control continued to escalate in the west.[123] But others saw it as a "waste of breath to urge upon the people of the country the acceptance of the Aldrich Plan of Currency Reform so long as one national bank, through a holding company, may control twenty, fifty, or a hundred of the national banks."[124]

Inflamed by the National City Company imbroglio, Congressmen Charles A. Lindbergh, Sr., of Minnesota introduced a resolution calling for a congressional investigation of the "Money Trust." In doing so, Lindbergh voiced the sentiment of populists and small country bankers: "Wall Street brought on the 1907 panic, got people to demand currency reform, brought the Aldrich-Vreeland currency bill forward and, if it dares, will produce another panic to pass the Aldrich central bank plan. We need reform, but not at the hands of Wall Street."[125] The Aldrich Plan was no more than a "wonderfully clever" scheme that invited "capture by Wall Street as soon as it should get into operation." Moreover, if Congress approved the plan, "the country banks would all be compelled to come under the control of Wall Street."[126]

On 25 April 1912, after rejecting the Aldrich Bill, the House Committee on Banking and Currency set up a special subcommittee "to investigate the concentration of money and credit." The subcommittee was headed by Arsene Pujo of Louisiana, but the actual investigations were conducted by Samuel Untermyer, a lawyer with known, and apparently personal, antipathies toward New York bankers.[127] Untermyer's highly publicized findings, drawn from over eight months of hearings, confirmed populists' worst suspicions: New York banks, through ties and interrela-

---

[121] John V. Farwell to Paul M. Warburg, 20 July 1911, National Citizens' League Files, James Laurence Laughlin Papers.

[122] McCulley, *The Origins of the Federal Reserve Act*, p. 400.

[123] Paul M. Warburg to John V. Farwell, 24 July 1911, National Citizens' League Files, James Laurence Laughlin Papers.

[124] *New York Times*, 4 November 1911.

[125] Charles A. Lindbergh, *Banking and Currency and the Money Trust* (Washington, D.C.: National Capital Press, 1913), p. 94. See also Bruce L. Larson, *Lindbergh of Minnesota: A Political Biography* (New York: Harcourt Brace Jovanovich, 1971), pp. 107–29.

[126] Quoted in McCulley, *The Origins of the Federal Reserve Act*, p. 414.

[127] Carosso, *The Morgans*, p. 626.

tionships that were far more extensive than previously known, "were the most active agents in forwarding and bringing about the concentration and control of money and credit in the United States."[128]

The "Money Trust" hearings had two important effects on banking reform. First, they eroded the delicate consensus among bankers by driving a wedge between New York and Chicago bankers. By July 1912, this division threatened to bring the reform drive to a "complete standstill."[129] By September, small bankers were in open revolt. At the annual convention of the ABA in 1912, in marked contrast to the unity of the delegation one year earlier, interior bankers expressed strong reservations about the Aldrich Plan. As a result, the ABA Currency Commission would not formally endorse the Aldrich measure, but merely resolved to "cooperate with any and all people in devising a sound financial system for this country."[130] The National Citizens' League, itself a tenuous coalition of east and west, also began to distance itself from the Aldrich Plan.[131]

In addition, the hearings further mobilized farmer and small business sentiment against the policy control features of the Aldrich Plan. By this time, it was no secret that the agents behind the plan were the same as those being discredited in the hearings and daily press. As the hearings continued to expose financial concentration in Wall Street, the Aldrich Plan became the subject of "a slow, creeping, deadly hostility. Neither party would have anything of it, nor does any politician seeking votes dare to speak a good word for it."[132] President Taft, a previous backer of the Aldrich plan, had his treasury secretary announce that reporters had "misquoted" his earlier statements of support.[133] Republicans, in their platform of 1912, omitted any reference to the Aldrich plan and declared only that "our banking arrangements today need further revision to meet the requirements of current conditions."[134] When Roosevelt bolted the party to form the Progressive party, he took with him many western Republicans who were the plan's most severe critics. In their platform, Progressives declared: "The issue of currency is fundamentally a Gov-

[128] U.S. Congress, House, Subcommittee of the Committee on Banking and Currency, *Report of the Committee Appointed . . . to Investigate the Concentration and Control of Money and Credit,* 62d Cong., 3d sess., 1913, 131.

[129] *Journal of Commerce,* 16 July 1912.

[130] McCulley, *The Origins of the Federal Reserve Act,* p. 424.

[131] Warburg, *The Federal Reserve System,* 1: 76–77.

[132] James, *The Growth of Chicago Banks,* p. 805.

[133] Taft endorsed the Aldrich plan before the New York State Bankers' Association. *New York Times,* 23 June 1911. For Taft's recant, see Laurence Laughlin to Paul Warburg, 28 October 1911, box 4, James Laurence Laughlin Papers.

[134] Kirk H. Porter and Donald B. Johnson, *National Party Platforms, 1840–1964* (Urbana: University of Illinois Press, 1966), p. 185.

ernment function. . . . The control should be lodged with the Government and should be protected from domination or manipulation by Wall Street or any special interest."[135] The plank of the victorious Democratic party was even more strongly worded: "We oppose the so-called Aldrich bill or the establishment of a central bank; and we believe the people of the country will be largely freed from panic and subsequent unemployment and business depression by such a systematic revision of our banking laws as will render temporary relief in localities where such revision is needed with protection from control or domination by what is known as the Money Trust."[136] In broader terms, the reaction reflected populist distrust of concentrating monetary power in the hands of groups most inclined to favor hard money over competing macroeconomic objectives. The subsequent debate was over who could be trusted to exercise money creating powers, which reflected the diverse inflation preferences of the public and the understanding that the new central bank's internal decision-making structures would have redistributive consequences.[137]

The Federal Reserve Act

Although the Aldrich plan did not receive the favorable attention of Congress, the campaigns waged by the National Monetary Commission and the National Citizens' League prepared the ground so thoroughly that, when the Democrats gained control of both houses of Congress and the presidency in 1912, reform along similar lines, but sponsored by Democrats, was almost assured. Congress might have delayed action further, had only bankers favored the program, but the support of powerful business organizations and the league's popular constituencies created broad, cross-sectoral pressure that reelection-minded politicians of either party could not ignore. Yet the Federal Reserve Act was not all the initial proponents of the Aldrich Plan had hoped for. Its essential difference was that it established not a central bank with branches controlled at every level by bankers, but a designated number of separate and semi-autonomous regional central banks operated by private bankers, and supervised and controlled by a central board in Washington, composed of government officers and appointees. The Wilson administration brokered this compromise.

Despite the change in the partisan landscape and the failure of the

[135] Ibid., p. 179.
[136] Ibid.
[137] Jon Faust, "Whom Can We Trust to Run the Fed? Theoretical Support for the Founders' Views," *Journal of Monetary Economics* 37, 2 (July 1996): 267–84.

Aldrich bill, the movement for banking reform did not lose much of its earlier momentum. This was due largely to the continuing efforts of the National Citizens' League, which, in recognition of the Aldrich Plan's political liabilities, began to focus exclusively on promoting "general principles," rather than on any tangible plan.[138] To ensure that Democrats would not let the matter slide, the league coordinated a mass letter-writing campaign to Congressman Carter Glass of Virginia, the new Democratic chairman of the House Banking and Currency Committee, and the head of a special subcommittee charged with reporting a banking reform measure. From November 1912 to February 1913, thousands of letters from individual businessmen, manufacturers, merchants and bankers, and hundreds of resolutions passed by commercial organizations, were sent to Glass, condemning the National Banking System and urging Glass to take the lead in reforming the system.[139] This widespread and seemingly grass-roots demand convinced Glass that banking reform should be a top Democratic priority. Glass, in turn, communicated the intensity of the popular demand to Wilson and received the president-elect's approval to develop a bill. Wilson wrote back in agreement and pledged to give currency reform his most serious and immediate attention.[140]

The political problems that befell the Aldrich plan did not arise from its core financial features. Indeed, the general provisions for establishing a discount market, creating rediscounting facilities, legalizing acceptances, and allowing foreign banking elicited remarkably little comment and certainly no organized opposition. In July 1913, Warburg could claim:

> Both parties have now recognized that it is not the "currency" which is the exclusive and main factor that needs reform, but that indissolubly interwoven with this question is the problem of rendering available and efficient the now immobilized reserves of the country, and of mobilizing and modernizing the now illiquid American bills of exchange, by creating a "discount market" and "bank acceptances." Both parties are thus in agreement as to the ends to be striven for; more than that, they are agreed even as to the technical means by which they must be attained.[141]

[138] Warburg, *The Federal Reserve System*, 1: 76–77.
[139] See boxes 25–27, miscellaneous correspondence, 1912–13, Carter Glass Papers (no. 2913), Manuscripts Division, Special Collections Department, University of Virginia Library; and Link, *Woodrow Wilson and the Progressive Era*, pp. 43–44.
[140] Woodrow Wilson to Carter Glass, 14 November 1912, box 25, miscellaneous correspondence 1912–13, Carter Glass Papers.
[141] Paul M. Warburg, "The Owens-Glass Bill as Submitted to the Democratic Caucus," [1913], in Warburg, *The Federal Reserve System*, 2: 237–38.

Instead, the dominant issue in the west and south, where the radical wing of the Democratic party found its strongest support, was who would control policy once the system was established. What was contentious was the administration of monetary policy, not the proposed payments system. As Glass put it, the principal objection to the Aldrich scheme was that it was "saturated with monopolistic tendencies" and faced an "absolute lack of governmental control."[142] Wilson concurred: "The Aldrich bill was probably about 60 to 70 percent correct but the remainder would have to be altered."[143] To those close to Wilson, it was clear that "the matter of control and the Board of Governors was the one question still undecided in his mind."[144] The challenge for Democrats was to incorporate the basic financial features of the Aldrich plan, but strip away the possibility that New York banks would gain policy control. Democrats seized upon the regional reserve bank idea, developed earlier by Victor Morawetz, in which both reserves and control were more decentralized than in the Aldrich measure.[145]

Carter Glass and H. Parker Willis (the economist who worked with Laughlin in the National Citizens' League) presented such a plan to Wilson on 26 December 1912. The plan called for a decentralized, yet still privately controlled, system of as many as twenty independent reserve banks with the power to hold the reserves of member banks, to issue notes backed by commercial assets and gold, to provide rediscounting services, and to conduct foreign operations. The object was to "provide for local or home control" over reserves, rediscounting, the issue of bank notes, and the international movement of gold, instead of the politically obnoxious "centralized control" of the Aldrich Plan.[146] Autonomy of the individual reserve banks was meant to assure local banks and their customers that they would have direct influence over credit policies in their districts. To provide some cohesion between the independent units of the system, Glass proposed to give the comptroller of the currency some very limited "supervisory" powers.

Wilson, however, would not go so far in the way of decentralization as Glass and Willis. In previous consultations with Warburg and Hepburn, Wilson and members of his inner circle, such as William G. McAdoo, Henry Morgenthau, and Colonel House, converted to the idea that some

---

[142] U.S. Congress, *Congressional Record*, 63d Cong., 1st sess., 1913: 4642.
[143] Quoted in Willis, *The Federal Reserve System*, p. 140.
[144] Dinwiddle to Paul Warburg (26 January 1912), cited in Stephenson, *Nelson W. Aldrich*, p. 403.
[145] For Morawetz's contributions to the organizational elements of the Federal Reserve System, see West, *Banking Reform and the Federal Reserve*, pp. 66, 95.
[146] Willis, *The Federal Reserve System*, p.145.

central agency had to be established to coordinate and conduct the domestic and international operations of the entire system.[147] The President, Willis wrote to Glass, recognized that a central bank was politically impossible even if economically desirable and that the goal should be to provide those central banking powers which were unmistakably desirable.[148] Wilson's solution was to establish a "capstone to be placed on the structure," a central board with substantial powers to coordinate and control the individual reserve banks.

Willis and Glass bent to the president's will on the matter of a central board, even though they recognized "this is where the bombardment will be directed" when set before western radicals in Congress.[149] But before tackling this challenge, Glass decided to conduct public hearings to see whether bankers would support a regional reserve system, if capped by a central controlling board. During the hearings, conducted between 7 January and 17 February 1913, bankers warmed to the idea.[150] Although Willis found that in "the majority of cases an unwilling and tentative approval was extended [by bankers] to the local reserve idea, the evident view being that in the absence of a central bank such an institution would be better than nothing."[151] Warburg, Hepburn, and Reynolds understood that a powerful controlling board would give a regional system much the same level of centralization as in the Aldrich Plan, but with a cosmetic veneer that might sidetrack populist opposition to central banking. As a member of the currency committee of the ABA put it, "even if it were called 'central supervisory control' rather than a central bank . . . it will be a central bank in the final analysis."[152]

When it was clear that major bankers were receptive to the idea of regional banks with overarching central control, Glass and Willis prepared a tentative draft of a bill and presented it to Wilson on 30 January 1913.[153] It proposed at least fifteen regional "Federal Reserve Banks," con-

[147] According to Glass, "It is clear to me that Mr. Wilson has been written to and talked to by those who are seeking to mask the Aldrich plan and to give us dangerous centralization." Carter Glass to H. Parker Willis, 29 December 1912, box 25, miscellaneous correspondence 1912–13, Carter Glass Papers. For evidence of such consultations, see Kolko, *Triumph of Conservatism*, pp. 224–25.
[148] H. Parker Willis to Carter Glass, 31 December 1912, box 25, miscellaneous correspondence 1912–13, Carter Glass Papers.
[149] Carter Glass to H. Parker Willis, 29 December 1912, box 25, miscellaneous correspondence 1912–13, Carter Glass Papers.
[150] U.S. Congress, House, *Hearings before the Subcommittee on Banking and Currency Charged with Investigating Plans of Banking and Currency Reform*, 62d Cong., pt. 1–17 (Washington, D.C.: GPO, 1913).
[151] Willis, *The Federal Reserve System*, p. 160.
[152] Kolko, *Triumph of Conservatism*, p. 226.
[153] The original Glass Bill is reprinted in Willis, *The Federal Reserve System*, pp. 1151–53.

trolled almost entirely by bankers. All but one of the directors were to be chosen by the member banks according to electoral procedures that closely mirrored those of the Aldrich Plan. The remaining director, designated the "Federal Reserve Agent," was to be selected by the central organization and would act as its representative at each reserve bank. As for the central organization itself, the Glass bill proposed a "Federal Reserve Commission" situated in Washington. Like the National Reserve Association, the commission would have only token government representation: while thirty members would be selected by the reserve banks (i.e., by bankers), just six would be political appointees. These six would include the secretary of the treasury, the secretary of agriculture, the comptroller of the currency and three others chosen by the president on the condition that they have practical banking experience. Bankers would also form the majority of the commission's executive committee, the "Federal Reserve Board." This nine-member board would be composed of three members chosen by the reserve bank representatives from among their ranks, the three presidential appointees with banking experience, the secretary of agriculture, the comptroller of the currency, and the secretary of the treasury (chairman).

The Federal Reserve Commission's power over the regional banks was as great as that of a central bank over its branches. It could fix each reserve bank's discount rate, it could apportion government deposits among the reserve banks, it could suspend reserve requirements in an emergency, it could impose a penalty tax on reserve deficiencies, and it could force or permit the reserve banks to rediscount the paper of other reserve banks. This last provision was the commission's most important instrument, as it enabled the central body to mobilize the reserves of the entire system and direct them where needed. Willis maintained that "it is evident that this power is not different in nature from that which is exerted by the head office of a central bank possessing several branches."[154]

The original Glass bill was thus not much more decentralized nor governmentally controlled than its predecessor. As such, it stood little chance of passing a Congress imbued with strong populist sentiment. In the wake of the "Money Trust" investigations and the National City Company controversy, anti-Wall Street forces were in no mood for the minimal government role provided for in the Glass-Willis plan. Indeed, before the bill was introduced, significant concessions were granted to these forces, headed as they were by William J. Bryan, Wilson's new secretary of state. In Willis's appraisal, "the adoption of the Glass bill in

---

[154] Ibid., p. 322.

the House of Representatives might well be abandoned unless the Bryan element could be induced to be friendly or neutral."[155]

When Woodrow Wilson entered the presidency he "knew practically nothing about the details of the matter, had made no commitments on the basic issues, and stood free to serve as a mediator among the rival Democratic factions."[156] Representing the agrarian wing of the party, Bryan insisted that the government control the central banking system from top to bottom and issue the nation's currency as well. Louis Brandeis agreed: "The conflict between the policies of the Administration and the desires of financiers and big business, is an irreconcilable one."[157] According to Arthur Link, Brandeis's admonition persuaded Wilson that concessions to the populist element had to be made.

At a series of White House conferences between 11 June and 18 June 1913, Democratic leaders modified the bill so that it conformed to Bryan's populist doctrine that control over the money supply "is a function of government and should not be surrendered to banks."[158] The revised bill, known as the Glass-Owen Bill, was introduced in both houses of Congress on 26 June 1913. Its most significant change, the one destined to "alter in no small degree the attitude of the banking community toward the measure," concerned the composition of the central organization.[159] The original plan had proposed a large national board and a smaller executive committee, both dominated by bankers or their representatives. In the Glass-Owen Bill, the commission was eliminated altogether, leaving only the board to set policy for the entire system. More importantly, bankers were stripped of nearly all representation on this board. The new seven-member board would consist of the secretary of the treasury, the secretary of agriculture, the comptroller, and four members chosen by the president with the advice and consent of the Senate. Of these four, only one had to be experienced in banking. In short, the impact of the country bank/agrarian contingent in Congress was "to make the change from a business to a political control of the federal reserve system."[160] This manner of constituting the Federal Reserve Board was acceptable to at least one rural banker, who noted that by placing responsibility for the general financial situation upon the incumbent administration, self interest would encourage the most patriotic ef-

---

[155] Ibid., p. 210.
[156] Link, *Woodrow Wilson and the Progressive Era*, p. 45.
[157] Cited in Link, *Woodrow Wilson and the Progressive Era*, p. 48.
[158] William J. Bryan and Mary Bryan, *The Memoirs of William Jennings Bryan* (Philadelphia: John C. Winston, 1925), pp. 370–71.
[159] Willis, *The Federal Reserve System*, p. 250.
[160] Ibid., p. 256.

fort.[161] Although not all small bankers had as much faith in the wisdom and impartiality of executive officials, they nevertheless feared political control less than Wall Street control. As a Wisconsin country banker concluded, "We are more willing to take our chances with the Government" than with big bankers.[162]

Money-center bankers, on the other hand, were naturally distressed with the "Bryanized Banking Bill." While amenable to a modest level of government oversight, bankers saw that a powerful board with only one member of technical banking experience on it, would be subject to political pressure and party trading in its make-up, and would fail to assume the sound money responsibilities of a central bank.[163] Bankers feared that political appointees would have electoral incentives to sacrifice price stability and external balance. In a well-circulated memorandum, Warburg clearly recognized how this structure, giving control to the majority, could lead to suboptimal policies: "In our country, with every untrained amateur a candidate for any office, where friendship or help in a presidential campaign, financial or political, has always given a claim for political preferment, where the bid for votes and public favor is ever present in the politician's mind, where class prejudice and antagonism between East and West and North and South run high . . . a direct government management, that is to say, a political management, apt to change every few years, would be a national disaster."[164]

In the debates of 1913, Wall Street bankers worked to reduce the level of government control and get more banker representation on the Federal Reserve Board. These efforts, however, were only marginally successful. In the bill that passed the House on 18 September, the only concessions of consequence were (1) of the four members appointed by the president, not more than two could be of the same political party, and (2) adding a "Federal Advisory Council" to the Board. This council was to be composed entirely of bankers elected by the directorates of the reserve banks and, although its purpose was to give the financial community voice in policy formation, its powers were strictly advisory. The bill that passed the Senate one month later also included changes that leaned

[161] W. S. Fant to Carter Glass, 2 August 1913, box 25, miscellaneous correspondence 1912–13, Carter Glass Papers.
[162] U.S. Congress, Senate, Committee on Banking and Currency, *Hearings on H.R. 7837,* 63d Cong., 1st sess., 1913, 1549.
[163] Frank A. Vanderlip to Carter Glass, 24 July 1913, box 16, miscellaneous correspondence, 1913–14, Carter Glass Papers.
[164] Paul M. Warburg, "The Owen-Glass Bill as Submitted to the Democratic Caucus," p. 240. For a model endogenizing central bank structure that is based on distributional conflict between the winners and losers of surprise inflation, see Faust, "Whom Can We Trust to Run the Fed?"

in the direction of the bankers' position. First, it removed the secretary of agriculture and the comptroller from the board, leaving the secretary of the treasury as the only *ex officio* member. This was a nod to the bankers, since it reduced the probability that the system would become simply the monetary arm of the executive, subject to electoral cycle pressures and pressures from easy money constituencies in the majority. Second, of the six remaining presidential appointees, at least two (rather than one) had to be experienced bankers. In the conference committee's report, which was accepted by both houses on 23 December 1913 and signed by Wilson on the same day, the comptroller of the currency was returned to the board. The five remaining appointed members, however, were given longer terms (ten years, rather than six as in the Senate version) which were also staggered, so that no president could appoint all the members during a normal two-term presidency. This, too, increased the prospects for monetary policy independence—the basic organizational goal of those who wanted sound money to be the central bank's primary objective. Finally, the conference struck out the clause in the House bill which gave the secretary of the treasury the power to supervise the active executive officer of the board, titled the "Governor" in the final act.

While bankers lost the battle to gain full private control over the Federal Reserve System, most considered the compromises obtained in the House, Senate, and in conference acceptable alternatives. As Warburg concluded, these changes "demonstrated progress of great significance in that they gave the Reserve Board at least a fighting chance for freedom from politics and governmental control."[165] In the short term, the issue depended upon Wilson's choice of appointees and, while bankers evidently trusted Wilson's discretion, they feared future presidents might abuse this power for short-term political gain. In correspondence with Glass, the head of the National Citizens' League considered it unlikely that Wilson, an exceptional president, would use political criteria in making his choice of appointees, but worried that the average president would be easily seduced.[166] Wilson, however, did not disappoint the bankers.[167]

Despite the intensity of the bankers' demand for more private representation on the board, this should not be construed as evidence that

[165] Warburg, *The Federal Reserve System*, 1: 127.
[166] John V. Farwell to Carter Glass, 2 July 1913, box 20, miscellaneous correspondence 1913, Carter Glass Papers.
[167] See Murray N. Rothbard, "The Federal Reserve as a Cartelization Device," in *Money in Crisis: The Federal Reserve, the Economy, and Monetary Reform*, ed. Barry N. Siegel (San Francisco: Pacific Institute for Public Policy Research, 1984), pp. 108–9.

they were opposed to the overall measure. Kolko argues that the bankers exaggerated their hostility to the bill in order to secure concessions on the control issue.[168] Vanderlip, an intractable critic of the bill in public, wrote privately that "it is workable and I think bankers should recognize the difficulties of getting an ideal measure and give such support as they can. Possibly that is the wrong way to put it; perhaps if bankers would show opposition to it there would be more chance of passage. However that may be, I shall be frank in saying that I think the measure is vastly better than the present law under which we are operating."[169] Indeed, in most important areas, the Federal Reserve Act was in broad sympathy with the Aldrich Plan, which was, of course, the bankers' pet measure.[170]

In terms of its international aspects, the Federal Reserve Act was nearly identical to the Aldrich Plan. There was no organized opposition after Chicago bankers were drawn into the coalition on the need to make the dollar an international currency and to improve international banking facilities. Taking every opportunity during the congressional hearings to press these matters, and all the while casting these arguments in terms of the national interest, New York bankers dominated the discussion.[171] Bankers' international concerns must have puzzled many members of Congress, since reform was widely perceived as growing out of domestic financial problems. In fact, during Conant's appearance before the Senate Banking and Currency Committee, Senator Joseph Bristow of Kansas noted with dissatisfaction that "most of our experts who come here are more interested in the foreign banking business than in our domestic banking business."[172] This is no surprise, given the large per capita benefits New York bankers were destined to receive.

The Federal Reserve Act installed the institutions that currency internationalists were seeking. To encourage the financing of international trade and discourage lending on call at the stock exchange, section 13 gave member banks the power to accept drafts or bills of exchange based upon the importation or exportation of goods.[173] To ensure that the

[168] Kolko, *Triumph of Conservatism*, pp. 217–54.
[169] Frank A. Vanderlip to J. M. Smith, 19 June 1913, part B, series 1, box 5, Frank A. Vanderlip Papers.
[170] See Warburg's juxtaposition of the complete texts of the Aldrich bill and the Federal Reserve Act in Warburg, *The Federal Reserve System*, 1: 178–368.
[171] See the testimony of Charles Conant, Fred Kent, Frank Vanderlip, and James Cannon in U.S. Congress, *Hearings on H.R. 7837*.
[172] Ibid., p. 1394.
[173] While the Federal Reserve Bill limited acceptances to the foreign field, the Aldrich Plan would have allowed national banks to accept both foreign and domestic bills of exchange. The justification for restricting acceptances to international transactions—a restriction that

liquidity of this paper would be sufficient to make it attractive as an outlet for bank funds, or, put another way, to develop a discount market in international bills of exchange denominated in dollars, section 13 allowed the Federal Reserve Banks to discount such acceptances. To enable banks to compete on a global scale, section 25 allowed any national bank with capital and surplus of over $1 million to establish branches in foreign countries and dependencies of the United States. (By restricting the benefits of foreign branching to only the very largest banks, this provision had a privatizing effect: in 1909, only 160 of nearly 7,000 national banks met the capital requirement necessary to establish foreign branches).[174] To manage and influence short-term capital and gold flows with, as Fred Kent of the National City Bank put it, the "idea of being in a position to cooperate with other nations and to use our own resources to best advantage," section 14 granted each Federal Reserve Bank extensive foreign powers.[175] The Reserve Banks were authorized to purchase from and sell to foreign banks, firms, or corporations bankers' acceptances, bills of exchange, and cable transfers; to deal abroad in gold coin and bullion and to make loans thereon; to exchange Federal Reserve notes for gold, gold coin, or gold certificates; and to open and maintain accounts in foreign countries, appoint correspondents, and establish foreign agencies for the purpose of purchasing, selling, and collecting bills of exchange.

These international features were nearly identical to those of the Aldrich Plan, with one important exception. Instead of a single central bank conducting the entire system's foreign operations, each Federal Reserve Bank was given such powers. To New York bankers, decentralization in this area was especially problematic, since "the eight to twelve regional banks may each establish agencies without number defined, in any and all foreign countries, and without uniformity of purpose or action."[176] With many reserve banks, each of varying financial strength and with necessarily different (or opposing) foreign exchange needs, a coher-

---

discriminated in favor of foreign finance and the money-center banks that were well versed in foreign operations—was that small banks might abuse the privilege and extend loans far beyond the safety of their resources. Benjamin H. Beckhart, *The Discount Policy of the Federal Reserve System* (New York: Henry Holt, 1924), pp. 117–20.

[174] Smaller national banks obtained an amendment to the Federal Reserve Act on September 17, 1919, which allowed *any* national bank, whatever the amount of its capital, to cooperate with other national banks to form a foreign banking corporation, or invest in the stock of such a corporation. See Clyde W. Phelps, *The Foreign Expansion of American Banks: American Branch Banking Abroad* (New York: Ronald Press, 1927), pp. 105–6.

[175] U.S. Congress, *Hearings on H.R. 7837*, p. 2982.

[176] Benjamin Strong to Fred Kent, 13 December 1913, Benjamin Strong Papers, Archives Division, Federal Reserve Bank of New York.

ent national policy could not develop. Moreover, the diffusion of resources and confusion of policy would undermine cooperative relations
with European central banks. As Kent saw it, "If we have 12 regional
banks, no one of them could have sufficient capital and power to command the credit that would be necessary in order to have direct dealing
with the European central banks, whereas in the case of a central bank it
would command such respect that it could take part with the great European banks in protecting each other."[177] To Warburg, decentralization undermined almost the entire international agenda, as it would lead to "the
destruction of a reliable and strong discount market, the weakening of
the reserve power of the country, the undoing of the hope of developing
the American bank acceptance and the sacrificing of a strong and effective foreign-exchange and gold policy."[178]

The solution that the bankers proposed was to limit the number of
reserve banks to four or five, so as to make coordination in the foreign
field easier to achieve. But in the existing political environment, bankers
were unable to reduce the number below a maximum of twelve (some
radicals wanted one in each state!). Nevertheless, Strong accurately predicted the inevitable: "It may well be that the bank of the region where
most of our foreign operations are conducted [the New York Federal
Reserve Bank] will be able to exercise a predominating influence in that
class of business."[179] Indeed, after Strong was selected to head the New
York Fed, he worked strenuously to bring about a high level of de facto
centralization in the system's foreign operations.[180]

Conclusion

From a public interest perspective, financial instability during the National Banking era involved wasted resources, as panics and extreme
seasonal fluctuations in credit markets rebounded negatively on financial
intermediation services and real economic activity. Over thirty million
Americans had money in the bank, and hence an interest in the soundness of the banking system. Happily, a small subgroup of society was
willing to expend resources lobbying for improvements to the financial

---

[177] U.S. Congress, *Hearings on H.R. 7837*, 2980. See also Benjamin Strong to Senator Theodore E. Burton, 5 December 1913, Benjamin Strong Papers.
[178] Warburg, *The Federal Reserve System*, 2: 253–54.
[179] Benjamin Strong to Fred Kent, 13 December 1913, Benjamin Strong Papers.
[180] Lester V. Chandler, *Benjamin Strong, Central Banker* (Washington, D.C.: Brookings Institution, 1958); U.S. Congress, House, Committee on Banking and Currency, Subcommittee on
Domestic Finance, *Federal Reserve Structure and the Development of Monetary Policy: 1915–
1935* (Washington, D.C.: GPO, 1971).

system. Why this group worked to make all of society better off is explained by the joint products model. Internationalizing the dollar and reducing internal financial instability were two complementary goods that differed in "publicness": the former offered excludable, localized benefits, while the latter presented diffuse, general benefits. Society benefited because the two goods were inseparable: consumption of the concentrated private benefits required consumption of the general public benefits. Hence, it was rational for the small group seeking the private (international) benefits to design an institutional manifesto that simultaneously advanced the provision of both goods, and then lobby on its behalf. Institutions that provide general benefits can indeed rest on the self-seeking interests of the few.

This chapter has focused on the second-order collective action dilemma that existed *within* the internationalist coalition. Just as a sounder banking system was a public good for society as a whole, internationalizing the currency was a public good for the smaller group of beneficiaries who made up the internationalist coalition. Hence, any lobbying effort to remake the financial system had to confront the free-rider problem. I argue that the severity of intra-coalitional collective action problems reflects not only the characteristics of the group itself, but political institutions which define the size, scope, and strategies of successful collective action. In this case, the distribution of benefits was sufficiently concentrated in the small number of very large money-center banks to privilege the entire internationalist coalition. This was particularly useful in the bill-formation stages of the legislative process, as New York could concentrate on overcoming the initial obstacle posed by midwestern pressure for an asset currency bill in committee. Bringing Chicago banks into the overall coalition, however, created additional collective action problems resolved only as clearinghouse associations were modified to act as monitoring and enforcement agents.

Unity among organized interests was but the first requirement dictated by political arrangements. The final approval of a majority of legislators meant that other constituencies had to be drawn into the coalition. The efforts of the National Citizens' League to build a wider political base were quite successful in terms of the basic principles of reform (e.g., broadening the discount market and central banking), but foundered on the issue of who would control central bank policy. Ultimately, Wilson mediated a compromise between the anti-monopoly forces and large metropolitan bankers. By dispersing decision-making authority between the central board in Washington and the regional reserve banks, and by replacing private actors on the central board with governmental appointees, Wilson convinced most populists that large banks could not dominate the system. Moreover, this compromise was acceptable to the advocates of banking reform in New York, largely because the Federal Reserve bill still fully incorporated the externally-oriented financial structures that were at the heart of their original institutional agenda. In a statement that Kolko misinterprets, Carter Glass captured the essence of the joint products interpretation of the Federal Reserve Act, shortly after its dual benefits became manifest:

> The proponents of the Federal Reserve Act had no idea of impairing the rightful prestige of New York as the financial metropolis of this hemisphere. They rather expected to confirm this distinction, and even hoped to assist powerfully in wresting the scepter from London, and eventually making New York the financial center of the world. Eminent Englishmen with the keenest perception have frankly expressed apprehension of such result. Indeed, momentarily this has come to pass. And we may point to the amazing contrast between New York under the old system in 1907, shaken to its very foundations because of two bank failures, and New York at the present time [April 1917], under the new system, serenely secure in its domestic banking operations and confidently financing the great enterprises of European nations at war.[181]

[181] U.S. Congress, *Congressional Record* 53, pt. 14 (1917), p. 755, cited in Kolko, *Triumph of Conservatism*, p. 254.

6/

The Origins of
Other Central Banks

C entral banks in existence prior to the Federal Reserve are
poorly explained by the broad societal public goods they
provided. Like the Federal Reserve Act, the charters of
these central banks contained a mix of general (public) and actor-specific
(private) benefits, and it is the existence of these joint goods which explains how they came into being. Though the particular joint benefits
were quite distinct from those involved in the founding of the Fed, the
basic analytics are the same: The interdependence of the multiple goods
provided a discrete subgroup of social actors with the incentives to design, promote, and maintain the early central bank charter.

Unlike the Federal Reserve, the early forerunners of modern central
banks were not born of society's need for a lender of last resort or monetary services. For early central banks, like the Bank of England and the
First and Second Banks of the United States, the main societal public
good was *fiscal* in nature and involved improving government creditworthiness during wartime. Recently, scholars working in the new institutionalist tradition have argued that these central banks were part of a
mechanism intended to make the state creditworthy, and, thereby, capable of financing necessary wars in a socially efficient manner.[1] The argu-

---

[1] Douglass C. North and Barry R. Weingast, "Constitutions and Commitment: The Evolution of Institutions Governing Public Choice in Seventeenth-Century England," *Journal of
Economic History* 49 (December 1989): 803–32; Barry R. Weingast, "Institutional Foundations
of the 'Sinews of Power': British Financial and Military Success Following the Glorious
Revolution," Working Paper, Hoover Institution, Stanford University, 1992. See also the

ment is most fully developed in the British case, where war-related fiscal crises in the seventeenth century prompted the constitutional, judicial, and financial innovations of the Glorious Revolution of 1688—liberal democratic changes that limited the arbitrary and confiscatory power of the Crown. The rise of Parliamentary power at the behest of society's wealth-holders increased the security of a broad range of private rights, while the creation of the Bank of England in 1694 institutionalized mechanisms limiting the state's ability to renege on its loan contracts. Britain did not default on its debt during the hundred years following the Glorious Revolution, which reflected the existence of institutions intended to make the state creditworthy.

The Bank of England was an important part of the mechanism committing the government to pay its debts. The bank obtained virtual monopolies in managing government debt and in issuing notes, and these monopolies were central to the commitment mechanism. Previously, lenders were incapable of imposing a general boycott on new lending to a government in default, because the government could tempt individual lenders to defect from such a boycott by offering new debt on preferential terms. For example, new loans were given priority over outstanding loans in terms of repayment, and the government could play one lender against another by offering very attractive interest rates to select creditors. The temptation for individual lenders to defect meant that the sanction of a credit boycott was not an effective means of committing the government to pay its debts.[2] The Bank of England's various monopolies, however, helped solve this collective action problem among lenders.[3] According to Barry Weingast:

> The beauty of this scheme is that by centralizing the loan decisions in a single agent rather than among a large and diffuse community of agents, the Bank's charter allowed it to enforce a community credit boycott. By using the courts, this arrangement provided a means to prevent defections that would previously occur when the sovereign defaulted. Because it improved the ability of lenders to coordinate their actions, it raised the pen-

---

collection of essays in *Fiscal Crises, Liberty, and Representative Government, 1450–1789*, ed. Philip T. Hoffman and Kathryn Norberg (Stanford: Stanford University Press, 1994).
[2] For a related analysis, see Avner Grief, Paul Milgrom, and Barry R. Weingast, "Coordination, Commitment, and Enforcement: The Case of the Merchant Guild," *Journal of Political Economy* 102 (August 1994): 745–76.
[3] For earlier interpretations of the Bank of England as a commitment mechanism, see Thomas B. Macaulay, *The History of England from the Accession of James II*, vol. 3 (Boston: DeWolfe, 1831); and John R. Hicks, *A Theory of Economic History* (Oxford: Oxford University Press, 1969), pp. 93–95.

alty they could impose on the government in the event of default. This, in turn, greatly improved the government's access to credit.[4]

The bank, in short, became a central player in all public loans, serving as the agent of the "large and diffuse community" of investors by coordinating their lending activities. And, as J. R. Jones notes, "by institutionalizing those who provided long-term finance in the Bank of England, Parliament effectively tied the hands of later Parliaments and administrations."[5]

This improvement in the government's credit standing advanced overall societal welfare in at least two respects. First, easier access to credit allowed the state to finance long, costly, and presumably necessary wars, which enhanced its competitive position in the international system. As John Brewer and others have shown, Britain's ability to finance wars on a massive scale after the Glorious Revolution, and ultimately to triumph over a more populous rival with a larger economy, stemmed from its superior mechanisms for raising loans (and revenue).[6] Second, it allowed for a policy of "tax smoothing": using debt to smooth distortionary taxes over time. Economists have long argued that tax smoothing has beneficial effects on the long-term health of an economy, since it allows a government to avoid imposing excessively high taxes to fund abnormally high current expenditures.[7] For example, financing wartime expenditures by borrowing, then servicing and amortizing the debt by taxation in peacetime—the policy England successfully pursued after 1688—lowers the total costs of raising revenue, because it produces fewer distortions in the investment decisions of private economic agents.[8]

The implicit logic of the institutionalist account is that the aggregate social gains of improved government creditworthiness are sufficient to

[4] Weingast, "Institutional Foundations of the 'Sinews of Power,'" pp. 34–35.

[5] J. R. Jones, "Fiscal Policies, Liberties, and Representative Government during the Reigns of the Last Stuarts," in *Fiscal Crises, Liberty, and Representative Government*, ed. Philip T. Hoffman and Kathryn Norberg, p. 82.

[6] John Brewer, *The Sinews of Power: War Money and the English State, 1688–1783* (New York: Knopf, 1989); P. G. M. Dickson, *The Financial Revolution in England* (London: Macmillan, 1967); Michael D. Bordo and Eugene N. White, "A Tale of Two Currencies: British and French Finance during the Napoleonic Wars," *Journal of Economic History* 51 (June 1991): 303–16.

[7] Robert J. Barro, "On the Determination of Public Debt," *Journal of Political Economy* 87 (1979): 940–67; Robert J. Barro, "The Neoclassical Approach to Fiscal Policy," in *Modern Business Cycle Theory*, ed. Robert J. Barro (Cambridge: Harvard University Press, 1989), pp. 236–64.

[8] The growth of a stable market for public debt may also have had a large and positive effect on the development of *private* debt markets. See North and Weingast, "Constitutions and Commitment," pp. 824–28.

explain the origins of early central banks, like the Bank of England.[9] The focus on collective goods, however, is incomplete almost by definition. Given the alternatives, the development of a public debt market is certainly one of the clearest examples of a societal public good, which suggests collective action problems on both the demand and the supply sides of institutional innovation. The demand side is problematic since a large number of diffuse individuals will have *insufficient incentives* to organize to demand institutions such as central banks, whose benefits accrue to all members of society, whether they contribute to its provision or not. As such, any benefit that derives from institutionalizing a set of contractual relationships will extend undiminished to all members of a given community, even if they do not share in the costs of obtaining them. Analogous problems exist on the supply side, as governments cannot charge the users of the good its true cost. While the institutionalist view is quite persuasive on the welfare-improving relationship between early central banks and government creditworthiness, it is virtually silent on the collective dilemmas surrounding institutional innovation itself.

A separate body of research looks at early central bank charters and the monopolies they established from an entirely different perspective, ignoring the general fiscal advantages stressed by institutionalists. The point of this "free-banking" literature is that central banks were not necessary, in any strictly economic sense, to the optimal operation of banking systems and the production of money.[10] Indeed, the focus here is on the distortions in *money* and *banking* markets that resulted from vesting a single bank with monopoly powers in these areas. In other words, the concern is with the market distorting privileges (private goods) granted to central banks, and the evolutionary consequences of legal cartels in banking and money production. Free bankers make the case that government-regulated cartels in banking biased developments away from the more efficient outcomes of free entry in banking, and freedom of currency issue by private banks.[11] For example, of English developments,

[9] Other examples that fit the "fiscal" central bank model, in addition to the two American cases discussed below, are the Bank of France (1800), the National Bank of Belgium (1850), the Bank of Spain (1874), and the Reichsbank (1876). See Charles Goodhart, Forrest Capie, and Norbert Schnadt, "The Development of Central Banking," in *The Future of Central Banking*, ed. Forrest Capie, Charles Goodhart, Stanley Fischer, and Norbert Schnadt (Cambridge: Cambridge University Press, 1994), pp. 1–231.
[10] George A. Selgin and Lawrence H. White, "How Would the Invisible Hand Handle Money?" *Journal of Economic Literature* 32 (December 1994): 1718–49; Vera C. Smith, *The Rationale of Central Banking* (Indianapolis: Liberty Press, [1936] 1990).
[11] Lawrence White, *Free Banking in Britain* (Cambridge: Cambridge University Press, 1984); Kevin Dowd, ed., *The Experience of Free Banking* (London: Routledge, 1992); Hugh Rockoff,

George Selgin writes: "The free-bankers' view is this: by stripping privileges from other English banks and concentrating them in the Bank of England, the Act of 1694 and other legislation that followed ruined any prospect for the development of a healthy and self-regulating competitive English-banking industry. By securing the use of its own notes as other banks' reserves, the Bank gained unprecedented lending power— power that allowed it to involve the entire English monetary system in inflationary episodes."[12]

The differences between institutionalists and free bankers derive from the analysts' distinct areas of specialization and concern. Institutionalists have a fiscal focus and are concerned with the structures that underlie public debt markets, while free bankers have a banking and monetary focus, and their purpose is to challenge the widespread belief that outcomes in these areas are inherently prone to market failure. As such, they speak past each other in terms of *explaining* early central banks: free bankers ignore the fiscal public goods associated with these banks, while institutionalists are blind to the rents and distortions created by their charters.

Joint Production and Early Central Banking

The joint products model is the analytical "bridge" that connects these disparate literatures. As noted above, the weakness of the institutionalist account is that it ignores collective action problems. That is, it remains unclear how maximizing individuals coordinated their actions to produce the institution that improved aggregate social welfare. Establishing a government central bank to advance the general good is costly and difficult, given that the product is a public good, which individuals can enjoy for free. Institutional formation is thus beset with problems of collective action on both the demand and supply sides, and progress requires an understanding of how such problems are overcome. On the demand side, improving government creditworthiness by developing a central bank to coordinate all creditors, monitor public debt contracts, and enforce a credit boycott in the event of reneging is certainly a nonex-

---

The Free Banking Era: A Reconsideration (New York: Arno Press, 1975); Arthur J. Rolnick and Warren E. Weber, "New Evidence on the Free Banking Era," *American Economic Review* 73 (1983); and Lawrence H. White, "Banking without a Central Bank: Scotland before 1844 as a 'Free Banking' System," in *Unregulated Banking: Chaos or Order?* ed. Forest Capie and Geoffrey E. Wood (London: Macmillan, 1991), pp. 49–59.

[12] George Selgin, "The Rationalization of Central Banks," *Critical Review* 7, 2–3 (1993): 342–43. See also Kevin Dowd, "The Evolution of Central Banking in England, 1821–1890," in *Unregulated Banking: Chaos or Order?* pp. 159–95.

cludable good. Hence, individual creditors, as well as the wider set of beneficiaries, will have insufficient incentives to organize to demand it. On the supply side, the government has great difficulty determining how much each individual beneficiary values the public good, and then taxing them accordingly.[13] This is because each citizen has powerful inducements to understate how much he or she values the good, and the amount he or she is willing to pay for it, given the public nature of the good. This lack of incentive to participate in paying for the public good is another manifestation of the free-rider problem.

The simple beauty of the joint products resolution is that it directs attention to the cartel aspects of the exchange stressed by free bankers: Organize a discrete subgroup of creditors by offering significant private benefits as an incentive to lobby for, and participate in, the central bank venture, and then "tax" this cartel by requiring subsidized loans to the government on demand. In the exchange with the government, this manageable subgroup internalizes part of the public benefits of improved government creditworthiness, thereby resolving the thorny collective action dilemmas that constrain institutional creation.

The most important analytical implication is that a broad and diverse group of individuals who share interests in the provision of a public good may actually *benefit* from the rent-seeking activities of a narrow segment of society. This claim is counterintuitive, since the core logic of the rent-seeking literature is that the activity is inherently wasteful—a form of what Jagdish Bhagwati calls "directly-unproductive, profit-seeking" behavior.[14] As such, the least expected outcome concerning rent-seeking is one where social welfare actually *increases*. Nevertheless, I advance this counterintuitive claim on the following foundations: Since actors in a given economic sector realize that government has the ability to limit the competitive forces in a market that restrain profits to normal, economy-wide levels, they will expend resources trying to obtain legal barriers on such forces. Economic rents, or supernormal profits, are made possible by governmental restriction of entry into a market through legal monopolies, regulated cartels, licenses, and the like. The government, however, recognizes that its monopoly position as supplier of rents has value, forming the basis of exchange. When the rent-seeking lobby has something the government needs, e.g., credit to finance the provision of necessary public goods, the government may accommodate the lobby out of mutual interest. Social welfare is advanced when such

[13] See the chapter on public goods in any good public finance textbook. A classic is Richard A. Musgrave, *The Theory of Public Finance* (New York: McGraw-Hill, 1959).
[14] Jagdish Bhagwati, "Directly-Unproductive, Profit-Seeking (DUP) Activities," *Journal of Political Economy 90* (1982): 988–1002.

exchanges yield aggregate benefits larger than the deadweight costs of the market restrictions, on net.

The specific argument about the formation of early central banks has a demand and a supply side. On the demand side, the actors are a subset of all creditors, seeking government regulation as a means to earn rents. The primary goal of these rent-seekers, which facilitates their organization into a lobby for the central bank, is the legal market restriction. The lobby expects the government to grant substantial rents on future financial transactions, by promising a monopoly on the marketing of government bonds and/or a regulated banking cartel. While the lobby may justify the plan on the basis of the general good (e.g., that the cartel enhances the government's creditworthiness and war-making capacity), these are external effects of its more narrow private incentives. Nevertheless, demand-side collective dilemmas are overcome through the organization of a select subgroup that internalizes a share of the general benefits of government creditworthiness.

The government composes the supply side by virtue of its mandate to provide necessary public goods *and* its authority to limit competitive forces in a market. When a government is accountable to, and depends for its continuance in office on, the whole of society, it internalizes aggregate welfare.[15] Democratic accountability thus creates incentives for governments to supply public goods-producing institutions that minimize the deadweight loss of some inefficient prevailing arrangement. In the case of fiscal central banks, the government seeks to reduce the distortions associated with financing abnormally high (wartime) expenditures with high current taxes (or the inflation tax). The better policy is tax smoothing, which requires institutions that improve the government's creditworthiness. Inasmuch as the government cannot obtain sufficient credit to spread the tax burden over time without offering the plum of a monopoly franchise, it has incentives to participate in a "cartel for credit" exchange. In return, the creditor cartel agrees to lend money to the government on demand. Both sides are mutual hostages to the original exchange, since the government depends on the creditor cartel for its borrowing, and the cartel depends on the government for its cartel rents. The bargain cannot be dissolved without making both sides worse off.

The following evidence and empirical observations are consistent with this argument. First, I expect to find a subgroup of the wider community

---

[15] Gary S. Becker, "The Theory of Competition among Pressure Groups for Political Influence," *Quarterly Journal of Economics* 98 (1983): 371–400; Gary S. Becker, "Public Policies, Pressure Groups, and Dead Weight Costs," *Journal of Public Economics* 28 (December 1985): 329–47.

of creditors at the head of the societal effort to create early central banks. If the possibility of earning rents is driving the demand for institutional change, then pressure for a fiscal central bank-qua-cartel should come primarily from an organized subset of the general class of net creditors, and not from the entire community. Second, this subgroup should have at the head of its institutional agenda a set of explicit barriers to entry or special privileges in mind (e.g., a monopoly on government issues and/ or special privileges in banking). The government, in turn, should be more receptive to the exchange, the deeper is its fiscal crisis. Third, to the extent that political conflict arises over the institutional agenda, it should be *intrasectoral* in nature. The market restrictions which the subgroup wants the government to create can be expected to provoke opposition from other firms in the regulated industry, who will not be so favored. More broadly, collective political action should revolve around the regulatory elements of the program that redistribute wealth to the cartel, rather than its public good component.

There are further implications that add dynamism to the theory. If the rent-seeking lobby is successful and government repeatedly limits competitive forces in its market, the market power of the favored firm will increase. In money and banking, granting and strengthening the special privileges of a single firm can result over time in the creation of a true central bank—a bank so dominant that it can influence general monetary conditions. With such monetary capacities lodged in a single institution, *intersectoral* political conflict should arise. With power over the state of the macroeconomy, central bank policies will have wide-ranging distributional effects that cut across sectors of the economy, affecting, for example, all nominal debtors and creditors, regardless of occupation. So, in addition to the ongoing opposition of financial firms who are disadvantaged vis-à-vis the central bank in the banking business, nonfinancial actors who lose (or gain) by the central bank's monetary policies should also politically confront (or support) the cartel arrangement.

In the following sections, I evaluate the argument against three well-known cases involving substantial variation: the founding and repeated rechartering of the Bank of England to 1819; the founding and subsequent dismantling of the First Bank of the United States (1791–1811); and the trajectory of its similarly fated successor, the Second Bank of the United States (1816–1832). Among the advantages of the argument is its ability to endogenize the evolution of government banks with fiscal powers into central banks with monetary and lender-of-last-resort powers. Moreover, the logic also helps solve the puzzle as to why the Bank of England persisted, while its American counterparts did not. The durability of the exchange depended first and foremost on the capacity of the central government to protect and enforce the central bank cartel. In the United States, this capacity was constrained by strong federalism, which allowed state legislatures to charter banks, giving rise to the state banking system. This difference in political institutions meant that American central banks faced powerful state-chartered rivals, who used some of their resources to undermine the national banks. The last section is the conclusion, which summarizes the findings and considers the implications for positive theories of institutions.

The Founding and Maintenance of the Bank of England

The case of the Bank of England fits the expectations reasonably well. Prior to the Glorious Revolution, repeated violations of existing government loan contracts by militarily insecure, and fiscally strapped monarchs severely limited the creditworthiness of the English state. Nearly continuous war created intense financial problems for the state, which responded by acceding to the plan of a small group of creditors, who were seeking both important monopoly privileges and mechanisms for ensuring debt repayment. In exchange for explicit monopoly rights in government issues and banking, the bank lent money to the government at preferential terms. As predicted, the bank's early history revolved around its monopolistic position and the political struggles to retain it— intrasectoral conflict predominated in the eighteenth century. Over time, and as a direct result of the bank's ability to retain and extend its monopolistic privileges, it became a modern central bank, which gave it power to affect monetary conditions. This development led to wider, intersectoral conflicts over the monetary orientation of the central bank in the nineteenth century.

The Bank of England was established in 1694, in the midst of a major war with France. At the time, the government was an extremely poor credit risk, due to previous repudiations of debts and confiscations of wealth. In the most egregious examples, the government seized the monetary wealth of its citizens outright. In 1640, Charles I shut the London Mint and confiscated the funds of private citizens that had been stored there. In 1672, Charles II surpassed this perfidy by expropriating £1.3 million deposited with the treasury by London goldsmiths. Charles II later acknowledged half of this debt, but reneged on the promise to pay. Interest payments were kept current only between 1677 and 1683. The direct loss to creditors (goldsmiths) and their roughly 10,000 depositors was nearly £3 million, "to say nothing of the frightful expense of such protracted litigation."[16]

These actions against the property rights of creditors had predictable consequences: creditors became exceedingly wary about loaning to the government at a time when war with France required ever higher government expenditures. Under William III, some imaginative and attractive borrowing schemes were developed, but with little success. In 1692, for example, a life annuity paying a tempting 10 percent brought in only £108,000 of an intended £1 million loan. This failure led the government to boost the interest payment to 14 percent, but the offering still remained undersubscribed. Just how low the credit of the state had fallen is illustrated in the following account: "The Government were obliged to revert to the humiliating plan of borrowing from every one in the city they could. They were obliged to solicit from the Common Council of London for so small a sum as £100,000, and if they granted it, the Councilmen had to make humble suit to the inhabitants of their respective wards, going from house to house for contributions, and for these advances had to pay, in premiums, discount, and commission, from 30 to 40 percent."[17]

With the war effort languishing for lack of funds, Parliament accepted a plan for a government bank—the Bank of England—put forth by William Patterson in 1694. Charles Montagu, Chancellor of the Exchequer, considered over seventy schemes before he decided to take Patterson's plan to Parliament.[18] Patterson, a Scottish entrepreneur, represented a small group of creditors—"that powerful group in the background"— whose intention was to get an inside track on the business of financing the government and on the banking business.[19] In effect, a deal was cut: the state would get badly needed loans at preferential rates in exchange for granting extensive legal privileges to a private banking corporation. As a necessary concomitant, the plan included a set of mechanisms designed to limit the government's ability to renege on its loan agreements.

Patterson's plan invited subscribers to a loan to the exchequer of £1.2 million to incorporate the Company of the Bank of England. In other words, the bank was founded with a capital of £1.2 million, which was immediately loaned to the government. The loan was a perpetuity, pay-

---

[16] Henry D. Macleod, *The Theory and Practice of Banking*, vol. 1 (London: Longmans, Green, 1923), p. 444.

[17] Ibid., p. 446.

[18] R. D. Richards, *The First Fifty Years of the Bank of England* (New York: Augustus M. Kelly, 1965).

[19] John H. Clapham, *The Bank of England: A History*, vol. 1 (Cambridge: Cambridge University Press, 1944), p. 15.

ing 8 percent interest plus £4,000 annually in management fees. In return, the bank's subscribers received the following rights: (1) the exclusive right to hold all government loans, (2) the exclusive right to lend money to the government, (3) the right to form a joint-stock banking company, (4) the exclusive privilege of limited liability in banking, and (5) the right to issue banknotes backed by government bonds in an amount not exceeding the bank's capital (in practice, the note issue was not limited to this amount). The terms were sufficiently attractive and the entire loan was subscribed within twelve days.[20]

Repayment of the original loan and interest was secured by earmarking new taxes (ships' tonnage and liquor taxes). Yet, apart from the guarantees behind the initial loan, the bank's monopoly rights played a more lasting role in improving government creditworthiness—a public good.[21] As the sole holder of loans to the government, the bank was used by all wealth-holders interested in lending money to the government as an intermediary for purchasing bonds, annuities, and the like. This prevented the government from seeking alternative sources of credit, and thus made default less likely. In addition, with the exclusive right to lend money to the government, the bank obtained the legal power, enforceable by the independent judiciary, to prevent other lenders from breaking a credit boycott, which enhanced the bank's ability to punish opportunism on the part of the government.

The idea that the bank *originated* to resolve these collective action problems among creditors raises an antecedent collective dilemma. Inasmuch as the bank offered generalized, nonexcludable benefits to be enjoyed by *all* government creditors, organization and participation in the scheme should have been extremely difficult. Viewing the bank's charter from the angle of the rents it sanctioned, however, offers the solution.

If the founders and subscribers of the bank were motivated first and foremost by supernormal profit considerations, their participation was understandable. Indeed, if the subgroup of creditors involved in the bank could obtain privileges that would give them an immense superiority over all competitors in both public finance and in the general banking business, it was rational for them to contribute. Rereading the charter in terms of the *competitive* advantages it conferred upon this favored group yields the following incentives: (1) The exclusive right to hold all government loans meant that the bank had a lock on managing the government's finances—a very large business—and, thereby, earned com-

---

[20] Ibid., p. 19.
[21] Weingast, "Institutional Foundations of the 'Sinews of Power,'" pp. 34–35; Brewer, *Sinews of Power*; Dickson, *Financial Revolution*.

missions and fees that, in a free market setting, would be allocated competitively. (2) The exclusive right to lend money to the government gave the bank a similar advantage over rivals as originators of loans. (3) The right to form a joint-stock banking company combined with, (4) the exclusive privilege of limited liability in banking meant that, among all creditors, the bank's shareholders were liable for the debts of the bank only to the amount of their investment, and not for its entire liability. Most important, (5) the right to issue banknotes meant that the bank was able to loan money in excess of deposits, by reason of the circulating notes it could issue against the government debt.[22] On the assumption that £1.2 million in banknotes could be loaned to private borrowers at the same rate as to the government (8 percent), the bank earned £96,000 from private borrowers, in addition to the £100,000 from the government, for a total return of 16.33 percent on their capital. Hence, the "precise purpose which the Government had in view in permitting their circulation [i.e., the circulation of Bank of England notes] was that of subsidizing the banker in return for the facilities he provided."[23] The bank's goldsmith-banker competitors, by contrast, were not only excluded from government lending and financial management, but restricted to *deposit* banking, which meant lending coin, or credit for which they held coin in reserve.[24] Ten years later, an opponent of the bargain argued against the note-issuing advantages of the bank:

> The power to extend their [the Bank's] credit, and upon so good a foundation as the security of an Act of Parliament is perhaps a more considerable article of their profit than an interest at 8 percent, payable by the state on its initial loan of £1.2 million. . . . It gave to them a power to issue bills of credit equal to that sum, making itself the security for all those who thus far trusted the Bank. . . . By virtue of that privilege, they have a further power of issuing what further credit of theirs now passes amongst us; and all this passes as currency upon the bottom of public sanction and security.[25]

As expected, opposition to the bank came from rival creditors, who felt that the legal advantages allotted to the bank gave it a superior com-

[22] Clapham, *The Bank of England*, pp. 21–22.
[23] Ellis T. Powell, *The Evolution of the Money Market, 1385–1915* (New York: Augustus M. Kelly, 1966), p. 126.
[24] Charles A. Conant, *A History of Modern Banks of Issue* (New York: G. P. Putnam's Sons, 1915), p. 84.
[25] John Broughton, *Remarks upon the Bank of England* (1705) cited in H. V. Bowen, "The Bank of England During the Long Eighteenth Century, 1694–1820," in *The Bank of England*, ed. Richard Roberts and David Kynaston (Oxford: Oxford University Press, 1995), p. 12.

petitive position. "Ever since the foundation of the Bank of England . . . political and economic interests excluded from participating in state financing complained bitterly about the special advantages enjoyed by holders of the public funds and tried to muscle their way into the action."[26] Indeed, "much of the Bank's early history revolved around its monopoly position, and political struggles to retain it."[27] According to John Brewer:

> The competition to hold a large part of the public debt is not difficult to explain. The acquisition of substantial public funds guaranteed their holder a regular income in the form of tax revenues assigned to service the national debt. This security, in turn, conferred enormous power in the private money market. Backed by the large sums of money which made up public finance, an incorporated creditor could also dominate private borrowing. *The prospect of financial hegemony in both the public and private spheres was the glittering prospect offered by corporate dominance of the national debt.*[28]

Even in 1694, competing creditors were at the forefront of the opposition: "The new Bank had also to meet the opposition of the goldsmiths and money-lenders who were deprived of their most obvious profits by the new undertaking."[29] Rival creditors' arguments in Parliament stressed the distortionary effects of the market restrictions. They "alleged that the Bank . . . would absorb all the money in the kingdom and would subject commerce to usurious exactions."[30] They talked of the risks to "honest merchants if they got into the clutches of this harpy."[31] The opposition was ineffectual, however, due to the urgency of war: "The project was only passed because the Government needed money and could not obtain it otherwise."[32]

War was the usual context in which the bank's charter was renewed.[33] Between 1688 and 1815, England was involved in seven extended wars, as well as in other military crises, such as the Jacobite uprisings of 1715 and 1745. For most of the bank's first 120 years, the nation was "either preparing for war, waging war, or seeking retrenchment after war," and

---

[26] Brewer, *Sinews of Power*, p. 120.

[27] Mark R. Brawley, "The Afterglow Hypothesis: The Role of Central Banks in Cycles of Hegemony," unpublished manuscript (1992), p. 79.

[28] Brewer, *Sinews of Power*, pp. 121–22 (emphasis added).

[29] A. Andreades, *History of the Bank of England, 1640–1903* (London: P. S. King, 1924), p. 68.

[30] Ibid.

[31] Thorold Rogers, *The First Nine Years of the Bank of England* (Oxford, 1887), pp. 9–10.

[32] Andreades, *History of the Bank of England*, p. 70.

[33] The bank's charter was extended in 1696, 1697, 1713, 1742, 1764, and 1781.

the bank's future was always negotiated during a military emergency.[34] The terms of each charter never extended for more than twenty-nine years and, on each occasion, provision was made for the expiration of the charter twelve months after a given date. "This brought a particular pattern of development to the Bank that was ultimately dependent upon the rhythm of war and peace . . . the Bank needed the state [for rents] as much as the state needed the Bank [for public finance]."[35]

Throughout the period, the bargain was renewed despite the opposition and intrigues of competing financial interests. In 1695, these competitors lent their support to the scheme of a Land Bank, which was chartered, but never began operations because of the hostility of the Bank of England and the promoters' failure to raise the funds for its cheap loan to the government.[36] The Land Bank's competitive challenge prompted the Bank of England's directors to negotiate a series of agreements with the House of Commons, the principle in each case being that in return for subsidized or even interest-free loans, "no other Bank or Constitution in the nature of a bank be erected or established, permitted or allowed by Act of Parliament during the Continuance of the Bank of England."[37] In addition to obtaining a genuine legal monopoly, which effectively tied the hands of the government to maintain the bargain, the bank was exempted from paying taxes and got an extension of its other privileges.[38]

In 1708, during a new war with Louis XIV and again in exchange for cheap loans, the bank obtained its most significant barrier to entry: the legal prohibition of associations of more than six individuals from carrying on a banking business in England. According to White, "This was crucial in restricting competition with the Bank, because public holding of banknotes was the major source of bank funding in the eighteenth and nineteenth centuries."[39] The Act of 1708 thus gave the bank "a monopoly over joint-stock *note issue*."[40] Despite the lack of a legal prohibition against joint-stock deposit banking, "there can be no question that the intention was to give the Bank of England a monopoly of joint-stock banking, and had any other institution of more than six partners at-

---

[34] H. V. Bowen, "The Bank of England During the Long Eighteenth Century," p. 5.
[35] Ibid., p. 6.
[36] Keith J. Horsefield, *British Monetary Experiments, 1650–1710* (Cambridge: Harvard University Press, 1960), chaps. 14–16; Brewer, *Sinews of Power*, p. 153.
[37] Clapham, *The Bank of England*, p. 47. Clapham writes that "the General Court [the directors of the Bank of England] wanted no more Land Banks."
[38] Andreades, *History of the Bank of England*, pp. 111–12.
[39] Lawrence H. White, *Competition and Currency* (New York: New York University Press, 1989), p. 73.
[40] Steven Russell, "The U.S. Currency System in Historical Perspective," *Federal Reserve Bank of St. Louis Review* 73, 5 (1991): 43 (emphasis in original).

tempted to carry on a banking business in England in any matter what-ever at any time during the first half of the century it would have been suppressed."[41] This authority thus prevented the formation of strong joint-stock banks and kept private (nonchartered) banks small and weak relative to the Bank of England.

The bank regarded its paper currency monopoly as critical to its prof-itability, and was willing to make large financial concessions to the gov-ernment in order to protect and extend it. The government, in turn, was willing to grant the bank a monopoly, because it needed the bank's fi-nancial assistance, in particular, to help it finance foreign wars. Just prior to the expiration of this charter in 1742, the bank provided an interest-free loan to the government in return for receiving a confirmation of its monopoly powers (the privilege of issuing circulating notes was rein-forced) and a lengthening of its charter to 1764. In that year, the bank gave the government an outright gift of £110,000, plus a loan at 3 per-cent. In 1781, another extension was granted in return for yet another loan, giving the bank a charter until 1812.

That the bank's shareholders were repeatedly willing to provide subsi-dized credit to the state is evidence of the private benefits (rents) they expected to receive from the many artificial barriers to competition the government provided. From the bank's perspective, its monopoly privi-leges had a price, which, presumably, was something less than the bank's transfers to the government. Not all the gains of this institutional arrangement were private and distortionary, however. The broader com-munity of creditors and the government also benefited from the deals the proprietors of the Bank of England cut with Commons.[42] As a conse-quence of the bank's ability to enforce a credit boycott in the event the government attempted to renege on its debts (along with new parlia-mentary provisions for financing debt service), the sanctity of govern-ment loan contracts improved markedly. Thus, the growing ranks of in-vestors found ample and secure outlets for their funds. In addition, the predictability of government lending, along with the bank's nongovern-mental banking transactions, facilitated the expansion of private capital markets, thereby linking savings with investment to finance a wider range of productive activities.[43]

With creditors' rights more secure, the government was able to borrow to finance wars on a scale that the Stuarts could only dream of. By 1720, government debt was over fifty times the 1688 level, and approximating

[41] Albert Feavearyear, *The Pound Sterling* (Oxford: Clarendon Press, 1963), pp. 167–68.
[42] This is the story told by North and Weingast, "Constitutions and Commitment."
[43] Ibid., pp. 824–28; Brewer, *Sinews of Power*.

GNP.[44] Moreover, the costs of borrowing also fell markedly, from 14 percent in the early 1690s to 3 percent by the 1730s, indicating that the risk of lending to the state had fallen. Thus, the state's ability to finance wars by pursuing a policy of tax smoothing (a public good), and the enormous expansion of private capital markets (another public good), paradoxically, went hand-in-hand with the rent-seeking origins and early expansion of the Bank of England. While this foundation was efficient, in the sense that it enhanced the state's ability to finance massive military undertakings, it came at the cost of having foisted a dominant bank onto an embryonic financial structure that suffered from its dominance.

Henry Macleod recounted some of the deadweight social losses associated with the "original sin of the monopoly of the Bank of England" at the time the industrial revolution was gathering steam:

> The prodigious development of all these industrial works demanded a great extension of the Currency to carry them on. What was required was to have banks of undoubted wealth and solidity issue such a Currency. Bank of England notes had no circulation outside London. Its monopoly prevented any other great banks being formed, either in London or the country, and it would not extend its branches into the country. . . . England required a Currency, and if it could not have a good one, it had a bad. Multitudes of miserable shopkeepers in the country, grocers, tailors, drapers, started up like mushrooms and turned bankers, and issued their notes, inundating the country with miserable rags.[45]

Since the only banks not affected by the Bank of England's monopoly were those having less than six partners, weak banks proliferated in the provinces to meet the heightened demand for banking services. In 1750, there were only about twelve banks outside London, but by 1790, the number had risen to around 400. These banks tended to collapse at the first unusual demand for cash. The panics of 1793, 1797, 1810, and 1812 were "due to the defective organization of the provincial credit," which itself was a direct result of the monopoly powers of the Bank of England.[46] "The six-partner rule of the Act of 1708 prevented England from experiencing the rise of strong nationally based joint-stock banks such as those whose branches superseded local and private banks in Scotland."[47] The centralization of banking privileges thus had its costs, as one would ex-

[44] North and Weingast, "Constitutions and Commitment," p. 822.
[45] Macleod, *The Theory and Practice of Banking*, pp. 506–7.
[46] Andreades, *History of the Bank of England*, pp. 171–72.
[47] Lawrence H. White, *Free Banking in Britain* (Cambridge: Cambridge University Press, 1984), p. 40.

pect: "(1) The banks outside of London were artificially stunted and fail-
ure-prone; and (2) the Bank of England as sole London issuer occupied a
position of unrivaled hegemony over the currency system as a whole."[48]
It was this second distortion which transformed the Bank of England
into an institution with monetary powers—a central bank—and so
transformed the political landscape.

Inter-Sectoral Conflict Over Monetary Policy

By virtue of its accumulated monopoly rights, the Bank of England obtained the power to affect general credit conditions, a power the government took advantage of to ill effect during the Napoleonic wars. The
government prevailed on the bank to help finance the wars through inflation, which was no less a violation of creditors' rights than that perpe-
trated by Charles II in 1672. This form of expropriation, however, had
more diffuse macroeconomic effects, adding a new political dynamic to
the politics surrounding the Bank of England. No longer were the battles
primarily intrasectoral (between the bank and other less privileged financiers). Since the redistribution was intersectoral, political alignments
followed suit, with divisions between creditors and debtors, and tradables and nontradables producers being preeminent.

Vera Smith argues that the origins of the Bank of England fit a more
general pattern: early central banks were "founded for political reasons
connected with the exigencies of State finance," and hence, central banking "is not a natural product of banking development. It is imposed from
outside or comes into being as a result of government favour."[49] The
British case defines the pattern. With the accumulation of so many privileges, the bank outperformed all competitors and became the dominant
bank in England, with nascent central banking powers. As Walter Bagehot observed, "With so many advantages over all competitors, it is quite
natural that the Bank of England should have outstripped them all. Inevitably it became *the* bank in London; all other bankers grouped around it
and lodged their reserve with it. Thus our one-reserve system of banking
was not deliberately founded upon definite reasons; it was a gradual
consequence of many singular events, and of an accumulation of legal
privileges on a single bank."[50]

The bank's monopolies as the government's bank and the issuer of

[48] Ibid., p. 59.
[49] Smith, *The Rationale of Central Banking*, pp. 167, 169.
[50] Walter Bagehot, *Lombard Street* ([1873] Westport: Hyperion Press, 1979), pp. 66–67.

notes were crucial to this development.[51] When the government borrowed, the bank identified the sources of credit. The government left balances with the bank, and a large part of its assets consisted of advances to government departments. These connections with state finance were what made the Bank of England so secure, and, thereby, induced other financial institutions to lodge deposits with it.[52] Moreover, its control over note issue gave the bank the power to exercise discretionary influence over the general credit situation and, thereby, justifies the use of the term "central bank."[53]

During the bank's first century, however, its ability to impart discretionary influence over the money supply was constrained by a de facto gold standard rule. The voluntary agreement the bank made with people who held its notes was inherently anti-inflationary, and the guarantee took the form of a contract to redeem bank notes at a fixed price in gold. If bank notes were issued to such an amount as to cause their market price in terms of gold to fall below the price promised by the bank, people would arbitrage the difference by trading gold for notes in the market at the low price and exchanging the notes for gold at the bank at the higher price. Specie convertibility, in other words, acted as the dominant constraint on the over-issue of Bank of England notes. Indeed, for the century in which this mechanism was in place (1694–1793), the annual average rate of inflation in England was just .01 percent.[54]

In the early stages of the Napoleonic Wars, however, the bank suspended gold payments. A drain of gold from the bank's reserves brought about by heavy government expenditures on British fleets and armies, subsidies and public loans to allies, and bad harvests was the proximate cause, but the intense government demand for credit to finance the war effort was the main cause. Since the bank's contract with its customers to redeem its notes in gold stood in the way of this interest, the king and Privy Council ordered the bank to suspend specie payments on 26 February 1797.[55] Although considered a temporary wartime

---

[51] Charles Goodhart, *The Evolution of Central Banks* (Cambridge: MIT Press, 1988).
[52] Tim Cogdon, "Is the Provision of a Sound Currency a Necessary Function of the State?" *National Westminister Bank Quarterly Review* (August 1981): 16.
[53] Smith, *The Rationale of Central Banking*, p. 148; Kevin Dowd, *The State and the Monetary System* (Oxford: Philip Allan, 1989).
[54] G. J. Santoni, "A Private Central Bank: Some Olde English Lessons," *Federal Reserve Bank of St. Louis Review* 66 (April 1984): 19.
[55] Feavearyear, *The Pound Sterling*, pp. 179–83; Phyllis Deane, *The First Industrial Revolution* (London: Cambridge University Press, 1965), pp. 173–77; and Victor E. Morgan, *The Theory and Practice of Central Banking, 1797–1913* (London: Cambridge University Press, 1943), pp. 23–24.

measure, suspension lasted until 1821, and in the interim brought monetary issues to the forefront of politics.

Suspension of gold payments eliminated constraints on note expansion on the part of the bank and, after a period of restraint, it became little more than the monetary arm of the exchequer.[56] The result was inflation and the depreciation of sterling against other currencies. By violating the contract to redeem its notes on demand for a fixed weight of gold and then bowing to the government's financial pressures, the bank, by suspension, usurped the property rights of all persons whose wealth consisted of money. In addition, depreciation worked to the advantage of tradables producers by raising the prices of traded goods relative to nontradables.[57] This set the stage for the intersectoral conflict over the terms of the monetary settlement.

Suspension had more general political ramifications than previous government repudiations, as its consequences—inflation and depreciation—brought about a redistribution of wealth from *all* creditors and producers of nontradable goods to *all* debtors and tradables producers. No longer was the Bank of England controversial because its legal monopolies privileged one group of creditors against all others (intrasectoral conflict). Since its notes were now fiat currency and the government chose to finance the war through inflation, two great intersectoral coalitions formed. The key beneficiaries of suspension were farmers and manufacturers. Tenant farmers, in particular, found strong incentives to support the existing state of monetary affairs, since "the price of the farmers' crops was rising whilst they were continuing to pay the same rents in depreciated notes."[58] The price of wheat, for example, jumped from 6 shillings 9 pence per bushel in 1797 to 16 shillings in 1800, while rents on agricultural land remained fixed at pre-inflation levels by long-term leases.[59] As David Ricardo observed in 1810, "He [the farmer] more than any other class of the community is benefited by the depreciation of money, and injured by the increase in its value."[60] Debtors of all classes gained by the long period of suspension, as they made interest and prin-

[56] Andreades, *History of the Bank of England*, pp. 195–202.
[57] For the exchange rate's distributional implications, see Jeffry Frieden, "Invested Interests: The Politics of National Economic Policies in a World of Global Finance," *International Organization* 45 (Autumn 1991): 425–51.
[58] Andreades, *History of the Bank of England*, p. 236.
[59] T. S. Ashton, *Economic Fluctuations in England, 1700–1809* (Oxford: Oxford University Press, 1959), p. 181.
[60] David Ricardo, *The Works and Correspondence of David Ricardo*, vol. 3 ([1816] Cambridge: Cambridge University Press, 1951), pp. 136–37.

cipal payments in a currency worth about 17 percent less in gold than when their debts were contracted.[61]

In addition, the monetary attitude of manufacturers and industrial labor tended to correspond with that of the farmer, as industrial demand, prices, and wages all rose as a result of the depreciation of sterling and the general stimulus of war.[62] The expansion, however, brought habits attuned to price, profit, and wage levels that were difficult to sustain after the final defeat of Napoleon. With war's end, demand dropped off, import competition increased (as blockades were lifted), and prices dropped dramatically. Domestic manufacturers, represented most vocally by organized Birmingham industrialists, sided with farmers in seeking monetary relief from the deflation/appreciation.[63] In addition, "the great exporting centers [e.g., Manchester] were just as antagonistic."[64] The coalition's anti-gold standard platform alternatively called for the continuation of suspension or a return to gold convertibility at a rate substantially lower than the prewar level, because "depreciation would effect a redistribution of wealth in favour of the productive classes— manufacturers, merchants and farmers."[65]

In contrast to the views of farmers and manufacturers, depreciation was injurious to England's creditor, rentier, and saver groups: "A creditor of 1800 might, because of the depreciation, be a debtor in 1819, and consequently be twice legally robbed."[66] Ricardo laid out the principle: "The depreciation of the circulating medium has been more injurious to monied men. . . . It may be laid down as a principle of universal application, that every man is injured or benefited by the variation of the value of the circulation in proportion as his property consists of money, or as the fixed demands on him in money exceed those fixed demands which he may have on others."[67]

The position of the landed aristocracy is instructive. From the late seventeenth century, landlords built ever larger estates and rented their acres to tenant farmers in larger units on long leases.[68] But during the

---

[61] Andreades, *History of the Bank of England*, p. 237.
[62] Morgan, *The Theory and Practice of Central Banking*, pp. 23–48.
[63] Boyd Hilton, *Corn, Cash, Commerce: The Economic Policies of the Tory Governments 1815–1830* (London: Oxford University Press, 1977), pp. 31–97; Frank W. Fetter, *Development of British Monetary Orthodoxy, 1797–1875* (Cambridge: Cambridge University Press, 1965), pp. 73–76, 99–106; Feavearyear, *The Pound Sterling*, pp. 224–26.
[64] Hilton, *Corn, Cash, Commerce*, p. 57.
[65] Ibid., p. 63.
[66] Ibid.
[67] Ricardo, *The Works and Correspondence of David Ricardo*, 3:136–37.
[68] Michael Tracy, *Government and Agriculture in Western Europe, 1880–1988*, 3d ed. (New

inflationary war years, landlords found they were receiving only about two-thirds of their rent in real terms.[69] Unable to raise rents in line with the upward trend in commodity prices, and prevented by Parliament from requiring tenants to pay rents in gold, rentier lords' monetary interests were in deflation and an early return to the gold standard.[70]

Landlords were joined by a powerful new economic group that emerged as a result of the wars. This group was composed of the owners of British government bonds, which had been issued in vast quantities to finance the wars at a time of high prices and interest rates.[71] There were roughly 17,000 of these "fundholders," a group that Leland Jenks considered to be "nearly synonymous with the governing classes."[72] Depreciation was costly to bondholders, because it reduced the purchasing power of a bonds' dividends and, through the rise in interest rates, reduced its capital value as well.[73] If the trend could be reversed, fundholders, who had bought into the national debt with depreciated currency, would receive repayment in a currency with much greater purchasing power. In effect, deflation—the requisite of the return to gold payments—would produce a large bonus for fundholders, as the real value of the war loans and interest payments would rise. Indeed, after resumption of gold payments in 1821, interest on the war debt came to absorb over half the government's total revenue by 1827, redistributing wealth from taxpayers to investors.

Granted, collective action problems should have constrained the political capacities of both coalitions, consisting, as they did, of large numbers of individuals. To some extent this is accurate, since the parliamentary debates surrounding Peel's Act of 1819 (which officially reestablished the convertibility of Bank of England notes into gold at the prewar rate), show little in the way of mass political pressures. Four classes of witnesses, weighted heavily toward the financial community, appeared before the Bullion Committee in 1810: Bank of England directors, private bankers, merchants, and financial specialists (political economists). One solution consistent with the argument, but needing further evaluation, is that the entire gold standard coalition was *privileged* by the existence of a

---

York: Harvester Wheatsheaf, 1989), p. 37; J. D. Chambers and G. E Mingay, *The Agricultural Revolution* (Cambridge: Cambridge University Press, 1966).

[69] Andreades, *History of the Bank of England*, p. 237.

[70] In 1811, a landlord tried to get his tenants to pay in gold, but a bill was promptly introduced that made it a misdemeanor to make any difference in payments between gold and bank notes. The bill passed Lords by a vote of 43 to 16 and Commons by a vote of 95 to 20. Conant, *A History of Modern Banks of Issue*, p. 111.

[71] Brian Johnson, *The Politics of Money* (London: John Murray, 1970), pp. 38–39.

[72] Leland Jenks, *The Migration of British Capital to 1875* (New York: Knopf, 1927), p. 26.

[73] John Maynard Keynes, *Monetary Reform* (New York: Harcourt, Brace, 1924), pp. 7–21.

single dominant creditor—the Bank of England itself. This is consistent with G. J. Santoni's claim that, "the gold standard came about largely as a result of the Bank's continuous prods to an unwilling Parliament."[74] Moreover, if the large bonus the bank stood to gain from having its outstanding government loans revalued is considered a form of rent, the argument is even stronger, for here, too, institutional creation hinged on narrow redistributive motivations. While the Act of 1819 benefited all creditors by limiting the bank to issue notes only in relation to the ebb and flow of gold, this protection came about as a secondary consequence of the rent-seeking behavior of the bank.

In summary, the collective dilemmas British society faced in the early 1800s were fundamentally different from those of a century earlier. In the 1690s, the core problem was government opportunism in relation to its debt obligations, while in the latter period it was government opportunism in relation to its currency obligations. Paradoxically, the solution to the first problem created the second. As the Bank of England grew in relation to other banks upon its anti-competitive foundations, it gradually assumed central bank capacities, which the government promptly seized during the Napoleonic Wars, when it depreciated the currency. To limit future recourse to this option, lenders and landlords, perhaps privileged by the position of the bank in credit and capital markets, rallied to obtain a legal commitment to the gold standard.

Central Banking in the United States, 1791–1834

Early central banking arose in the United States during War of Independence, as the fledging government simultaneously undermined the sanctity of its debt obligations and its monetary covenant with its citizens. Unable or unwilling to raise taxes to finance the war, the Continental Congress took to the printing press to outfit the army, and the resulting depreciation destroyed both confidence in paper money and the government's credit. As in Britain, a bargain was struck between the government and a select group of wealth-holders: the government promised substantial rents of financial transactions by granting a monopoly of government issues/balances, in return for the creditor cartel agreeing to lend to the government. The exchange was formalized in the charter of the First Bank of the United States, and had the external effect of restoring public confidence in both lending to the government and the currency. The bank also developed into a central bank with regulatory powers, again largely due to the legal privileges it obtained in the ex-

---

[74] Santoni, "A Private Central Bank," p. 15.

change. Yet, unlike the Bank of England, America's first public-qua-central bank could not perpetuate itself. When the First Bank's rechartering effort failed in 1811, confidence problems in debt and money reappeared, severely constraining the government's ability to prosecute the War of 1812. This wartime fiscal crisis brought forth a successor bank—the Second Bank of the United States—but like its predecessor, it, too, was politically unsustainable.

For these developments to fit the expectations of the theory, the following should be observed: (1) The processes of central bank creation and change should show evidence of micro-level political action, since large encompassing coalitions face high costs of collective action due to their size, heterogeneity, and diffusion. To the extent that the free-rider problem is overcome, rent-seeking on the part of subgroups of a more general constituency should be elemental to the origins of the central bank exchange with government. (2) Yet, since government creditworthiness and currency debasement arose simultaneously in this case, political divisions over central banking should entail intra- *and* intersectoral patterns—the central bank's monopoly status animates rival creditors, while monetary policy excites a wider and more general population. More specifically, since the effects of currency repudiation are general (macro-political) and indiscriminate, individuals should hold positions on the issue according to (a) their positions in credit markets, with net debtors advocating some form of inflationary, soft money institutions, while creditors seek the reverse, and (b) their positions in the global economy, with tradables producers seeking soft money/depreciation and nontradables producers seeking the reverse. (3) The "cartel-for-credit" exchange should be durable only so long as both parties are able perform according to the contract. Should the government be unable to maintain the favored bank's cartel, for example, the bargain may be dissolved. I propose that dissolution occurred in the United States due to strong federalism, which gave state governments the right to charter banks within their domains, creating strong economic and political rivals to the national central bank.

During the War of Independence, the Continental Congress issued $242 million in "Continentals," and the states issued their own paper to the amount of $209 million—all this superimposed over a preexisting money supply of only $12 million. In the end, the war was paid for overwhelmingly by the issue of such unsecured paper money. Taxation was limited, because Congress lacked the legal authority, the infrastructure, and, most of all, the will to tax. In John Kenneth Galbraith's pithy terms, Americans "were opposed to taxation without representation, as greatly remarked, and they were also, a less celebrated quality, opposed to taxation *with* representation."[75] So, like Parliament under William Pitt, Congress used its nascent monetary powers as a critical source of war finance. Patterns of early American monetary politics were thus remarkably similar to those of England at the time of the Napoleonic Wars. In both cases, war was the catalyst for major institutional change, as it led to fiscal and monetary disturbances (inflation in the British case; hyperinflation in the American case) that brought central banking to the foreground.

Since currency was issued far in excess of any increase in specie, prices rose sharply. By 1781, the phrase, "not worth a Continental" was common currency. In that year, a pair of shoes cost $5,000 in Virginia; a full set of clothes, $1 million. As common wisdom had it, "a wagon-load of money would scarcely purchase a wagon-load of goods."[76] For people with substantial amounts of property in the form of money, the effects of the price inflation were severe. Since the paper was granted legal tender status, the dramatic fall in its purchasing power had the usual effect of transferring wealth from creditors and people on fixed incomes to debtors. As is well recognized, debtors of all kinds—frontier farmers, manufacturing entrepreneurs—reveled in the situation and scrambled to repay their obligations in the nearly worthless money. Creditors, in turn, took to hiding out to avoid receiving repayment in the depreciated notes.[77] These groups were also involved in the production of tradable goods, so the relative price effects of depreciation were to their advantage.

As in England after the defeat of Napoleon, conditions were ripe for political conflict over money. Creditors and rentiers wanted a paper currency only if it was convertible into specie, so as to avoid receiving interest and principal payments in money of inferior purchasing power. Holders of public securities—the American equivalent of the "fundholders"—were particularly interested in deflation and stable money, since the bonds and certificates of indebtedness they held would rise sharply in value if made payable at their full face value in currency redeemable in specie. Moreover, speculators picked up these securities at large discounts on the gamble that interest and principal would be repaid at par and in specie.[78] The creditors of the American Revolution,

---

[75] John K. Galbraith, *Money: Whence It Came, Where It Went* (Boston: Houghton Mifflin, 1975), p. 46.
[76] Galbraith, *Money*, p. 59.
[77] Norman Angell, *The Story of Money* (New York: Frederick A. Stokes, 1929).
[78] James E. Furgeson, *The Power of the Purse: A History of American Public Finance, 1776–1790* (Chapel Hill: University of North Carolina Press, 1961); Curtis P. Nettels, *The Emergence of a National Economy, 1775–1815* (New York: Holt, Rinehart, and Winston, 1962).

just like the creditors of Pitt and George III, stood to receive a hefty premium from monetary orthodoxy.

Behind the movement for stable money were creditors of both the states and the new national government, as well as debt speculators who believed that the new government would have to honor all wartime commitments in hard money or seriously weaken its credit standing. For the young government, the need to enhance public credit was critical, due to the war emergency. In casting about for a remedy, treasury officials Robert Morris and Alexander Hamilton took their lead from the Bank of England, which was an exemplary model for building credibility. In an early recommendation for a government bank, Hamilton noted that America's independence was the main object, and that object would be achieved "not by gaining battles, but by introducing order into our finances—by restoring public credit."[79] The need was to preserve and enhance government credit by showing that lending to the state entailed little risk of expropriation by currency debasement.

Hamilton argued that, by installing a central bank as the foundation of government debt, the pecuniary interests of society's wealthiest and most influential elements could be tied to the future success of the new national government. The problem lay in convincing creditors to venture wealth on a government whose short history was rife with monetary expropriations. The solution was to offer a central bank (along with credible mechanisms for funding the public debt) with substantial special privileges, that offered opportunities for earning rents in the banking market. To the favored cartel, who lent their credit to that of the government, went the spoils of monopoly rights.

Like the Bank of England, the institutional design of the First Bank served to enshrine it both as the dominant bank in the nation, able to out-compete all rivals, and as an important aid to the government. And, like its English counterpart, the First Bank acquired so much business, that its "public [fiscal] function was to many persons quite unapparent except as usurpation and privilege."[80] Nevertheless, it granted loans to the treasury—by the end of 1792, the government's debt to the bank was $2.6 million; by the end of 1795 the figure was $6.2 million—and assisted in both the collection of taxes and the administration of the public finances. By allowing subscribers to pay for their capital stock one-fourth in specie and three-fourth in government securities, the bank not only attracted sufficient capital to support extensive lending operations, but

---

[79] Fritz Redlich, *The Molding of American Banking*, vol. 2 (New York: Johnson Reprint Company, 1968), p. 47.
[80] Bray Hammond, *Banks and Politics in America from the Revolution to the Civil War* (Princeton: Princeton University Press, 1957), p. 249.

also enhanced the market price of government bonds and, thereby, improved public credit. For Hamilton, the "national bank" was "an institution of primary importance to the prosperous administration of the finances, and would be of the greatest utility in the operations connected with the support of the public credit."[81] In the event of future military threats, Hamilton argued that the government could look to the bank, rather than to the printing press. In addition to taking government debt, it would also serve as the government's fiscal agent, facilitating the collection of revenues and the distribution of expenditures.[82] But the bank's artificial advantages, not its public functions, were the sufficient conditions for its establishment.

The bank was given an exclusive national charter—Congress could authorize no other bank during the bank's twenty-year charter. Because it was the only national bank, the bank's note issue had a national character that other state-chartered and unincorporated banks could not match.[83] Additionally, it had a lock on the deposits of the federal government, a very good thing, given that the government was the single largest transactor in the market. These special advantages were necessary to cajole an organized and intensely interested core of support out of the disorganized and opportunistic mass of constituents, who would benefit from sound public credit. In other words, the inducement to collective organization was the possibility of earning rents, not the nonexcludable benefits of the plan. Hence, on the day subscription to the bank was opened in July 1791, the entire amount ($8 million) was oversubscribed within an hour.[84] Among the subscribers were the state of New York, the Bank of Massachusetts, Harvard College, thirty members of Congress, merchants, and professionals. Eventually, much of the stock came to be held by foreign investors.

Hamilton was not shy about the need to grant substantial concessions to participants in the project: "Those who are most commonly creditors of a nation are enlightened men . . . enlightened friends of good government . . . who took the risks of reimbursement, a hazard which was far from inconsiderable . . . and each security holder deserved to reap the

---

[81] Annals of Congress, *Report on a National Bank*, 1st Cong., 2d sess. (14 December 1790), cited in J. Z. Rowe, *The Public-Private Character of United States Central Banking* (New Brunswick: Rutgers University Press, 1965), p. 9.

[82] Richard H. Timberlake, Jr., *The Origins of Central Banking in the United States* (Cambridge: Harvard University Press, 1978), pp. 4–11; John T. Holdsworth, *The First Bank of the United States* (Washington, D.C.: GPO, 1910).

[83] Redlich, *The Molding of American Banking*, p. 98.

[84] Margaret G. Myers, *A Financial History of the United States* (New York: Columbia University Press, 1970), p. 68.

benefit of his hazard."[85] More telling is a passage from Hamilton's *Report on a National Bank*:

When the present price of the public debt is considered, and the effect which its conversion into bank stock, incorporated with a specie fund, would in all probability, have to accelerate its rise to the proper point, it will easily be discovered, that the operation presents, in its outset, *a very considerable advantage to those who may become subscribers; and from the influence which that rise would have on the general mass of debt, a proportional benefit to all the public creditors, and, in a sense which has been more than once adverted to, to the community at large.*[86]

Hamilton recognized that the bank's public benefits were derivative of the exclusive benefits that accrued to current bondholders, original lenders, and speculators alike. Of course, this was just the initial private benefit; in addition to the boost in value of outstanding government debt (much of which was contracted at deep discounts with depreciated currency), backers could expect to earn rents in the banking business, due to the legal advantages lodged in the bank. The general point is that the public goods components of the institution were, in a sense, external to the original transaction.

The First Bank as a Central Bank

The bank was not only a superior competitor to the state banks, "it was also their master."[87] While it took the Bank of England nearly a century to realize the position of a central bank, the rise of the First Bank was remarkably rapid in this respect. There are differences in the details, but the fundamental cause in both cases was the initial set of legal privileges: the bank's role as financier and fiscal agent to the government, its predominance in note issue, and its subsequent accumulation of reserves.[88]

In the United States, the form of influence over the money supply was peculiar, stemming from the fact that state governments could, and did, charter note-issuing banks (I return to this important difference below).

[85] Cited in E. A. Johnson, *The Foundations of American Economic Freedom* (Minneapolis: University of Minnesota Press, 1973), p. 148.
[86] Reprinted in Herman E. Krooss and Paul A. Samuelson, eds., *Documentary History of Banking and Currency in the United States*, vol. 1 (New York: McGraw-Hill, 1969), pp. 258–59 (emphasis added).
[87] Galbraith, *Money*, p. 74.
[88] The First Bank held specie reserves of $15 million by 1809, fully half the specie in the country. Redlich, *The Molding of American Banking*, p. 99; Hammond, *Banks and Politics in America*, p. 202.

Because the First Bank was the government's fiscal agent, it received the notes of state banks in payment for taxes. This made it constantly the creditor of the state banks, thereby giving it an immediate claim upon them for specie. The relationship enabled the bank to exercise control over the banking system and, thereby, to act in the manner of a central bank. Indeed, the First Bank kept state banks in line by refusing to accept notes that were not redeemable in specie, and by returning the notes of questionable banks for redemption.

With the rapid expansion of state banking after the war, and the realization that creating liabilities in the form of bank notes and deposits could effectively serve the same expansive purpose as government-issued paper money, the point of controversy shifted from preventing government misuse of money to regulating the money-creating power of banks. Because the First Bank could influence the issues of state banks, it soon became the focal point of monetary contention and, for reasons given below, lost the battle to obtain another charter in 1811.

The Fall of the First Bank

The first American central bank, like its English counterpart, came into existence to aid the government, but when it began to exercise monetary control over bank credit, its charter was allowed to lapse. To explain this variation across the cases, I invoke the structure of political institutions, which influenced the rent-seeking dynamic of institutional politics. The most important difference was the *federal* structure of the American political system and the consequent semi-sovereign proprietary powers of state governments, versus England's higher degree of political centralization. Federalism in the United States meant that the national government faced competition from the states in chartering note-issuing banks. The subsequent rise of state-chartered joint-stock banks in the United States helps to explain the failure of central banking to perpetuate itself. Unlike the Bank of England, the First Bank faced an organized body of established competitors, a core that easily mobilized to defeat rechartering efforts.

Although states lost the power to issue currency at the Constitutional Convention, they did not lose the power to charter banks. Like the national government, states viewed banks as sources of revenue and, therefore, coveted the power to charter them. In fact, during this period several states derived close to half their revenue from bank sources.[89] Since

---

[89] John W. Wallis, Richard E. Sylla, and John B. Legler, "The Interaction of Taxation and

the very existence of banks depended on the favor of state governments, and states depended on banks for meeting their fiscal needs, exchanges between state governments and favored banks were common. This meant that, unlike the Bank of England's monopoly, which limited competition to firms of less than six partners, large banks of issue could arise across the banking landscape in the United States, even though the First Bank operated as the only nationally chartered bank.

States and states' rights advocates coveted the power to charter banks for the same reason as Congress: they were ready sources of credit and revenue. These exchanges were, in fact, modeled on the charters of the Bank of England and the First Bank: that is, state governments got large payments or loans on favorable terms, in return for monopoly rights in note issue.[90] As Steven Russell notes, "the motives (and actions) of the states in this regard were similar to any license-granting monopolist. . . . Bank charters would be more valuable to their holders, and thus issuing charters would be more lucrative for the states, if the charters conveyed an *exclusive* right to issue paper currency."[91] An American variant of this exchange was that state governments often required bank promoters to cede the state an equity interest, in return for granting a bank charter. Sometimes the interest was ceded *gratis*, and sometimes merely on favorable terms. The practice was most common in the Southeast, where bank dividends accounted for a substantial portion of state revenues.[92] Hence, "States that owned a substantial equity interest in banks had an incentive to maximize the value of that interest by restricting competition."[93]

States thus set up their own versions of the First Bank within their respective jurisdictions. These were monopolistic franchises that performed public services in government finance, in exchange for prohibiting the banknote issue of potential banking competitors. This is reflected in the fact that, until the charter of the First Bank expired in 1811, most states chartered just one or, at most, a handful of banks. When the First Bank was founded in 1791, there were only four other banks in existence, the idea being a government bank with monopoly rights for each

Regulation in Nineteenth-Century U.S. Banking," in *The Regulated Economy*, ed. Claudia Goldin and Gary Libecap (Chicago: National Bureau of Economic Research, 1994), p. 122.
[90] "The charters of many of the earliest state banks were virtual carbon copies of the Bank of England's charter." Russell, "The U.S. Currency System in Historical Perspective," p. 48.
[91] Ibid.
[92] Richard Sylla, John B. Legler, and John J. Wallis, "Banks and State Public Finance in the New Republic: The United States, 1790–1860," *Journal of Economic History* (June 1987): 391–403; J. Van Fenstermaker, *The Development of American Commercial Banking, 1787–1837* (Ohio: Kent State University Press, 1965), pp. 17–20.
[93] Wallis, Sylla, and Legler, "The Interaction of Taxation and Regulation in Nineteenth-Century U.S. Banking," p. 142.

state. Each was the exclusive banking institution in its state. Each issued paper money in the form of bank notes, accepted deposits and transmitted funds by check or draft, and granted either secured or unsecured loans on promissory notes. In addition, each of these banks held state funds and provided loans to its state government.

States valued their power to charter banks, but ultimately dissipated it. At first, they set up single bank monopolies in their respective domains in exchange for loans, equity stakes, bribes, and political favors. What began as the sale of the states' proprietary interest "advanced with the increase in the number of banks till the interest was wholly abandoned."[94] In short, there was movement from one equilibrium policy in 1800 (state-chartered monopoly banks) to another by around 1860 (an open and competitive banking industry).[95] Most banking historians see the movement as driven by rival rent-seekers: "One group after another pleaded, cajoled, fought, and bribed its way to a bank of its own."[96] Yet, variation in the *way* states regulated entry into banking also helps to explain variation in their propensity to grant charters across states and over time.[97] When states owned or held equity stakes in banks, their incentives were to limit new charters, since restricting competition maximized the value of that stake. In contrast, when states taxed inputs, such as bank capital, the incentive was to grant many charters, since this maximized the use of that input. Over time, the trend was toward taxing inputs and, thus, toward open entry. By 1815, 212 note-issuing state banks were in business.[98]

The growth of the state banking system occurred in tandem with the growth in the monetary powers of the First Bank. The introduction and diffusion of banking allowed for the extensive creation of money liabilities in the form of notes—commercial banking offered the possibility of excessive money creation and, thus, inflation. The First Bank, however, derived the power to regulate the issues of other banks, because its role as fiscal agent for the government made it a creditor of the other banks. The government's receipts came to the First Bank in state bank notes, so the state banks were usually in debt to it. If it thought that the state banks were expanding their loans and investments too rapidly and wished to retard the progress of credit expansion, the First Bank pre-

---

[94] Hammond, *Banks and Politics in America*, pp. 144–71, 191.
[95] Instead of a strict secular trend toward general incorporation laws in banking, there was substantial variation across states and over time. See Wallis, Sylla, and Legler, "The Interaction of Taxation and Regulation in Nineteenth-Century U. S. Banking."
[96] Ibid., p. 67.
[97] Ibid.
[98] Fenstermaker, *The Development of American Commercial Banking*, p. 401.

sented state bank notes to the banks that had issued them for redemption in specie.[99] This put pressure on commercial bank reserves, limiting the amount of credit they could extend and constraining their ability to continue to expand their liabilities. This central banking function, which Albert Gallatin called "securing with certainty" a stable currency, demonstrated the public advantages of monopoly as a method of credit control.[100]

The First Bank deliberately regulated state banks in this manner. Not surprisingly, state legislators, acting as agents for state banks, strongly opposed the First Bank. "These bodies wanted the First Bank compromised so that the state banks, in which the states themselves had extensive stock holdings, would profit by the deposit of federal moneys."[101] Incensed by the check the First Bank put on their operations, and jealous of the bank's lock on Federal money, state banks led the movement that prevented the First Bank from obtaining a renewal of its charter in 1811.[102] The bank's privileged position in handling the Federal government's business was central to their opposition, for they sought greater access to government deposits; the First Bank "stood in their path both as a government depository and as a regulator of the currency."[103]

On the fringe of this mobilized and active anti-bank core was a larger, heterogeneous group of unlikely allies: the banks' borrowing clients, whose demands for money and credit generally outpaced the available supply, and the anti-banking agrarian element, who opposed all banks and wanted a pure commodity standard (preferably silver). These farmers were extremely suspicious of fractional reserve paper money, having been forced to accept worthless Continentals during the War of Independence.[104] Standing behind the First Bank were conservative state banks (e.g., Hamilton's Bank of New York), which acknowledged the benefits of having a central bank to control the less prudent behavior of their peers; Philadelphia banks, which believed that having the bank headquartered on Chestnut Street contributed to the financial primacy of their city after it should have passed to New York City; and another faction of the farm sector, which saw in the national bank a way to curb

---

[99] Richard H. Timberlake, *Monetary Policy in the United States* (Chicago: University of Chicago Press, 1993), pp. 10–11.
[100] Cited in Hammond, *Banks and Politics in America*, p. 305.
[101] Timberlake, *Monetary Policy in the United States*, p. 12.
[102] Hammond, *Banks and Politics in America*, pp. 197–226.
[103] Ibid., p. 220.
[104] Marcello de Cecco, "Modes of Financial Development: American Banking Dynamics and World Financial Crises," in *Development, Democracy, and the Art of Trespassing*, ed. Alejandro Foxley, Michael S. McPherson, and Guillermo O'Donnell (Notre Dame: University of Notre Dame Press, 1986).

the state banks and, thus, to protect the credit system from abuses and domination by an urban "money power."[105] In the end, renewal was prevented by the single-minded opposition of state banks—a rival group of rent-seekers—who were readily organized and had strong support in Congress from their respective legislators. Nevertheless, the issue of the bank's constitutionality, and worries about its British shareholders, contributed to the one-vote margin by which renewal was defeated.[106]

The liquidation of the First Bank in 1811 began, but did not complete, the process that was to differentiate the development of the American financial system from the English system. This event only momentarily suspended the American experiment with central banking. In 1816, Congress established a second Bank of the United States, setting in motion a course of political events that was similar to that which had sealed the fate of the First Bank.

The Second Bank of the United States

Demand for a new central bank began only three years after the fall of the First Bank, prompted once again by the fiscal exigencies of war. When war broke out between England and the United States in June 1812, the federal government was forced to conduct its fiscal and monetary policies without the aid of a national bank. The heavy resource demands of the war caused government expenditures to increase sharply, while regular revenues (i.e., customs) declined. Congress attempted to finance the rising fiscal deficit by authorizing sales of government securities, but banks and the public shunned the offering. Without the First Bank, the government's creditworthiness had fallen, and the loan was subscribed very slowly.[107] One congressman found it "difficult to conceive of a situation more critical and perilous than that of the government at this moment, without money, without credit, and destitute of the means of defending the country."[108]

In this environment, the government chose the inflation tax as the means to finance the war. Between 1812 and 1815, the treasury issued $36 million in "notes" that were, in effect, money. The treasury notes were ostensibly nonmoney, interest-bearing debt instruments, but, because they could be used as legal tender for payment of federal taxes,

---

[105] Ibid., pp. 209–26.
[106] On the constitutionality and foreign ownership issues, see Redlich, *The Molding of American Banking*, p. 99–101.
[107] Timberlake, *Monetary Policy in the United States*, p. 14.
[108] Alexander C. Hanson of Maryland, cited in Hammond, *Banks and Politics in America*, p. 230.

they became widely acceptable as bank reserves. Richard Timberlake estimates that treasury notes outstanding came to equal 39 percent of all bank reserves by 1813, and 65 percent by 1816."[109] In short, "the issues of treasury notes were the fuel that moved the inflation vehicle" between 1814 and 1817.[110] All state banks, except those in New England, suspended specie payments in 1814, and the federal government, whose credit was already extraordinarily weak, now had to accept depreciated state bank notes as payment for its securities and taxes. In short, the loss of the First Bank, which left the state unable to float a sufficient volume of loans, created quite a monetary pickle.

Despite the pressures, the treasury did not organize the campaign for a new national bank. Instead, a small group of rent-seeking investors, led by Stephen Girard and John Jacob Astor, were the primary movers in the story. Girard, the largest stockholder in the First Bank at the time of its liquidation, bought up the bank's Philadelphia headquarters and its remaining assets in the expectation that the federal government would soon need a successor bank.[111] His group then purchased much of the $16 million war loan of 1813, but when the government's credit fell, and the price of these bonds fell with it, the group promoted a new national bank, as a means to protect the value of its holdings.[112] The weakness of the government's financial position, combined with the eagerness of Girard's group to underwrite a new central bank venture, led to the reconstitution of the Bank of the United States in 1816. Monopoly privileges in banking served both the bank's promoters and the government's interests well.

The Second Bank's monopoly powers were superior to those of its predecessor in one important respect: it received de jure recognition as sole depository of the treasury. For this and its other advantages, the bank paid a "charter fee" to the government of $1.5 million. Girard himself took up $3 million of the bank's capital stock. Yet, the charter of the Second Bank, unlike that of the Bank of England, carried with it no restrictions on the note-issuing powers of *all* other commercial banks: banks chartered by the states retained this authority. As a result, powerful competitors could again mount a political threat to the bank's existence. The bank's directors were aware of this and, during the period

---

[109] Timberlake, *Monetary Policy in the United States*, p. 15.
[110] Ibid., p. 17.
[111] Kenneth L. Brown, "Stephen Girard, Promoter of the Second Bank of the United States," *Journal of Economic History* 2 (November 1942): 125–32; Phillip H. Burch, Jr., *Elites in American History: The Federalist Years to the Civil War*, vol. 1 (New York: Holmes and Meier, 1981), pp. 88, 97, 116–21.
[112] Redlich, *The Molding of American Banking*, p. 101.

when the treasury retired the excess of treasury notes issued during the war (1816–1820), causing a contraction of bank reserves and the money supply, the bank attempted to soften the pain by practicing "forbearance"—limiting its presentation of state bank notes for redemption in specie. Indeed, Timberlake found that one of the core tenets of the bank was to "make concessions to the state banks to prevent invidious feelings on their part."[113] The bank moderated its regulation of state banks for political purposes and, later, cultivated some additional support by providing lender of last resort services. But in the aftermath of the War of 1812, the policy of forbearance had definite limits. The treasury's full-scale retirement of its notes was the major factor affecting the macro-economy, the equivalent of a modern, open-market sale that erases bank reserves, and the bank could do little more than tinker with the structure of bank credit. Given the treasury policy, contraction was inevitable. Deflation began in 1818, and prices fell 30 percent in the next three years.[114] But, because the bank was involved in the treasury's policy of contracting the money supply—as the government's bank, it managed the debt retirement—it became the "target for complaints from the people most immediately injured, namely, banks that issued bank notes and people who used bank notes."[115] The Second Bank got much of the blame for the wave of bank failures and business hardship of the recession that began in late 1818.

Under Nicholas Biddle, the Second Bank parlayed its most-favored fiscal position into monetary powers, which it employed conservatively to make the U.S. dollar "as good [a currency] as the best in the world."[116] The bank's charter gave it licenses to be the government's fiscal agent and a profit-making commercial bank. The bank collected money for the treasury, making it a depository for public funds. As a depository, it had large amounts of government money in it and flowing through it, which gave it the opportunity to manipulate the money stock. And, as a profit-making firm with monopoly privileges, the bank had clear incentives to use its monetary powers conservatively. Sound currency was a precondition to earning rents, for, if other banks did not play by the rule of specie convertibility, the bank's legal privileges could not yield above-average returns, as any gains would quickly be lost to over-issuing state banks. In other words, the bank kept a tight rein on the money supply, but not because it "subordinated profit to stability and public duty"—a view

---

[113] Timberlake, *Monetary Policy in the United States*, p. 23.
[114] U.S. Bureau of the Census, *Historical Statistics of the United States, Colonial Times to 1957* (Washington, D.C.: GPO, 1960), series E-1, p. 115.
[115] Timberlake, *Monetary Policy in the United States*, pp. 24–25.
[116] Hammond, *Banks and Politics in America*, p. 307.

fundamentally inconsistent with the bank's organization as a profit-making firm.[117] Instead, it followed a hard money rule in order to maximize the returns that derived from its legal advantages.

Biddle employed the Second Bank's monetary powers conservatively throughout his tenure, using the foreign exchanges as a guide for policy.[118] When the dollar depreciated to the gold export point, Biddle would redeem more state bank notes for specie and reduce the bank's own discounts. For this, he aroused the enmity of those state banks that were over-issuing, and their easy-money clientele. Biddle resisted their demands for expansion and continued sending their notes in for redemption, leading these bankers to resent the very privileges which gave the Second Bank the capacity to regulate them. Yet, state bankers were not uniformly opposed to the bank. For banks that were not habitual over-issuers, Biddle continued the practice of forbearance, which probably won some acceptance for Biddle's view, that the bank was "a stern but gentle shepherd."[119] In addition, under Biddle, the bank acted as a lender of last resort on at least one occasion (1831–1832), combining forbearance with an expansion of loans and note issue, and allowing its specie reserve to fall by 41 percent.[120] These supportive activities may help to explain why 61 of 394 state banks (15%) formally petitioned Congress in support of the Second Bank during the rechartering battle of 1832.[121]

The Second Bank not only frustrated many competing state bankers, it also raised the ire of Wall Street bankers. Indeed, Bray Hammond considers New York's opposition the crux of the bank's downfall.[122] This is a puzzle in that it is the only case I know where the largest and soundest banks of a country *opposed* a central bank with an excellent monetary record. The explanation lies in the logic of rent-seeking. The Second Bank was a powerful and privileged competitor of Wall Street in two major respects. First, as the government's bank, it received all federal deposits, a crucial competitive advantage. New York's position as the hub of the nation's international trade meant that customs revenues from the port of New York were larger than those of all other American ports combined. The fact that the Second Bank received and controlled these huge deposits antagonized New York bankers, who eyed these deposits as a source of profit. With the Second Bank eliminated, millions of

[117] Ibid., p. 324.

[118] Redlich, *The Molding of American Banking*, pp. 135–37; Timberlake, *Monetary Policy in the United States*, p. 32.

[119] Timberlake, *Monetary Policy in the United States*, p. 41.

[120] Ibid., pp. 38–39.

[121] John M. McFaul, *The Politics of Jacksonian Finance* (Ithaca: Cornell University Press, 1972). See also Jean A. Wilburn, *Biddle's Bank* (New York: Columbia University Press, 1964).

[122] Hammond, *Banks and Politics in America*, pp. 355–61.

dollars of customs receipts would necessarily be paid into the city's commercial banks, acting as government depositories. Second, the bank was also in the same business as any ordinary bank—issuing bank notes and making commercial loans—and the New York banks coveted the bank's commanding position in these areas. The conservative New York banking community thus led the fight against the Second Bank, because, if it could be brought down, "all the benefits arising from deposits and also the whole profits of the very great circulation of the United States Bank notes would be transferred from the United States to the state banks—without compelling them to increase their own capital to the amount of a single dollar."[123]

While the leaders of the anti-bank movement were competing bankers, farmers were the coalition's "masse de maneuvre."[124] It was not, however, the bank's prudent regulation of the money supply that aroused farmer opposition. Instead, Andrew Jackson attained the presidency in 1828 on a ground swell of hard money agrarianism of the Jeffersonian kind (no banks, no paper money). Ever since they were forced to accept worthless paper as payment during the War of Independence, farmers had retained a skepticism about fractional reserve money. Jackson's bullionism spoke to this fear and the agenda was to get rid of all banks and all paper money, and establish a pure specie standard. As the first object of the assault, Jackson went after the most powerful bank of all. However, agrarians' distrust of banking and paper money was seized upon by concentrated groups, who wanted to get rid of the central bank for competitive reasons. While Jacksonians viewed the destruction of the bank as but the first step in a broader program to get rid of all banks, abolishing the Second Bank was the end point for New York bankers and some other state bankers. These people saw the Second Bank as a privileged rival and coveted its government business—eliminating fractional reserve banking was the last thing they wanted. Yet, as Hammond argues, bankers exploited that element in the agricultural mind that was fearful of banks in general, and concentrated this powerful political energy on the "monster" in Philadelphia. The attack was thus presented as being for farmers and against capitalists, for the poor and against the rich, and for the people and against the "money power." Throughout the propaganda campaign, the bank's opponents kept their particular interests in the background, and having Jackson and the popular majority behind them, won the so-called Bank War. The locus of

---

[123] Jabez D. Hammond, *History of Political Parties in the State of New York* (Syracuse: Hall, Mills, 1852), pp. 350–51. Cited in Hammond, *Banks and Politics in America*, p. 357.
[124] De Cecco, "Modes of Financial Development."

opposition, however, was not Jackson and his mass agrarian constituency, but "Wall Street, the state banks, and speculative borrowers dressing up for the occasion in the rags of the poor and parading with outcries against oppression by the aristocratic Mr. Biddle's hydra of corruption, whose nest they aspired to occupy themselves."[125]

The legacy of this experience was that central banking was left with no "natural" financial constituency in the United States. For about seventy-five years thereafter, Wall Street bankers opposed moves toward monetary and financial centralization. It was not until the turn of the century, when New York's prospects of becoming an international financial center entered their calculations, that Wall Street's attitudes finally changed.

Conclusion

As with the Federal Reserve Act, the charters of early "fiscal" central banks contained public and private goods, which would have been difficult, if not impossible, to produce separately. On the one hand, governments facing military challenges needed to restore public credit (and in the U.S. case, confidence in the currency as well), which had been tainted by past expropriations. The objective was to construct institutions that improved government creditworthiness, which is a public good from the standpoint of society. On the other hand, a segment of the broader group of abused government creditors and issuers of banknotes wanted government-sanctioned rents—a private good—which the government was in a unique position to provide. This formed the basis of mutually beneficial exchange in the chartering of early central banks, an exchange in which the public benefits were partially internalized by rent-seekers. In the exchange, a subgroup of private creditors extracted monopoly rights in banking and government finance for large payments or subsidized loans to the government. The granting of special privileges to a single bank was the selective incentive that was necessary for the production of the public good, establishing an institution that allowed the government to raise funds during periods of war to finance abnormally large expenditures with a policy of tax smoothing.

Since the argument runs headlong into the idea that rent-seeking is bad for society because it wastes resources, it is not surprising that it generates interesting and counterintuitive findings. First, a more effective banking monopoly may actually *improve* the prospects for public goods provision. Contrast the Bank of England with the Bank of the

[125] Hammond, *Banks and Politics in America*, p. 443.

United States in this respect. The former's monopoly was nearly complete for over a century, due to England's centralized political system, and the only banks that arose were small and restricted. The consequence was that political competition with rival rent-seekers was limited, and the bank was able to sustain its dominance as banker to the government and, ultimately, in money creation. The government's credit was never stronger and this, in turn, aided Britain in its military competition with France. In contrast, federalism in the United States meant that the Bank of the United States was unable to prevent the rise of large and powerful state-chartered rivals, who used some portion of their resources politically to undermine the national bank. And liquidating the First Bank of the United States was costly to the nation. Without a central bank to support it, the government's credit fell, and the treasury was compelled to resort to the inflation tax to finance the War of 1812. The cycle of inflation, the breakdown of the specie standard, then deflation and resumption, might have been avoided, had the First Bank been rechartered. (A similar story could be told for the Civil War finance). The point is that there appear to have been large positive externalities to monopoly in money and banking. To the extent that the gains derived from public creditworthiness exceeded the sum of the deadweight costs associated with rent-creating distortions and the wasteful use of resources implied by the cartel's "directly unproductive" lobbying activity, the process was welfare improving. In our examples, the costs of banking cartels, measured in terms of distortions in the banking market, could hardly have been greater than the general benefits that derived from the production of the public good of enhanced public credit. The weakness of the free banking critique is that it overlooks these important positive externalities of rent-seeking.

A second apparent paradox is that a monopolistic, profit-maximizing central bank will have stronger incentives to adhere to a low inflationary rule for money production (e.g., specie convertibility), than the general class of commercial banks. Inasmuch as all commercial banks are tempted to exploit the informational asymmetries that limit the ability of note-holders and depositors to constrain them effectively, there is always an incentive for banks to increase their return and risk by reducing their reserve ratio.[126] Profit-making central banks, however, are different by virtue of the monopoly element of charters. On the one hand, their monopoly in government issues, and large capital investment in fixed-interest government securities, gives them a strong incentive to seek price

---

[126] Goodhart, *The Evolution of Central Banks.*

stability.[127] On the other, their favored position as monopoly note issuer provides them with sufficient rents to make them more risk averse than the average bank. Over-issuing currency may be the dominant strategy for all banks *except* the dominant, extracompetitive bank whose monopoly position is undermined by it. Moreover, to the extent that rents cannot be maximized if other banks are playing by a looser set of money-creating rules, the central bank has incentives to use its influence to get other banks to maintain convertibility. All these predictions flow from the model, and are consistent with the behavior of central banks in the period. In short, the "circumstances of the (government-authorized) establishments of these special commercial banks may be seen as reinforcing their owners' and managers' commitment to the maintenance of convertibility."[128]

Finally, free bankers' emphasis on the cartel arrangement, with its implicit demand-side story, adds a necessary component to the new institutionalists' view. The key puzzle lies in how large groups of rational, but socially disconnected masses of individuals arrive at the cooperative outcomes and select the institutional public goods that govern their behavior. My point is that distributional considerations are essential to explaining the early central bank charter. Government creditworthiness makes everyone better off, but the distribution of the improvement is concentrated when cartels are part of the exchange. It is this concentrated distribution that gives individual agents the incentive to lobby for it.

[127] Santoni, "A Private Central Bank."
[128] Goodhart, Capie, and Schnadt, "The Development of Central Banking," p. 7.

Summary, Observations, and Implications

The original charters of central banks share a basic feature in common: they contain a mixture of public and private goods. The charters of the Bank of England, the First and Second Banks of the United States, and the Federal Reserve System produced multiple benefits, some of which were enjoyed by the whole of society (i.e., government creditworthiness, payments system stability), and others that were consumed exclusively by a small subset of the overall community (i.e., restrictions on competition, international currency institutions). This was not mere happenstance or historical accident. Central bank charters were structured this way to resolve the classic collective action dilemmas that normally constrain the production of public goods to suboptimal levels.

Even before central banks developed their full panoply of modern monetary powers, which came in the twentieth century with the decline of the gold standard, they were already great success stories in administrative government. From the late seventeenth century to the early nineteenth century, central banks provided national governments with fiscal public goods. The earliest examples worked to improve the capacity of governments to borrow in wartime and allowed for tax-smoothing fiscal strategies. Thereafter, existing central banks and freshly created ones acquired new public functions, in addition to their role in government finance. From the middle of the nineteenth century to the early twentieth century, central banks provided the public good of regulating and stabilizing the payments system, offering lender of last resort and foreign exchange services for the communities in which they operated.

At each stage, the aggregate welfare gains had to be sanctioned by collective choice through the legislative process. What is unclear is how wealth-maximizing and free-riding individuals in and out of government coordinated their actions to produce these legislated improvements in their fiscal, financial, and monetary environments. Building institutions that advance the general good is costly, especially in collective choice situations involving very large numbers of people (i.e., in democracies). Since the social benefits are nonexcludable and nonrival in consumption, free-riding should have plagued the demand and supply of these public goods-producing institutions. With central banks, the benefits (e.g., government creditworthiness, banking stability) certainly have the characteristics of public goods. So how did they come into existence?

The venerable joint products model speaks to this conundrum with analytical cogency and historical accuracy. The bottom line is that by conjoining private benefits with the production of public goods, central bank charters internalized a portion of societywide benefits within a subset of the community, creating incentives for these individuals to demand and supply institutions that had wider social benefits.

The boundaries of the model are defined by the characteristics of the goods involved and by the nature of supply. First, when joint goods are complementary in consumption (i.e., they enhance one another's services) and difficult or impossible to produce separately, then failure to contribute suggests a smaller payoff than contributing, since the complementary private good is not then available. This is the basic logic behind my account of the Federal Reserve Act, but the situation is far more common.[1] For example, the establishment of socially-efficient property rights approximates the complements situation, since individuals cannot enjoy any redistributive private benefit unless they contribute to the collective activity: "Capturing a portion of the aggregate gains from mitigating common pool losses is a primary motivating force for individuals to bargain to install or to modify property rights arrangements."[2] Second, when an organization monopolizes the provision of the private good, then contributions are necessary, given a technology of supply that makes it hard to separate the private from the collective good. This is the

---

[1] See Todd Sandler, *Collective Action: Theory and Applications* (Ann Arbor: University of Michigan Press, 1992), pp. 59, 102–6.
[2] Gary D. Libecap, *Contracting for Property Rights* (Cambridge: Cambridge University Press, 1989), p. 19. See also Jack Knight, *Institutions and Social Conflict* (Cambridge: Cambridge University Press, 1992), pp. 108–11.

essence of my story of early central banking, but the situation may be ubiquitous. For example, when a government provides the service of police protection, the collective output of deterring crime that is available to all cannot be divorced from the locally-specific outputs arising from deployment decisions.[3] In such situations, a convergence arises between the private and social costs of institutional change, making it possible for societies to produce collective goods.

In the case of early central banks in England and the United States, the interdependence of multiple goals was sufficient to overcome the inherent collective dilemmas. The formation of the Bank of England clearly benefited aggregate social welfare, but the government's monopoly in supplying rents to favored citizens provided a subgroup of society with incentives to lobby and maintain it. The deal stuck because both the bank's shareholders and the government had no incentive to act opportunistically. As long as the government was needed to sanction and enforce the bank's cartel by legally restricting competition in banking, the bank was willing to extend credit to the government on favorable terms. The government, in turn, depended on the bank for its (wartime) borrowing, and the bank depended on the government for its cartel rents, making both sides mutual hostages. The bargain came unstuck in the United States because the federal government lacked a monopoly in supplying rents. Federalism allowed state governments to form similar contracts with other creditor cartels, creating strong economic and political rivals to the national bank in Philadelphia.

The founding of the Federal Reserve is also explicable from a joint products perspective. What follows is a summary of the findings, a brief look at how the Federal Reserve served in its early years to advance the international goals of its proponents, and some observations of broader significance to the study of international political economy.

Founding the Fed

To explain the movement from the old institutional regime to the new Federal Reserve equilibrium (the changes are thoroughly described in Chapter 1), I developed the joint products argument in three successive stages. In the first stage, I demonstrated that the international and do-

---

[3] Similarly, international alliances yield a public good (deterring common enemies) and private, nation-specific benefits (alliance armaments used for patrolling coastal waters, protecting colonies, providing disaster relief, curbing domestic unrest, pursuing nationalistic goals, etc.). John A. C. Conybeare and Todd Sandler, "The Triple Entente and the Triple Alliance, 1889–1914: A Collective Goods Approach," *American Political Science Review* 84 (December 1990): 1197–1205.

mestic outputs of the Federal Reserve Act differed in terms of their "publicness," or the degree to which consumption of the goods was either nonexcludable or nonrival in consumption. I showed that payments system stability approximates a societywide public good, while internationalizing the currency produces private, concentrated benefits of the kind sufficient to generate collective action. To produce the latter result, I appealed to the literature on international currency use, which identifies the international distribution of benefits and costs of issuing international money. Typically, issuing nations benefit from seignorage, denomination rents, and reduced cost and risk of foreign exchange, while sacrificing some degree of national monetary independence. With the exception of seignorage, these benefits and costs are not distributed evenly among residents in the issuing country, making it possible to draw inferences concerning collective action at the domestic level. The key winners are relatively small groups within the issuing country—for example, money-center financial firms and exporters of differentiated and standardized manufactured products. Unlike the societywide public good of banking stability, international currency status confers large concentrated gains upon a more restricted number of agents. Inasmuch as small groups are better able to control free riding amongst their members, collective action in support of international currency institutions is more likely than is support of institutions that promote banking stability.

The second stage addresses a basic theoretical challenge to the joint products model: the potential efficiency of separately producing the private and public goods. Inasmuch as agents are motivated to contribute by selective incentives, then some other organization not encumbered with supplying the public good might be able to supply the private good more efficiently. My claim is that the Federal Reserve's joint products could not be separately produced due to the inherent complementarity of the outputs. As a result, agents seeking the private benefits could not help but contribute to the production of the collective good, since the joint products were complementary in consumption. The failure to do so would have meant that the complementary private good was not then available.

To elaborate, the institutions required to enhance the standing of the dollar in international markets and to stabilize the payments system possessed just this sort of complementarity, as stabilizing the fractional reserve banking system and developing the dollar for international use rested upon a common set of institutions. Theory and experience indicate that certain domestic institutions are necessary prerequisites for internationalizing a currency. A country whose currency is used internationally must possess a large assortment of financial instruments, developed secondary markets in these instruments, and a reliable rediscount-ing mechanism. Together, these institutions give the domestic currency the "capital certainty" it needs to be held and traded internationally. That is, developed financial markets provide confidence that the proba-bility of loss from selling assets denominated in that currency is reasona-bly low. But it is axiomatic that capital certainty also complements do-mestic financial stability. Articulated home markets have a stabilizing effect on the payments system, since they give resident agents, as well as nonresidents, confidence that their assets will be liquid and safe. A wide range of financial instruments means banks and other lenders can diver-sify risk. Deep secondary markets mean that assets can be sold easily and without capital loss to obtain liquidity in normal times. Central bank rediscounting means an agency exists to support the markets in abnor-mal times by acting as a lender of last resort. Hence, the international goal could be obtained only by lobbying for institutions that comple-mented banking stability—the goals were inseparable. For currency in-ternationalists, failure to contribute to banking reform implied a smaller payoff than contributing.

In the third stage, I add dynamism to what would otherwise be a static framework. Since the objective is to explain institutional *change*, specifying the fixed preferences of individuals, groups, and potential co-alitions is necessary, but insufficient. Additional factors must be incorpo-rated into the analysis to explain movement from one equilibrium to another, and it is my claim that change in the nation's relative interna-tional economic position is the relevant variable.

The supplementary determinants of international currency use are systemic because they involve the relative extent, direction, and compo-sition of a nation's trade, as well as balance of payments considerations. The ultimate demand for a nation's currency reflects the size of markets in it, so that the larger the nation in world trade and payments, the greater the demand for its currency for international purposes. I allege that the process of institutional change within a nation is driven by change in that nation's international economic position, as changes in global position affect the number of agents benefiting from issuing inter-national currency, as well as the preference intensities of these agents. The rise of a nation to the upper levels of the world economy—as mea-sured by a large and increasing share of world trade, an increasing share of the world's manufactured product exports, an increasing share of its exports going to developing countries, and the onset of enduring current account surpluses—has a second-order impact on the necessary domes-tic institutions, by way of its first-order effect on the relative number and political enthusiasm of the pro-international currency agents in society.

Chapters 3 through 5 evaluated these claims, and the findings are supportive. Before 1913, international use of the pound, the reichsmark, and the franc followed changes in the relative international economic positions of England, Germany, and France, confirming the role of the supplementary international factors outlined in the literature on currency use. The U.S. dollar was the crucial exception. Even though the United States had grown to rival England and Germany, and to surpass France in the categories of world economic position relevant to currency use, the dollar had no standing in world markets (with the exception of the dollar reserves held by Canadian banks). The parochialism of the dollar before 1913 most clearly demonstrates the overriding importance of the necessary domestic determinants of international currency use. The domestic financial machinery, in short, was ill-adapted to the nation's advancing position in the world economy.

Evaluation of the response in the United States shows that members of the international currency coalition did internalize the costs of banking reform. The rapid rise of the economy gave these agents private incentives to contribute to changing domestic institutions. Within the coalition, the most active agents were members of the New York financial community. Money-center bankers understood that internationalizing the dollar offered the possibility of seizing a portion of the economic rents which English banks earned from sterling's international usage. The growing numbers of export-competitive manufacturers also recognized the advantages of invoicing trade in the home currency; yet bankers remained at the forefront of the reform movement. This reflected the greater per capita benefits going to bankers, as well as their already substantial collective action capabilities. Paul Warburg, in particular, stands out as the intellectual light and most active organizer and lobbyist for institutions designed to bring the domestic financial system into accordance with the nation's new stature in the international economy.

Warburg's writings, speeches, and correspondence read as an early statement and practical application of the modern literature on international currency use. For Warburg, the creation of a discount market and the legalization of American bankers' acceptances were prerequisites for establishing an international discount market in New York. In turn, a broad discount market offered joint benefits, some of which were private, destined to benefit certain internationalists, while others would be conveyed upon society at large. Warburg made it very clear that money-center bankers would benefit disproportionately, due to the enhanced demand for banking services in New York that would accompany international usage of the dollar. But in addition to listing these concentrated benefits, Warburg very persuasively itemized the broader social welfare gains attendant with the proposed changes. He detailed how a discount market in acceptances would allow joint-stock banks to invest in highly liquid bills of exchange, representing the foreign trade of the nation, as opposed to stock exchange call loans, thereby increasing the separation of the money and capital markets. He argued that the construction of a discount market would lead to greater economy in the use of gold to settle international payments imbalances, as Europeans would come to invest in American bills as readily as they did in each other's short-term paper. Most importantly, Warburg showed that an articulated discount market supported by a central bank rediscounting mechanism was at once an essential component of internationalizing the currency and a source of stabilizing expectations domestically. Warburg's frequent references to the "preliminary conditions" for currency internationalization reflect the dual and inseparable functions of the Federal Reserve Act: increasing the resilience and liquidity of the domestic payments system through a system of rediscounting reserve banks was necessary to make the dollar attractive as an international currency.

To summarize, unlike the nonexcludable societywide benefits of producing a stable domestic payments system, the benefits of internationalizing the dollar were concentrated, private, and relatively agent-specific. The more private character of this good increased the likelihood that contributions to the collective effort would result, as the establishment of New York as a global financial center on par with London offered to a narrow segment of society selective incentives to pay the costs of institutional change. The relative advance in the international economic position of the nation served as the tipping point to the new institutional equilibrium. With the nation's trade and payments invoiced and settled in foreign currencies (primarily sterling), relative international economic expansion meant ever greater benefits foregone to currency internationalists in the United States. By the early 1900s, the opportunity costs shifted in favor of lobbying for the necessary institutional changes. These efforts paid off handsomely, as the Federal Reserve, in conjunction with the financial effects of World War I, propelled the United States to the position of nascent world banker.

Internationalization of the Dollar

Measured on the scale of nations, the economy of the United States went from being merely large in 1870, to colossal by 1913. Its maturation as a modern industrial economy was reflected in its payments position, which, after 1896, showed persistent current account surpluses for the first time and corresponding exports of *long-term* capital. This much was to be expected: America financed its growing trade surpluses with capital outflows in the form of long-term loans and foreign direct investment. What is puzzling is that, despite the nation's strong capital position, neither the U.S. dollar nor the largest American commercial banks were in demand as international financial resources. The United States thus remained a peripheral nation, and its ambitious financial class resented this status and the lost profits it entailed.

A remarkably rapid transformation took place over the next five years. From 1914, the dollar began to compete seriously with the pound as an international currency, and New York began to displace London as the premier international banking center.[4] By 1916, the dollar had largely replaced sterling as the means of payment, not only for U.S. exports and imports, but also for most of Europe's trade with Latin America and the Orient. To provide the necessary financing facilities, American banks set up branches in the world's major trading centers. The New York discount market, in turn, eroded London's dominant position by offering relatively cheap credit facilities for borrowers, as well as reliable investment opportunities for foreigners seeking a stable store of value. Moreover, the United States began to play a significant role as stabilizer of the international monetary system through the indirect channels of Federal Reserve officials and, later, New York bankers, cooperating extensively with foreign monetary authorities and providing loans for stabilization purposes. In short, the United States emerged in this period as a nascent "world banker," providing dollar-denominated liquidity to the international system. Nonresidents accumulated dollar balances to maintain liquidity and/or to undertake investment, to pay for imports invoiced in dollars, and to service loans for capital development that were denominated in dollars. America's halting, tentative first steps as financial "hegemon" in global affairs date from this period.

The literature on the rising importance of the United States in global financial affairs pays insufficient attention to the role of domestic institutional factors in this transition. For most analysts, the exogenous shock that upset the international hierarchy was World War I. While the war greatly accelerated the pace of America's ascent in the world economy, the United States might not have seized the opportunity without the institutional innovations of the Federal Reserve Act. In other words, *two* factors combined to bring about the result: the onset of World War I and

---

[4] The best source is Paul P. Abrahams, *The Foreign Expansion of American Finance and Its Relationship to the Foreign Economic Policies of the United States, 1907–1921* (New York: Arno Press, 1976).

the opening of the Federal Reserve System. The war's impact was to hasten the relative advance of the U.S. economy, which was already well underway. The timely establishment of the Federal Reserve System, in turn, allowed the United States to realize earlier, and to an extent far greater than previously anticipated, the international benefits that had propelled members of the international currency coalition to lobby on its behalf.

The immediate factor in the rapid wartime advance in the American economic position was the insistent demand of the belligerent powers for American goods and services.[5] As Europe turned to America for war materials, the U.S. current account surplus grew rapidly. The war also cut off Latin America and other developing regions from European manufactures, thereby increasing the foreign demand for American goods. To settle accounts, Europeans liquidated American securities and borrowed heavily from American private investors and from the U.S. government. By war's end, the United States had accumulated nearly half the world's monetary gold. In just five years, the United States had not only eclipsed Great Britain as the world's greatest trading nation, but had also been transformed into a mature creditor nation, a change so rapid that it is considered "perhaps the most dramatic transformation in economic history."[6]

A longer view reveals that the war merely compressed into several years trends that were already well established in decades prior to the war. U.S. current account surpluses date from the mid-1890s, a function of the nation's industrial maturation and successful penetration of foreign markets. To finance accounts with the United States, foreign governments and corporations began long-term borrowing in the New York market, with the flotation of foreign securities peaking between 1901 and 1905. At the long end of the credit market, long-term interest rates in New York were as low, if not lower, than rates in other markets from 1880 on.[7] In addition, the United States accumulated an ever larger proportion of the world's monetary gold, rising to 24 percent by 1913, from just 4 percent in 1875.[8] Understandably, but somewhat prematurely, Sec-

---

[5] The classic source here is William A. Brown, Jr., *The International Gold Standard Reinterpreted, 1914–1934* (New York: National Bureau of Economic Research, 1940).
[6] Alexander D. Noyes, *The War Period of American Finance* (New York: G.P. Putnam's Sons, 1926), p. 436.
[7] Milton Friedman and Anna J. Schwartz, *A Monetary History of the United States, 1867–1960* (Princeton: Princeton University Press, 1963), chaps. 4 and 10; Michael Edelstein, *Overseas Investment in the Age of High Imperialism* (New York: Columbia University Press, 1982), chap. 10, and pp. 295–96.
[8] Marcello de Cecco, *Money and Empire* (London: Oxford University Press, 1974), table 16, p. 247.

retary of State John Hay declared in 1902, "The 'debtor nation' has become the chief creditor nation. The financial center of the world, which required thousands of years to journey from the Euphrates to the Thames and Seine, seems to be passing to the Hudson between daybreak and dark."[9] Hence, the wartime period does not represent new trends in the nation's international payments position, but an acceleration of existing ones.

The revolution that *did* occur after 1914 involved the role of the U.S. dollar and the American joint-stock banking system in *short-term* international financial markets. Before 1914, domestic institutional factors, rather than financial or economic immaturity, were the barriers to greater U.S. participation in these areas.[10] Legal restrictions prevented the largest and most reputable banks from establishing overseas branches. Banks were also forbidden from accepting bills of exchange and drafts, which hindered the global rise of the New York market because acceptances were the principal instrument in international trade finance and in the world's short-term bill market. Finally, the absence of a central bank and a discount market for acceptances and other short-term instruments before 1914, "meant that the United States could not compete on the field where the contest of international short-term finance was played."[11]

The Federal Reserve Act relaxed all these restrictions with the aim of internationalizing the dollar and the joint-stock banking system. In a speech to New York bankers in 1916, Warburg summarized how the Federal Reserve System worked to bolster the international standing of the dollar and of American banks in the unexpected context of the war:

> The far-reaching effects of the War as they worked in favor of the United States and to the disadvantage of Europe are apparent to all. The effects of the opening of the Federal reserve banks are not quite so easily discernible to the casual observer. The Federal Reserve System has created a condition of health and strength which is accepted by many as a natural state without thinking of men whose thought and energy brought it into life, at almost a providential moment, this remarkable piece of banking machinery. It is true, nonetheless, that without the steadying influence of this System, without the new machinery that it provided for the financing of our foreign trade, we should have sunk lower and should not have risen

---

[9] Cited in Cleona Lewis, *America's Stake in International Investments* (Washington, D.C.: Brookings Institution, 1938), pp. 338–39.

[10] For a corroborating account, see Vincent P. Carosso and Richard Sylla, "U.S. Banks in International Finance," in *International Banking, 1870–1914*, ed. Rondo Cameron and V. I. Bovykin (New York: Oxford University Press, 1991).

[11] Ibid., p. 53.

so far and so fast. Had it not been for this feeling of safety this country could not at one and the same time have absorbed its own securities and granted foreign loans estimated to aggregate together the staggering amount of one billion and a half to two billion dollars. And while these imposing transactions were being carried through, crops were moved at the lowest rates ever known. Without the usual seasonal fluctuations in interest rates and without a ripple of financial difficulty we passed through political situations which in years gone by might have caused violent financial disturbances. At the same time some hundreds of millions of dollars were provided to pay off long bills our bankers formerly drew on Europe for the moving of our imports and exports and for other credit operations, while simultaneously our own bankers' acceptances sprang into existence. They are being drawn today from South America, the Far East, and from Europe for the purpose of financing not only our own trade but also that of foreign nations.[12]

By allowing national banks to accept bills of exchange and to open foreign branches, and by establishing the Federal Reserve banks to give acceptances and other commercial paper a ready market of last resort, the Act helped to establish the kind of discount market upon which Britain's position as world banker had rested. The outbreak of the war and the establishment of the Federal Reserve System tended to reinforce each other in this respect: the war enhanced the attractiveness of international banking and the New York money market, just when the institutional foundations for global banking had been put in place. As Warburg suggested, there was nothing coincidental about the timing of the Federal Reserve Act; to the "men whose thought and energy brought it into life," the war merely compressed into a matter of years the evolution of the nation's international economic position that was already well underway.[13]

Under the stimulus of the war, American banks, dollar acceptances, and the New York discount market gained increasing international stature. National City Bank opened its first foreign branch in Buenos Aires in November 1914, less than a year after the Federal Reserve Act became law.[14] By 1920, American banks and banking corporations had established 181 foreign branches, which substituted dollar acceptances for

---

[12] Paul Warburg, "Some Economic Problems of the Day," address delivered before the New York Credit Men's Association, 16 January 1916. Reprinted in Paul M. Warburg, *The Federal Reserve System*, vol. 2 (New York: Macmillan, 1930), pp. 356–57.
[13] Ibid.
[14] Robert S. Mayer, *The Influence of Frank A. Vanderlip and the National City Bank on American Commerce and Foreign Policy, 1910–1920* (New York: Garland, 1987); Harold van B. Cleveland and Thomas F. Huertas, *Citibank, 1812–1970* (Cambridge: Harvard University Press, 1985).

sterling bills in the financing of world trade.[15] The war forced London acceptance houses to greatly reduce their international lending, thereby opening the door to U.S. banks. In addition, sterling's fall from the gold standard, and the imposition of exchange controls in England, left a "free field for the development of the dollar bill during a period when America's foreign trade reached unprecedented totals."[16] But the Federal Reserve Act provided the institutions required to seize the opportunities. As Clyde Phelps put it, "If the World War provoked the expansion it is also true that the American banking reforms permitted it, granting our banking institutions full freedom to enter the foreign field without those legal restrictions to which they had previously been subject."[17]

Dollar acceptances steadily encroached on the sterling empire in this environment. The acceptance provisions of the Federal Reserve Act, along with the liquidity guarantee provided by the Federal Reserve banks, allowed dollar exchange to substitute for sterling credits in international commerce, just as the war reduced the amount of English capital available for trade finance. Moreover, the Federal Reserve Bank of New York, the Federal Reserve Board, and the New York bankers all "endeavored in every way to encourage, not only the making of, but the investment in, bankers' acceptances at rates sufficiently low to make a draft on the United States the cheapest that can now be drawn anywhere in the world."[18] By April 1915, New York banks had created acceptance liabilities of $80 to $100 million; by 1919, the total volume of dollar acceptances outstanding had reached $1 billion, an amount approximating London's prewar levels.[19] Since attaining a position as world banker was one of the primary, yet relatively obscure, objectives of banking reform, it is not surprising that a committee of Federal Reserve officials viewed the rapid growth of dollar acceptances as "ample justification in itself for the enactment of the Reserve Act."[20]

Beyond enabling American banks and the dollar to expand overseas, the Federal Reserve Act also provided the United States with the institu-

---

[15] Lewis, *America's Stake in International Investments*, pp. 194–98.

[16] Benjamin H. Beckhart, *The New York Money Market: Uses of Funds*, vol. 3 (New York: Columbia University Press, 1932), p. 312.

[17] Clyde W. Phelps, *The Foreign Expansion of American Banks: American Branch Banking Abroad* (New York: Ronald Press, 1927), p. 132.

[18] Pierre Jay, *The Responsibilities of the Federal Reserve System for the Maintenance of Gold Payments* (New York: Trust Companies Association, 1917), p. 8. For the support given to the dollar discount market in acceptances, see Abrahams, *The Foreign Expansion of American Finance*.

[19] Abrahams, *The Foreign Expansion of American Finance*, p. 52; Beckhart, *The New York Money Market*, p. 310.

[20] Cited in Beckhart, *The New York Money Market*, p. 312.

tional means to become an active agent in international monetary affairs, a goal that had been in the minds of American internationalists since at least 1907.[21] In the prewar period, ad hoc collaborations between European central banks helped keep the international payments mechanism operating smoothly in the face of shocks—typically originating in the United States itself.[22] Indeed, before the war, New York bankers had already concluded that the U.S. economy had grown too large and too unstable financially to remain outside the circle of central banking nations. Shortly after the 1907 crisis, for instance, Warburg wrote:

> Our own system being absolutely inelastic, we have become accustomed to use as a substitute the power of the [New York] banking community to borrow in Europe. We thus use Europe as an auxiliary financial machine; but we forget that our weight has become so great as to threaten the safety of the European machinery when we are compelled to use it to its utmost capacity in order to provide for our needs. Europe, in sheer self-defense, refuses under these circumstances to let us borrow. . . . Thus, instead of securing additional means of assistance at the most critical moment, we find ourselves suddenly forced to dispense with a most important part of our machinery, upon which we are wont to rely in normal times. This is what happened in 1907, and history will repeat itself, unless we adapt our system to growth.[23]

The international dimensions of the 1907 crisis led other bankers to the same conclusion. In November of that year, a group of New York banks, led by J. P. Morgan and Company and National City Bank, began negotiations with the Bank of France for an emergency gold loan to the United States. This was an appeal to existing practice, as the Bank of France, which had explicitly adopted the role of international lender of last resort, regularly came to the aid of Britain in this way. The Bank of France, however, refused to grant similar direct assistance to the United States, on the grounds that the loan lacked sufficient institutional guarantees—that is, the guarantee of a central bank.[24] There is also evidence

[21] For a fuller treatment, see J. Lawrence Broz, "Wresting the Scepter from London: The International Political Economy of the Founding of the Federal Reserve" (Ph.D. dissertation, University of California, Los Angeles, 1993).

[22] Barry Eichengreen, *Golden Fetters: The Gold Standard and the Great Depression* (New York: Oxford University Press, 1992); de Cecco, *Money and Empire*, pp. 110–26.

[23] Paul M. Warburg, "The Discount System in Europe," in Warburg, *The Federal Reserve System*, 2:198–99.

[24] According to J. P. Morgan, Jr., the Bank of France "does not feel sufficiently acquainted [with] American affairs to be willing [to] deal with the Banks individually." Vincent P. Carosso, *The Morgans: Private International Bankers, 1854–1913* (Cambridge: Harvard Univer-

suggesting that Bank of France officials refused the loan because they feared it would delay the development of a central banking movement in the United States. According to one French participant, "One of the arguments used against the shipment is the absence of a State bank in America. The opinion is expressed in the highest quarters that if the plan goes through, there will be an end for a long time to come of banking reform in the United States. The bankers of America will say, 'See, they send us gold just as they send it to the Bank of England. Why change our present system?' "[25] In the end, the Bank of France made a direct loan to the Bank of England, which then allowed gold to flow from London to New York. Benjamin Strong noted the added costs of this indirect method of obtaining gold and attributed it to the absence of a central bank:

> In 1907 we were given to understand in this country by French bankers that the Bank of France would be glad to loan gold to this country if there were any way that it could do so. This meant that if we had a central bank, the Bank of France would have loaned gold to it directly. Not being able to do so, the Bank of France loaned gold to the Bank of England, and we then obtained gold from London—a roundabout and expensive method, for the Bank of England had to have its interest, which was un- doubtedly reflected in the Bank of England rate, which was up to 7 per- cent.[26]

These experiences led Warburg, Strong, and others to press for, and obtain, provisions in the Federal Reserve legislation that gave reserve banks the authority to deal with, and support, foreign central banks. Though I have no special evidence of this, it is plausible that these actors anticipated the increasing private benefits of promoting global financial stability as their international interests grew. The first application of this authority occurred in 1916, when the New York Federal Reserve Bank, acting as agent for all the other reserve banks, and with the approval of the board, established correspondent relations with the Bank of England.[27] This enabled the New York Fed and the Bank of England to maintain deposit accounts and represent each other in the purchase of bills of

sity Press, 1987), pp. 545–46. See also Maurice Patron, *The Bank of France in Relation to National and International Credit* (Washington, D.C.: GPO, 1910), pp. 144–46.

[25] *New York Times*, 15 November 1907, p. 1.

[26] Benjamin Strong to Senator Theodore E. Burton, 5 December 1913, Benjamin Strong Pa- pers, Archives Division, Federal Reserve Bank of New York.

[27] For the details, see Lester V. Chandler, *Benjamin Strong, Central Banker* (Washington, D.C.: Brookings Institution, 1958), pp. 93–98.

exchange, with the purpose of moderating wartime exchange-rate pressures and limiting the need for England to ship gold. In his account of the negotiations, Strong noted how the advent of the Federal Reserve made it possible to formalize such a relationship:

> Lord Cunliffe has undoubtedly consulted Grenfell and Norman, and I gathered from his statement that he and those of his associates with whom he has consulted see the wisdom of a close working relationship between the Bank of England and the Federal Reserve Banks with the view of exercising reasonable control over the exchange and over gold shipments. They have apparently discussed this in the past but have felt unwilling to make an arrangement with any one American bank, and would not care to have their business distributed among a number, so that the organization of the Federal Reserve Banks, corresponding in their functions with the Bank of England, gives them an opportunity to make an arrangement, the desirability of which had already been recognized.[28]

Similar agreements were concluded with the Bank of France and several other European central banks. These relationships formed the foundation for central bank cooperation in the 1920s, in which the New York Fed played a major role.[29] Here, the New York Reserve Bank's efforts were, for the most part, connected to the efforts of foreign countries to return their monetary systems to a gold basis. The growing importance of American foreign trade, the flood of gold into the United States, and the rise of the United States as a creditor nation made Strong and other American internationalists even more anxious to see international monetary order reestablished. The Federal Reserve Act, in turn, provided the institutional means to act on this agenda. Strong provided the clearest statement of this view when called upon to justify the New York Fed's large stabilization loan to the Bank of England in 1925:

> The provisions of the Federal Reserve Act relating to dealing in gold, to opening accounts in foreign countries, buying foreign bills and checks and cable transfers, had but one object in view, namely, to provide a stabilizing influence upon exchange rates and effect some regulation of the inflow and outflow of gold. . . . It is, of course, true that the authors of the Federal Reserve Act did not have in mind, when drafting it, that the world would be plunged into a great war which would result in universal ex-

[28] Benjamin Strong Diary, 30 March 1916, Benjamin Strong Papers, Archives Division, Federal Reserve Bank of New York.
[29] Chandler, *Benjamin Strong*; Stephen V. O. Clarke, *Central Bank Cooperation, 1924–31* (New York: Federal Reserve Bank of New York, 1967); Richard H. Meyer, *Bankers' Diplomacy: Monetary Stabilization in the Twenties* (New York: Columbia University Press, 1970).

change disorder, suspension of gold payment, and monetary disorganiza-
tion throughout the world. The powers granted to the Reserve Banks,
however, are fortunately those which are expressly applicable to dealing
with just such a situation, and they have been evoked for that specific
purpose, although it may, indeed, be true that the authors of the Act,
knowing nothing of the possibilities of the war, did not contemplate that
transactions of that character would necessarily be of the magnitude of
this one. They doubtless did have in mind such gold movements as that of
1907. The principle is no different, the powers are no different from those
that would have been required, nor are the objects to be obtained any
different, except that the circumstances calling for their exercise are more
grave and important in their considerations than would have been the
case without a war.[30]

In summary, during the war and immediate postwar period, the position of the United States in international financial affairs progressed far
along the lines envisioned by Warburg, Strong, Vanderlip, and other currency internationalists. The dollar acceptance increased in use as an instrument of trade finance, American banks formed a worldwide network
of foreign branch banks, and the New York discount market attained
worldwide status. In addition, the New York Fed became a focal point
for international monetary cooperation in a manner similar to what the
proponents of the Aldrich plan had sought through a single central
bank. However, the internationalism of the reserve bank and New York
bankers, in shoring up foreign currencies, and in matters related to war
debts, reparations, and European reconstruction, ran up against the iso-
lationism of broader American foreign economic policy, which ultimately
undercut efforts to stabilize the world economy.

The timely formation of the Federal Reserve System facilitated this
epic transformation by eliminating existing legal restraints and providing the broader domestic underpinnings for a prospective world banker.
While one historian of the Federal Reserve Act gives passing recognition
to these international goals, the foreign dimension is not central to his
causal story.[31] The present perspective, in contrast, gives international
factors explanatory primacy, and in so doing, fills logical and empirical
gaps in the allocative story. Inasmuch as my account addresses the issue
of how nation-states respond to international forces, I also speak to the
broader international political economic literature.

---

[30] Benjamin Strong, *Interpretations of Federal Reserve Policy* (New York: Harper and Brothers,
1930), pp. 273–74. The New York Fed also granted stabilization loans to banks of issue in
Belgium (1926), Poland (1927), Italy (1927), and Rumania (1929).
[31] James Livingston, *Origins of the Federal Reserve System: Money, Class, and Corporate Capitalism, 1890–1913* (Ithaca: Cornell University Press, 1986), pp. 119–20, 153, 193, 202–3.

Implications for International Political Economy

The argument rests on the precept, drawn from theories of collective action, that the allocative aspects of institutions are insufficient as explanations *of* institutions. Attempts to explain the demand and supply of particular institutions, based upon the collective benefits that such arrangements provide, usually run into intractable analytical problems. In contrast, a stalwart analytical theme in the collective action literature is that many real-world situations approximate the conditions specified in the joint products model. In these situations, public and private goods cannot be separately produced and consumed, meaning that collective action in support of both goods is more likely. My argument is that American payments system reform involved just this situation, creating the necessary overlap between the private and social costs of institutional change.

For international political economists, the important finding is that groups in American society responded to international forces by organizing, defining, and sustaining the drive for domestic institutions compatible with the external signals because of the concentrated (private) benefits involved. While theoretical considerations indicate that internationalizing a currency has clear-cut distributional effects *between* issuing and nonissuing nations, there need be no appeal to the amorphous "national interest," in explaining patterns of international currency use and the origins of institutions that buttress such a status.[32] This is because theoretical considerations also indicate that internationalizing a currency has straightforward distributional consequences *within* issuing and nonissuing nations. Inasmuch as the benefits (or costs) are asymmetrically weighted in favor (or against) certain subsets of society, propelling such agents to champion (or oppose) currency internationalism, positive analysis can yield testable predictions about preferences and coalition patterns. Though only suggestive, this approach implies that taking the national interest *out* of the study of international political economy can be a productive enterprise.[33]

---

[32] For a recent analysis of currency affairs in the "statist" tradition of international relations theory, see Jonathan Kirshner, *The Political Economy of International Monetary Power* (Princeton: Princeton University Press, 1995).

[33] For complementary approaches in the area of international finance, see Jeffry A. Frieden, "Invested Interests: The Politics of National Economic Policies in a World of Global Finance," *International Organization* 45 (Autumn 1991): 425–51; C. Randall Henning, *Currencies and Politics in the United States, Germany, and Japan* (Washington, D.C.: Institute for International Economics, 1994); and Frances McCall Rosenbluth, *Financial Politics in Contemporary Japan* (Ithaca: Cornell University Press, 1989).

Index

Aldrich, Nelson W., 148, 170–72, 173–85, 186–87
Aldrich Plan, 176–92, 201; defeat of, 190–94; international features of, 179–80, 201–2; relation to Federal Reserve Act, 193, 201–3
Aldrich-Vreeland Act (1908), 30, 172–73
Andrew, A. Piatt, 174, 176
Astor, John Jacob, 238

Balance of payments: international currency usage and, 69–70, 72, 81–82, 86, 88–90, 249; of U.S., 104–7
Baltimore Plan (of 1894), 169
Bank of England: as commitment mechanism, 206–9, 215–16; discount market and, 63, 115; fiscal aspects of, 206–9, 220–21; founding of, 214–22; free banking view of, 209–10; Glorious Revolution and, 207–8; gold standard and, 117–18, 223–24, 226–27; international role of sterling and, 63, 115, 117–18; joint products view of, 212, 216–17, 220–21, 247; monopoly powers of, 219–20, 222–24; new institutionalist view of, 206–9; political conflict over, 222–27
Bank of France: discount rate policy of, 120–21; gold devices and, 118–119; gold reserve of, 120; gold standard and, 117–18; as international lender of last resort, 49–50, 257–58

Bank regulation: of banknotes, 25–27, 53; of branching, 21–25, 52; destabilizing aspects of, 20–30; economic theory of, 24–25; of portfolios, 36, 52; of reserves, 27–28, 36, 52
Bankers: Bank of England and, 215, 217–22; Chicago, 33, 139, 168–69, 171–73, 174, 177, 184, 190, 192, 201, 204; First Bank of the United States and, 227, 228, 230, 233–37; international currency benefits to, 8, 76–77, 158–59, 161, 175; Midwestern, 168–70, 177–78; Second Bank of the United States and, 240–42; small country, 178–79, 181–82, 189, 192, 198–99; as supporters of Federal Reserve, 3, 139–42, 166–70, 185–90, 200–201. *See also* Creditors; Internationalists, economic; New York bankers; *entries of individual nations*
Bankers' acceptances: Aldrich Plan support for, 179, 194, 201n; Bank of England support for, 115, 137; defined, 6–7n, 38–40; English, 62, 110, 137; Federal Reserve support for, 7, 33–34, 45–48, 53, 55, 64, 201–2; French, 123–24; German, 110, 124–25; growth of dollar, 255–56; international currency aspects of, 62, 137–38; Japanese, 62; restrictions on, 41–42, 53, 137; transaction costs and, 6–7n, 42; Paul Warburg and, 142–50, 158–59.

Bankers' acceptances: (*continued*)
See also Bills of exchange; Commercial
paper; Discounting
Bankers' balances. *See* Correspondent
banking system
Banknotes: elasticity of, 26–27; Federal Reserve, 46, 53; National Banking System
restrictions on, 25–27
Belmont-Morgan Syndicate, 136
Biddle, Nicholas, 41, 49, 239–40
Bills of exchange, 6–7, 28, 39–41, 45–47,
55, 64, 83, 109, 119, 124–25, 137–38,
143–44, 147–52, 179, 194, 201–2, 251,
254–55, 258–59. *See also* Bankers' acceptances; Commercial paper; Discounting
Bloomfield, Arthur, 117–18
Branch banking: Canada, 20, 23–24; foreign, 35, 52, 79, 125–26, 128–29, 137–38,
179, 202, 252, 254; opposition to, 24–25;
restrictions on, 21–25, 35, 254; stabilizing aspects of, 22–23. *See also* Unit
banking system
Bretton Woods System, 75, 81
Brewer, John, 208, 218
Bryan, William Jennings, 61, 197–98
Bundesbank, 74–75

Call (demand) loans, 28, 43, 53, 64, 72,
146–48. *See also* Reserve "pyramid-
ing"
Calomiris, Charles, 24–25
Canada, banking in, 20, 23–24, 112
Capitalist class, founding of Federal Reserve and, 32–33
Carosso, Vincent, 54, 138
Cartelization, of banking: Bank of England
and, 215–23; early central banking and,
209, 211, 214; Federal Reserve Act and,
17–18, 31; First Bank of the United
States and, 227–28, 230–32; Second
Bank of the United States and, 238–39.
See also Rent-seeking
Central banking: alternatives to, 20–30,
33; discount market and, 45–50, 63–64,
115, 125, 137–38, 150–52, 176, 179, 194,
201–2, 251, 254–56; distortions of, 209,
221–22; fiscal aspects of, 206, 210–14; international advantages of, 7, 45, 49–50,
63–64, 142, 150–52, 243–44, 249, 255–60;
lender of last resort and, 1, 19, 21, 28–
29, 63–65, 125, 151, 183, 206, 239–40,
245–46, 249, 255, 257; tax smoothing
and, 208, 212. *See also entries for individual central banks*

Citibank. *See* National City Bank; Vanderlip, Frank
Civil War: evolution of discount market
and, 40–41, 49, 152; financing of, 77,
243; greenbacks and, 60–61; National
Banking System and, 25–26, 169
Clearinghouse associations: Aldrich-
Vreeland Act and, 30, 171–73; Federal
Reserve Act and, 11, 15, 65, 163, 180,
187–89; loan certificates of, 29; as private lenders of last resort, 28–30
Cohen, Benjamin, 8, 59, 72
Collective action: clearinghouse associations and, 187–89; early central banking
and, 207–17, 228, 245–47; government
creditworthiness and, 207–12, 216–17;
institutional change and, 1–2, 246;
lobbying coalitions and, 14, 24, 31, 54,
161, 204, 226–27; payments system reform and, 2–3, 6–8, 10–11, 55–56, 65,
72, 159–60, 185, 226, 245, 247–51; political institutions and, 15, 160–65, 173, 204.
See also Free-rider problem; Public
goods
Commercial paper: Aldrich-Vreeland Act
and, 172; described, 37–39; double-
name, 37–38, 49, 137; Federal Reserve
support for, 36–37, 45–50, 53, 179, 194,
201–2, 251, 254–56; liquidity of, 42–43,
46–47, 145–46; markets in, 40–44, 144–
45; secondary markets in, 6–7, 64;
single-name, 37–38. *See also* Bankers'
acceptances; Bills of exchange; Discounting
Committees, congressional, 136, 162–65,
168, 170–74, 191, 194, 200–201, 204
Continental Congress, 227–28
Continental currency, 228–29, 236
Correspondent banking system, 28–29, 35,
147–48; as substitute for branch banking, 42
Cortelyou, George, 167–68
Creditors, 207, 211–13; First Bank of the
United States and, 227, 229–31, 233–37;
founding of the Bank of England and,
214–226; Second Bank of the United
States and, 240–42. *See also*
Bankers
Creditworthiness, of government: as cause
of early central banks, 206–9, 214, 229–
30, 237–38; as public good, 209, 243

Davis, Lance, 42, 144n
Davison, Henry, 174, 177, 186–87

Debtors, 213, 222, 228; currency deprecia-tion in England and, 224–25; origins of First Bank of the United States and, 229–30
Democratic Party, and origins of Federal Reserve, 193–95, 198. *See also* Glass, Carter; Wilson, Woodrow
Denomination rents: distribution of, 76–77; Federal Reserve and, 10, 248; German mark and, 129; international currency issue and, 72–73, 75; money-center banks and, 8, 76–77, 80–81, 89, 137, 146; sterling and, 125–26, 146
Deposit insurance, 8, 19, 23n
Developing countries, trade with: demand for international currencies and, 9, 66–69, 71, 86, 88, 90; United States and, 98–99, 105, 153–57
Discounting, 36–45, 136–37, 158–59, 251; Aldrich Plan and, 177, 179, 194; defined, 36–38; in England, 62–63, 110, 115–18, 123, 137; Federal Reserve and, 35–37, 45–50, 64, 141–43, 172, 175, 194, 201–2, 251, 254–56; in France, 119–20, 123–24; in Germany, 109, 124, 128–29; interna-tionalization of U.S. dollar and, 144–50, 179–80, 251–56; in U.S. before Federal Reserve, 6, 28, 39–43, 55, 64, 125, 136–37. *See also* Rediscounting
Dual banking system, 34–36, 51

Eichengreen, Barry, 26n, 49n, 63, 115n, 168n, 257n
England: bankers' acceptances in, 62, 110, 115, 137; bankers in, 215, 217–22; cartel-ization of banking in, 215–23; creditors in, 214–26; debtors in, 224–25; discount-ing in, 62–63, 110, 115–18, 137; eco-nomic internationalists in, 116–17, 137; economic nationalists in, 113, 117, 130; exporters in, 116–17; farmers in, 224–26; gold standard in, 114–15, 226–27; infla-tion rate in, 222–26; landlords in, 225–26; rent-seeking in, 214, 216–17. *See also* Bank of England; Sterling (British pound)
Exchange-rate risk: distributional aspects of, 8, 73–75, 78–81, 84, 88; English ex-porters and, 116–17; French exporters and, 121–22; German exporters and, 125–26, 128–29; international currency usage and, 67–68, 88; U.S. exporters and, 140, 153–58; U.S. importers and, 155, 158

Exports: demand for international cur-rency and, 87–88; English, 91, 93, 98, 102, 116–17; French, 91, 93; German, 91, 93, 98; manufactured, 68, 92–93; spe-cialized, 68, 93, 97; U.S., growth of, 9–10, 79, 90–99, 153–56. *See also* Exchange-rate risk

Farmers: in England, 224–26; First Bank of the United States and, 229, 236; in France, 121–22; monetary centralization and, 182, 192; Second Bank of the United States and, 241–42
Farwell, John, 186
Federalism: bank regulation and, 24; fail-ure of early American central banking and, 214, 228, 243; First Bank of the United States and, 233–37; Second Bank of the United States and, 247
First Bank of the United States: demise of, 233–37; fiscal aspects of, 206, 227, 230; joint products and, 206, 242, 245; mone-tary aspects of, 232–33, 235–36; rent-seeking and, 213, 232–33. *See also* Federalism
Forgan, James, 169, 171–72, 177, 184
Fowler, Charles, 169–70, 172
Fowler Plan (of 1902), 169
Fractional reserve banking, instability of, 19–20; as cause of Federal Reserve, 19–21, 165–66
France: bankers' acceptances in, 123–24; discounting in, 119–20, 123–24; economic internationalists in, 121–23; economic nationalists in, 113, 121–22, 123, 130; exporters in, 121–22; farmers in, 121–22; global currency position of, 91–92, 108–9; gold reserve of, 120; gold standard in, 118–24; money markets in, 119–20; relative economic decline of, 112–13. *See also* Bank of France
Free banking: critique of central banking, 209–10, 244; defined, 20–21; view of bank regulation, 26–28
Free silver movement, 60–61, 133–34
Free-rider problem, 3, 5, 12, 15, 29, 161–63, 185, 187, 189, 204, 210–11, 228, 246. *See* also Collective action
Frieden, Jeffry, 75n, 79, 82n, 224n, 261n
Functional arguments, 17–18

Galbraith, John Kenneth, 228–29
Gallatin, Albert, 236

Germany: bankers' acceptances in, 110, 124–25; discounting in, 109, 124, 128–29; economic internationalists in, 113, 125–26, 128–29; economic nationalists in, 113, 125–26, 128–29; exporters in, 125–26, 128–29; global currency position of, 91–93, 109–11, 128–29; gold standard in, 126–27; panics in, 127, 191. *See also* Reichsbank

Girard, Stephen, 238

Glass, Carter, 141, 190, 194–98, 205

Gold reserve: Federal Reserve and, 49–50, of France, 120; Treasury management of, 136; of U.S., 104–5, 108, 134–35

Gold standard, 49, 61; in England, 114–15, 226–27; in France, 118–24; French franc and, 119, 123–24; German mark and, 128–29; in Germany, 126–27; gold devices and, 117–19, 127–28, 136; Gold Standard Act, 61; international cooperation in, 49–50, 256–60; internationalization of dollar and, 135–36; Napoleonic wars and, 223–24; sterling usage and, 113–15, 118; U.S. Treasury and, 134–36, 167–68

Goodhart, Charles, 29, 43

Gourevitch, Peter, 165

Hamilton, Alexander, 163, 230–32

Hammond, Bray, 240

Hay, John, 254

Hegemony, 11–12; global economic position of U.S. and, 90–105, 132–33, 250–53

Henning, C. Randall, 47n, 116n, 261n

Hepburn, A. Barton, 188, 196

House, Col. Edward M., 195

Importers, and currency politics, 67–68, 79–80, 155–58

Indianapolis Plan (of 1898), 169

Inflation rate: in England, 223; Federal Reserve structure and, 193, 198–201; gold standard and, 60–61, 223; international currency aspects of, 58–60, 65, 70, 74, 81; monopoly central banks and, 243–44; politics of, in England, 222–26; politics of, in U.S., 227, 229–30; seigniorage and, 72; in U.S., 229; war finance and, 212, 222, 228–29, 237, 243

Inseparable goods. *See* Joint products model

Institutional change: archaeology of, 17; Federal Reserve as case of, 2–4; functional theories of, 17–18; international

economic position and, 56, 84, 86, 130–31, 133; as public goods problem, 4, 245–46

Interest rate fluctuations, seasonal, 26–27, 132, 147, 149, 255

International currency: as cause of Federal Reserve, 7–10, 49–50, 55–56, 249–51; defined, 56–58; distributional effects of, 71–85; French franc as, 108–9, 118–24; German mark as, 109–11, 124–29; as impure public goods, 6–7; prerequisites for, 60–66; sterling as, 105–8; supplementary factors related to, 66–71, 86–87; transaction costs and choice of, 57–58; U.S. dollar as, 5–6, 56–59, 249–57

Internationalists, economic: Aldrich Plan and, 153–56, 177–80; in England, 116–17, 137; in France, 121–23; in Germany, 113, 125–26, 128–29; importers as, 78–80; manufacturing exporters as, 78–80; money-center bankers as, 76–77, 160–61, 250; preferences of, 8, 56, 76–80, 87–89; as supporters of dollar internationalization, 79–80, 83–84, 138–39; as supporters of Federal Reserve, 54, 140, 153–60, 201–4, 250–51. *See also* New York bankers

Jackson, Andrew, 241–42

Jacobs, Lawrence, 143–44, 154

Jekyl Island Conference, 176–78

Jenks, Leland, 226

Joint products model, 4–7, 50–51, 55–56, 159, 203–4, 206, 210–14, 246–48, 250. *See also* Collective action

J. P. Morgan & Co., 149, 171, 257

Kent, Frederick, 202–3

Kindleberger, Charles, 12–13, 66

Kolko, Gabriel, 32–33, 201, 205

Krugman, Paul, 57, 68

Kuhn, Loeb, & Co., 140–41

Laughlin, J. Laurence, 186, 189, 191

Lender of last resort. *See* Central banking; Clearinghouse associations

Lindert, Peter, 110–11

Link, Arthur, 167

Liquidity, of banking system, 12–13, 19, 26–27, 61–62, 146–47

Livingston, James, 18, 32–34

McAdoo, William, 195

Miron, Jeffrey, 26

Monetary policy: independence of, 61, 74–75, 79, 82, 84, 113–14, 195, 200; internationalization of currency and, 59; intersectoral conflict over, 222–27, 228; politics of, 2, 83–84, 120; tools of, 117, 122, 127. *See also* Gold standard
"Money Trust" hearings, 32, 191–92, 197
Morawetz, Victor, 195
Morgan, J. P., 141, 170, 172, 174, 176–77
Myers, Margaret, 41, 135

National Banking System/Acts (1863 and 1864), 18–19; bankers' acceptances and, 41, 47; banknote issue and, 25–26, 168; branch banking and, 21; foreign banking and, 138–39, 153; support for replacement of, 140, 152, 169, 194, 203
National Board of Trade, 185–86
National Citizens' League, 185–90, 192–94, 200, 204
National City Bank, 156, 190–91, 202, 257. *See also* Vanderlip, Frank
National City Company, as related to National City Bank, 190–91; controversy and impact on legislative change, 197
National Monetary Commission, 173–85, 190, 193
National Reserve Association, 178–82, 190–91. *See also* Aldrich Plan
Nationalists, economic: Aldrich Plan and, 180; in England, 113, 117, 130; in France, 113, 121–22, 123, 130; in Germany, 113, 127, 131; preferences of, 56, 76, 80–84, 113, 130;
New Institutionalism, 206–10, 244
New York bankers: Aldrich Plan and, 168–70, 175–76, 186, 191–92, 210–11; establishment of Federal Reserve and, 10–11, 15, 27–29, 31–33, 140, 154, 159, 199–200, 257–58; Second Bank of the United States and, 240–42
New York Chamber of Commerce, 140–41
North, Douglass C., 39n, 206n

Olson, Mancur, xi, 160. *See also* Collective action
Open-market operations: derivation of power to perform, 7, 37, 53, 64; prior to the Federal Reserve Act, 25, 41–42, 239; purposes of, 45, 47–50

Panics, 115; of 1893, 165; of 1907, 3, 6, 30, 31, 127, 131, 142, 149, 165, 191, 257; as cause of banking reform, 10–11, 18–20,

54, 152, 165–66; causes of, 1, 26–28, 132, 147, 203; dates of, 5, 29, 221; dollar internationalization and, 131; Germany and, 127, 191; institutions and, 20, 24, 165; international gold standard and, 136, 152; populists and, 191, 193; as public goods problem, 6–7; solutions for, 29–30, 65, 167, 170–71, 188
Patterson, William, 215–16
Payments system: defined, 2; before Federal Reserve, 2–3; as public good, 2
Perkins, George, 186–87
Portfolio restrictions, on banks, 36
Populists, and central banking, 25, 60–61, 191–93, 196–99, 204–5. *See also* Bryan, William Jennings
Price stability. *See* Inflation rate
Private goods. *See* Joint products
Privileged group arguments: defined, 4; of Federal Reserve Act, 161; international, 12. *See also* Collective action; Free-rider problem; Joint products model
Progressive Party, 192–93
Public goods: central banks as providers of, 206, 210–13, 216, 221, 232, 242–43, 248; lobbying for, 161–62; provided by the Federal Reserve Act, 1, 19, 82, 84; public debt market as, 209; theory of, 2–6, 12, 65–66, 159, 160–61, 210–14, 244, 245–49

"Real" bills (assets currency), 33, 168–69, 172, 177, 183
Rediscounting, 42–43, 47, 63–65, 125, 151, 183, 206, 239–40, 245–46, 249, 255, 257. *See also* Central banking; Discounting
Reichsbank, 117–18, 125, 127
Reisser, Jacob, 110, 124
Rent-seeking: Bank of England and, 214, 216–17; defined, 211; development of modern central banking and, 213, 219–20, 222–23; early central banking and, 212–13, 242, 247; Federal Reserve Act and, 31; First Bank of the United States and, 227–28, 231–32; Second Bank of the United States and, 238; social welfare and, 211, 242. *See also* Denomination rents
Reserve banks, 201–3
Reserve "pyramiding," 27–28, 35, 45–46
Reserve requirements: Federal Reserve Act and, 36, 197; National Banking System and, 27–28, 35–36
Reynolds, George, 174, 177, 196

Roosevelt, Theodore, 166, 192
Russia, banking in, 111

Schiff, Jacob, 140–41. *See also* Kuhn, Loeb & Company
Second Bank of the United States, 5, 15, 41, 213, 237–42; demise of, 228, 240–42; "forbearance" and, 239–40; joint products and, 245; as lender of last resort, 239–40; monopoly powers of, 238–39; note issue and, 238–39; origins of, 228, 237–38; public goods and, 206, 245; trade acceptances and, 41. *See also* Astor, John Jacob; Biddle, Nicholas; Girard, Stephen; Hammond, Bray; New York bankers; War finance
Seignorage: defined, 72; international currency issue and, 72–73, 75–76, 81, 248
Selective incentives. *See* Joint products model
Selgin, George, 27, 210
Seligman, Edwin, 142
Shaw, Leslie, 136n, 167
Smith, Vera, 222
State-chartered banks, 233–41. *See also* Dual banking system
Sterling (British pound): Bank of England and, 63; denomination rents and, 125–26, 137, 146, 161; displacement of, 112, 137, 148, 150–51, 159, 161, 251–52, 254–56; domestic financial markets and, 62, 113, 115, 123; global role of, 99, 105–8, 111–14, 115, 123, 250; gold standard and, 113–15, 118; as invoicing currency for U.S. trade, 109, 153–58; as safest international currency, 59; World War I and, 252–54
Straus, Isidor, 179–80
Strong, Benjamin, 175, 258–59
Swoboda, Alexander, 72

Taft, William Howard, 167, 192
Tavlas, George, 58, 72–73
Tax smoothing, 208; war finance and, 212, 221, 242
Tilly, Richard, 109
Timberlake, Richard, 238–39
Trade, international, and currency use, 66–67, 87–90
Trade acceptances: defined, 38; historical usage of, 40–41, 48; open-market operations and, 48
Transaction costs: bankers' acceptances and, 6–7, 13, 42, 143–44; international currency and, 58, 62

Treasury Department: Aldrich Plan and, 182; Aldrich-Vreeland Act and, 30; bank reform and, 167–68; banknotes and, 25–26; Federal Reserve Act and, 197–98, 200; gold devices and, 136, gold reserve of, 134–35, 167–68; quasi-central banking role of, 136, 167, 184. *See also* Cortelyou, George; Shaw, Leslie
Trust companies, 31–32

Unit banking system: after Federal Reserve Act, 34–35; reserve "pyramiding" and, 28; as result of anti-branching laws, 21–25
Untermeyer, Samuel, 191–92

Vanderlip, Frank: 186, 190, 260; on Aldrich Plan, 170, 175, 187; on banking / payments system reform, 140–41, 151, 164, 176–77, 187, 201; on foreign trade, 156–57; on the need for a central bank, 151; on supporting the Federal Reserve Act, 201. *See also* Jekyl Island Conference; National City Bank; National City Company; National Monetary Commission
Vreeland, Edward, 172–73

Wall Street. *See* New York bankers
War finance: Aldrich-Vreeland Act and, 30; Civil War, 25, 77, 243; Napoleonic, 222–23, 225, 227, 229; National Banking System and, 25; origins of central banks and, 206–9, 218–221, 237–38; tax smoothing and, 212, 221, 242; War of Independence, 228–29
War of Independence, 228–29
Warburg, Paul M., 142–53; on Aldrich Plan, 175, 177, 183, 185–87, 189–91, 196; bankers' acceptances and, 142, 143–53, 158, 194, 203, 255, 260; central banking and, 37, 41, 49, 142–43, 150–52, 158, 178, 183–84, 196, 199–200, 203, 251; discount market and, 37, 40–41, 137, 142–53, 158, 194, 203, 250; on German banking practices, 128; internationalization of the dollar and, 143–53, 158–59, 203, 250–51, 254–55, 260; and Kuhn, Loeb, & Co., 141; National Reserve Association and, 190–91; as supporter of banking reform, 141–53, 158–59, 177–78, 184, 185–87, 189–91, 194, 196, 199–200, 203, 250–51, 254–55, 257, 258, 260. *See also* National Citizens' League; National Monetary Commission

Weingast, Barry, 16n, 206n, 207
West, Robert, 31
White, Eugene, 23–24
White, Lawrence, 219
Willis, H. Parker, 165, 170, 189, 195–98

Wilson, Woodrow, 167, 193–200, 204–5
World War I: economic ascendancy of U.S. and, 86, 104, 130, 251, 252–57, 260; monetary and banking structures before, 176; rise of German mark before, 109, 130